for Maia and Kira

DMN METHOD AND STYLE

THE PRACTITIONER'S GUIDE TO DECISION MODELING WITH BUSINESS RULES

Bruce Silver

DMN Method and Style, the Practitioner's Guide to Decision Modeling with Business Rules

By Bruce Silver
ISBN 978-0-9823681-5-2

Published by Cody-Cassidy Press, Altadena, CA 91001 USA
Contact
        info@cody-cassidy.com
        +1 (831) 685-8803

Library of Congress Subject Headings
Industrial management--Decision making--Mathematical models
Information visualization
Process control -- Data processing -- Management.
Business -- Data processing -- Management.
Management information systems.
Agile software development.

Cover design by Leyba Associates
60129

TABLE OF CONTENTS

PREFACE IX

FOLLOWING THE PATH OF BPMN X

MAKE WAY FOR DMN XI

WHY I WROTE THIS BOOK XII

WHAT MAKES A DECISION MODEL "GOOD"? XIV

OBJECTIVES XVI

ORGANIZATION OF THE BOOK XVI

ACKNOWLEDGMENTS XVIII

A FINAL WORD XIX

PART I: BUSINESS DECISION MANAGEMENT 1

1. WHAT IS BUSINESS DECISION MANAGEMENT? 3

DECISIONS DRIVE BUSINESS 4

THE BUSINESS VALUE OF MODEL-BASED BDM 5

BDM, BIG DATA, AND PREDICTIVE ANALYTICS 7

BDM AND BPM 8

BDM, EVENT PROCESSING, AND INTERNET OF THINGS 10

PART II: THE DMN STANDARD 13

2. WHAT IS DMN? 15

WHAT IS A DECISION? 15

    Decision Tables 15

    No ORs or Parentheses 17

    Logic Transparency 17

ORIGINS OF THE STANDARD 18

DMN OVERVIEW 20

    1. Decision Requirements Diagram (DRD) 20

    2. Decision Table 21

    3. FEEL 22

    4. Boxed Expression 22

    5. Metamodel and Schema 23

WHAT'S NOT IN THE STANDARD 24

RELATING DRD TO DECISION TABLES AND BPMN 25

DECLARATIVE DECISION LOGIC 26

A Hierarchy of Decisions 28
    The Value of Hierarchical Decision Structure 28
DRD and the Business Decision as a Whole 29
    What Is the Business Decision as a Whole? 30
End-to-End Decision Logic and the DMN Method 33
    BPMN Describes Decision Implementation..............................36
    Does DRD Prescribe an Order of Execution?............................36
Three Meanings of "Decision" 38
Value Expressions.. 38
DMN Conformance Levels 39

3. Decision Requirements **41**
Decision Requirements Diagram (DRD) 41
Decision Services 47
Business Knowledge Models 48
Business Context and Motivation 49

4. Decision Logic at Conformance Levels 1 and 2 ....**51**
The Big Picture.. 52
    Variables..53
    Datatypes 53
S-FEEL.. 54
    Names 55
    Literals 56
    Ranges 57
    Expressions 57
Literal Expressions 58
Decision Tables... 59
    Variable Name and Output Label 60
    Input Expression 60
    Input and Output Values 61
    Input Entry 62
    Output Entry 64
    Decision Rules 64
    Compound Output 64
    Hit Policy 65
    Completeness Indicator 66
    Table Orientation 67
Business Knowledge Models 68

5. Decision Logic at Conformance Level 3 ....**71**
Boxed Expressions 71
Context.. 72
Function Definitions 73
Lists 74
Relations 75
FEEL.. 75

What Is FEEL? 76
FEEL Names 77
Datatypes 78
Ternary Logic 78
Path Expressions 79
Built-In Functions 79
FEEL Operators 83
IMPORTS 85
DMN Import 86
XSD Import 86
XML Import 87
EXAMPLE: COLLECTIONS OF CARS CHALLENGE 88

6.   LENDING EXAMPLE WALKTHROUGH 91
OVERALL DECISION FLOW 91
THE STRATEGY DECISION 93
Bureau Call Type 95
Pre-bureau Risk category 96
Eligibility 97
Application Risk Score 98
Pre-Bureau Affordability 98
Required Monthly Installment 101
THE ROUTING DECISION 103
Post-Bureau Affordability 105
Post-Bureau Risk Category 105
THE ADJUDICATION DECISION 106

7.   METAMODEL AND SCHEMA 109
ELEMENT REFERENCES 110
DMNELEMENT AND NAMEDELEMENT 110
DEFINITIONS 111
namespace 112
expressionLanguage and typeLanguage 113
exporter and exporterVersion 113
IMPORT 113
ITEMDEFINITION 114
DECISION 115
question and allowedAnswers 116
variable and typeRef 116
expression 118
informationRequirement 118
knowledgeRequirement 119
authorityRequirement 119
Other Info 119
INPUTDATA 120
BUSINESSKNOWLEDGEMODEL 120
DECISIONSERVICE 122
EXPRESSION 122

literalExpression 123

INVOCATION 124

DECISIONTABLE 126

    context 130

    list and relation 131

PART III: METHOD AND STYLE 135

8. WHAT MAKES A GOOD DECISION TABLE? 137

VANTHIENEN 137

    Sixteen Commandments 137

    Clear and Consistent 139

ROSS 141

    Layout 142

    Scope, Restrictions, Exceptions, and Defaults 143

    Structured Business Vocabulary 144

    Procedural Dependencies 145

    Anomalies 146

THE DECISION MODEL (VON HALLE AND GOLDBERG) 147

    TDM Notation 148

    TDM Style 149

NORMALIZATION 152

    First Normal Form 152

    Second Normal Form 153

    Third Normal Form 153

RECOMMENDATIONS COMPARED 154

    Condition Heading 155

    Conclusion Heading 155

    Orientation 155

    Scope, Restrictions, and Table Completeness 155

    Hit Policy 156

    Maximum Contraction 156

    Table Cells Optimized for Visual Scanning 156

    Standardized Business Vocabulary 157

9. DMN STYLE 159

NAMING 159

    Removing the Spaces 159

    Name Should Suggest the Type 160

DECISION TABLE STYLE 161

    Rules-as-Rows 161

    Input Entry Cell Merging 162

    Hit Policy 162

    Compound Output 162

    Maximum Contraction of Rules 163

    Input Expressions 164

    Input and Output Values 165

    Input Entries 165

    Output Entries 167

    Table Completeness and Null 167
    Null in Conditional Decisions 167
    Action Subtables 170

10. DMN METHOD **173**
  DECISION MODELING METHODOLOGIES 173
    "Decision Table Methodology" 173
    TDM – STEP Methodology 173
    FICO – Decision Requirements Analysis 175
    Similarities and Differences 176
  SYNTHESIS AND DEPARTURE 176
    Top-Down Decomposition 178
    Decision Logic vs Process Logic 179
  OUTLINE OF THE DMN METHOD 180

11. DECISION LOGIC PATTERNS **183**
  ARITHMETIC FORMULA PATTERNS 183
    Unconditional Computation 183
    Reusable Literal Expression – BKM Invocation 185
    Literal Function Invocation 185
    Conditional Computation 187
  CLASSIFICATION PATTERNS 187
    All-or-Nothing Pattern 187
    Category-Score Pattern 191
    Category with Reasons Pattern 191
  ITERATION PATTERNS 192
    Iteration without for..return 194
  TABLE LOOKUP AND QUERY PATTERNS 196
    Table Lookup Pattern - Filter Expression 197
    Table Lookup Pattern – Decision Table 198
    Table Join Pattern 199
    Adding, Removing, Renaming, or Rearranging Table Columns 202
  SORTING AND OPTIMIZATION PATTERNS 202
    Min and Max 202
    Meets a Threshold 203
    Sort Function 203
    Make a Burger Challenge 205
  ACTION SUBTABLE PATTERNS 207
  VALIDATION PATTERNS 208
    Invalid Data 208
    Validation Rules 208
    Error List Pattern 209

12. TOP-DOWN DRD DECOMPOSITION **211**
  DECOMPOSITION STRATEGY 211
  LENDING EXAMPLE REVISITED 213
    First Order Decomposition 214
    Role of BPMN in Decision Modeling 218

Priority of Supporting Decisions...219
Full Decomposition 222
Prequalification 223
Qualification 227
SUMMARY OF THE DECOMPOSITION 229

13. DATA MODELING AND BUSINESS GLOSSARY **233**
DATA MODELING FOR DMN 233
Logical Data Model...233
DMN Data Models 234
XSD Data Models 236
BUSINESS GLOSSARY 237
DMN Elements Supporting a Glossary and Data Model.............................239

14. EXAMPLE: AUTO INSURANCE PREMIUM **241**
USERV PRODUCT DERBY 241
Rules 242
Fact Model...245
Decision Process 247
First-Order Decomposition 247
Fact Model...248
EligibilityScore without Iteration 250
Premium without Iteration 253
Adding Iteration 256
LEVEL 2 SOLUTION 261

15. EXAMPLE: MORTGAGE RECOMMENDER **265**
Decision Process 265
DRD Decomposition..266
Fact Model...267
LoanTypes..269
Bankrates 270
MatchingProducts 271
FinancialMetrics 271
CUSTOMER REQUEST AND DECISION RESPONSE 273

16. DECISION ANALYSIS AND TESTING...**277**
COMPLETENESS 277
CONSISTENCY 279
DECISION ANALYSIS..280
ANALYTICS: COMPLETING THE CIRCLE 283

17. THE ROAD AHEAD..**285**
CHOOSING A DMN TOOL...286
IMPROVING THE STANDARD 287

APPENDIX A. A QUICK BPMN TUTORIAL **293**
APPENDIX B. REAL-WORLD EXAMPLE: DODD-FRANK REGULATORY COMPLIANCE **295**
    COMPREHENSIVE CAPITAL ADEQUACY REVIEW 296
    LIQUIDITY COVERAGE RATIO 296
        Example: HQLA Level 2B Classification 297
INDEX **299**
ABOUT THE AUTHOR **305**
    APPENDIX B AUTHOR 305

Preface

Decisions are so pervasive and deeply woven into the fabric of business that we often take them for granted:

- *What is the total price – including applicable discounts, surcharges, taxes, and shipping – for this order?*

- *Is the information on this form complete and valid?*

- *What upsell offer should be made to this customer?*

These decisions are more than arbitrary human judgment. They are based on some *defined business logic*. Optimizing operational performance, risk, and compliance in the face of a complex and ever-changing business environment requires the logic of these decisions to be determined and maintained by the business, not delegated to programmers. In the past that has not been easy. But things are changing.

Here we are talking not about strategic decisions – *Should we acquire company XYZ?* – but the *operational decisions* that occur every day. They perform calculations and approvals, check compliance, and suggest next-best actions... all based on some defined decision logic applied repeatedly in the course of business. The logic of operational decisions is fundamentally based on *business – not technical – considerations*. If you tried to explain it to someone outside your organization, you'd probably begin by saying, "Well, it depends on a number of factors..."

To explain the decision logic in complete detail, you'd have to list all of those factors, enumerate their possible values, and then specify all the rules that determine the decision result for any possible set of factor values. For years, organizations have tried to do this in lengthy "business requirements" documents handed off to programmers for implementation, either in a business application or a dedicated *Business Rule Engine*.

In applications such as underwriting, benefits administration, and risk management, companies have long relied on Business Rule Engine (BRE) technology to automate the decision logic. So-called *Business Rule Management Systems* (BRMS) surround the BRE with a proprietary rule language, a repository for ruleset versioning and test, and a governance/change control framework. While those systems were intended to give control over business logic to business analysts, in practice such control frequently remained a prerogative of software developers. Historically, the business stakeholders' role has been to try to specify the *requirements* for that decision logic, typically in spreadsheets and text-based requirements documents, which are then interpreted by technical architects and programmers (as best they can) and then translated into executable code. But that handoff is not an efficient or effective way of defining decision logic that is continually changing. *Because decision logic is business logic, business people should be able to define and maintain it themselves.*

Now, for the first time, we have an industry standard executable decision modeling language – *Decision Model and Notation (DMN* - designed for business users. DMN allows business analysts, business architects, and regular business people themselves to model and maintain the decision logic that impacts their daily operations, rather than simply write business requirements for programmers.

A *decision model* is not the same as a text-based requirements document. A decision model communicates through structured diagrams and tables, not unstructured text. Unlike text-based requirements, diagrams and tables can be reviewed simultaneously by all stakeholders. Moreover, since the model conforms to a defined structure and rules, it can define decision requirements more precisely, completely, and consistently than a business requirements document ever could. A DMN model can even be *directly executed* on a decision engine without requiring translation into the rule language of a proprietary BRE.

DMN is an *industry standard*, maintained by the Object Management Group (OMG).[1] That means its concepts and formats are not owned by a tool vendor or consulting company. In fact, DMN is supported by *modeling tools and decision engines from many vendors*.[2] Moreover, the DMN specification defines an XML format for interchanging decision models between tools. This promises not only to bridge the business-IT divide that has long gotten in the way of business agility in decision management, but also to disrupt the current market landscape, dominated by proprietary BRMS offerings. With a standard comes increased competition, new business-friendly formats and methods, and dramatically lower technology cost. This is the promise of DMN.

Following the Path of BPMN

We have a recent precedent for this in the case of *business process modeling*. Ten to fifteen years ago, in order to bring automation to a business process, business requirements were captured either in text-based requirements documents handed off to programmers or in modeling tools embedded within a proprietary *Business Process Management Suite* (BPMS). In other words, to do any business process modeling you had to buy a runtime system first.

---

[1] http://www.omg.org

[2] A Live Catalog of DMN Supporting Tools may be found at
http://openjvm.jvmhost.net/DMNtools/

The emergence of the BPMN standard in 2003-2005 revolutionized business process management. All of a sudden you could describe *any* business process – manual or automated – as a set of diagrams with precise meaning defined by an industry standard, not by a proprietary tool. Because it was business-friendly, BPMN 1.x was rapidly adopted by business and technical users alike, and proprietary process modeling tools quickly died out. The shift to model-based requirements based on standards led to radically new BPM project methodologies in which business users collaborated with developers directly in the implementation phase.

Although BPMN 1.x was not executable, it was believed at the time that mapping BPMN to a similar process execution language standard called BPEL would suffice, since many of the leading process automation suites, like IBM, Oracle, and SAP, already supported BPEL. But in the end, business users rejected that idea. There were BPMN diagrams that BPEL could not execute without redrawing them in a way that looked completely unfamiliar to the original modelers.

Consequently, in 2008-2009 those same BPEL vendors led the development of BPMN 2.0, which made BPMN both a diagramming language and a process execution language. Not only was modeling standardized, but much of the automation runtime was standardized as well. This led to a significant transformation of the BPM technology landscape, with an explosion of new tools, lower costs, open source software, and all the rest. It was nothing short of a revolution.

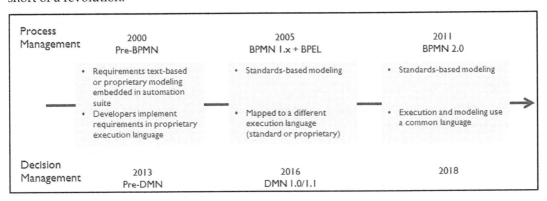

Figure 1. DMN following the path of BPMN

Make Way for DMN

Decision management is embarking now on that same path (Figure 1). With DMN we now have standards-based decision modeling geared to business analysts and ordinary business users. Instantly, that moves us past the problems of text-based decision requirements documents. In the longer run, it promises to make model-based decision execution pervasive in business systems.

DMN's two most prominent features are:

- *Decision requirements diagrams* (DRD), able to depict complex end-to-end business decisions as a hierarchy of decision nodes, supporting decisions, and input data, annotated with links to policies, business rules, and analytics models that provide an authoritative basis for the decision logic.[3]

- *Decision tables*, tabular specifications of the logic of an individual decision node in a DRD. Decision tables have been in use for decades, but DMN specifies a standard syntax and formats for them.

Unlike the first generation of BPMN, DMN already defines an *executable expression language* called FEEL, so DMN models, at least in principle, can be executed. I say "in principle" because, as of this writing, few FEEL-based DMN tools are available. So far, most have been substituting their own tool-specific expression languages with FEEL-like capabilities. In fact, several first generation DMN tools are content to serve as a modeling front end to commercial BREs such as IBM, FICO, and RedHat, requiring translation of DMN into a different rule language. But the arc of BPMN's history suggests that this is a temporary state of the market. Ultimately DMN/FEEL engines will exist with production-level performance and reliability, and the decision management revolution will be fully realized.

Why I Wrote This Book

When the DMN 1.0 specification was finalized in November 2014, I had been doing BPMN training for almost eight years. My book *BPMN Method and Style*[4] was in its second edition, translated into German, Japanese, and Spanish. Through all that experience I had learned the difference between an OMG specification and its effective use, which requires firm guidelines. My guidelines, based on the "Method and Style approach," is founded on a few basic principles:

1. What counts in the model is *what you can see in the diagrams*, not details buried in the nether reaches of a tool.

2. Modeling is fundamentally *a disciplined exercise not a creative one*. Creativity is critical to designing *better* processes or *better* decisions, but translating some given logic into a model should be as "mechanical" as possible.

3. While the spec may allow many different ways to model the same bit of logic, differing in compactness, ease of understanding and analysis, ease of change, and other factors, it's best for everyone to *standardize on one way* to model a particular type of scenario.

---

[3] DRD comes from a FICO methodology called Decision Requirements Analysis, detailed by Alan Fish in his book *Knowledge Automation*. Fish is co-chair of the DMN task force in OMG.

[4] Bruce Silver, *BPMN Method and Style 2nd edition* (Aptos: Cody-Cassidy Press, 2011), http://www.amazon.com/dp/0982368119/

On reading the DMN spec, I saw immediately that several factors that had made my previous BPMN work successful were in place again with DMN:

- The opportunity to transform an undisciplined text-oriented practice of specifying decision requirements into a disciplined model-driven effort. There is a widely held belief that business users cannot "follow the rules," but my BPMN experience had proven that to be false. You just need to show them how to do it.

- A specification extremely difficult to decipher, even upon close and extensive rereading. OMG specifications make no attempt to be "teaching" documents, and the DMN spec is no exception. Moreover, the diagrams and examples in the spec are often more confusing than clarifying.

- The complete absence in the specification of any methodology or practical guidance for how to use DMN's many features.

I had previously done an engagement or two with Larry Goldberg of KPI,[5] co-author with Barb von Halle of *The Decision Model*[6] (TDM), that showed the client how to apply decision modeling and process modeling in tandem based on a business-oriented methodology. TDM was, I believe, the first serious effort to make decision modeling a true business-oriented discipline, and a number of TDM ideas are incorporated in DMN. My original thought for the book was to take the DMN standard, which differs from TDM in several significant ways, and apply much of the TDM methodology and "style rules" to it.

But that is not the book I ended up writing.

As I was rereading the DMN spec for the umpteenth time, certain sections remained unclear or contradicted other sections. The only real example in the spec, a Lending decision, seemed to omit critical features of the standard. For example, all decision tables referenced only literal values, but the spec says they could reference variables, as well. That's a pretty big omission! Some chapters of the spec, like the one on FEEL, remained impenetrable after multiple attempts. The purpose of the "boxed expression" format was never really explained. To top it off, the XML schema – the key deliverable for DMN implementers – contained critical bugs.

I began firing off questions to the DMN LinkedIn group.[7] I quickly became such a pest that Gary Hallmark, a contributor to the group and co-chair of the DMN 1.1 Revision Task Force (RTF) in OMG, invited me to join the RTF. The main purpose of a "minor revision" RTF is to clarify the standard and fix bugs, so I was happy to do it. That turned out to be a transformative experience, as it gradually became clear, after six months of weekly

---

[5] Now Sapiens DECISION

[6] Barbara von Halle and Larry Goldberg, *The Decision Model* (Boca Raton: Taylor and Francis, 2010), http://www.amazon.com/dp/1420082817/

[7] https://www.linkedin.com/groups/4225568

teleconferences, what the spec was struggling to say.[8] In time I discovered aspects of the standard that even its original authors failed to appreciate. For example, I saw how a prominent feature of the standard, the *Decision Requirements Diagram* (DRD), makes DMN fundamentally different from TDM, and suggests not only a very different methodology but a relationship between DMN and BPMN that is different from the one discussed in the spec.

The DMN 1.1 RTF completed its work in November 2015. Official publication is in the hands of the editors at OMG. The bugs in the schema have been fixed and some vague passages in the spec text have been cleaned up. For example, it's clear now that decision table cells may reference variables! But while the interior plumbing has changed completely from DMN 1.0, the features modelers are most interested in, decision tables and DRDs, still look the same as they did in the original version. On the downside, the DMN 1.1 spec text still tends to obfuscate more than enlighten. The FEEL chapter is as impenetrable as ever, and the Lending example decision table cells still contain only literal values. It was impossible to fix those things by the DMN 1.1 deadline, and to be honest, *some RTF members like them just as they are*. So to dig beneath the surface of DMN, you'll just have to read this book.

Those endless re-readings of the spec text, edits to the metamodel and schema, and vigorous debates in the RTF meetings also produced an unexpected bonus, a much deeper understanding of *what DMN can be when it is fully implemented by tool vendors*. As of this writing, DMN tools have implemented only a portion of the specification. Full implementation should include two key features inadequately explained in the spec: FEEL and boxed expressions. I believe these hold the key to advancing, in the terms of Figure 1, from BPMN 1.x-like decision models to BPMN 2-like decision models: *a unified language supporting both modeling and execution*.

While boxed expressions and FEEL are critical to the long-term success of DMN as a standard, the world doesn't really know about them yet. And so, in addition to my original objective of teaching modelers how to use DMN effectively, the book has the additional goal of encouraging those modelers to demand that tool vendors fully implement these features of the spec.

What Makes a Decision Model "Good"?

DMN Method and Style is aimed at creating decision models that not only are "valid" according to the DMN specification, but that could be called "good DMN," models that communicate the decision logic clearly, completely, and consistently through printed diagrams and tables. But what makes a decision model "good"?

---

[8] I'm not the only one who was confused. Most first-generation tools also omit the ability to reference variables in decision table cells, and they ignore boxed expressions, which I have come to understand as an essential part of the DMN "notation."

There is a substantial literature describing what makes a good decision table, including publications (all predating DMN) by Vanthienen,[9] Ross,[10] and von Halle and Goldberg.[11] There is general agreement among these authors that a well-designed decision table should be *complete* (cover all possible combinations of input values), *consistent* (provide a single conclusion value for any particular combination of input values), and as *compact* as possible (within the defined table format). Also, there is some consensus that the table should be organized to facilitate analysis of completeness and consistency by visual inspection. The specific recommendations of these authors differ, of course, and they must be adapted to the decision table structure defined by DMN. *DMN style* applies those principles with specific recommendations applicable to DMN decision tables, and adds others – for example, concerning naming of decisions and input data – that attempt to communicate more meaning through the printed diagrams.

However, the literature provides little guidance on how best to decompose a complex operational decision into a DRD. This is the *DMN Method*, and it represents a new and original approach. The Method begins by understanding the *business decision as a whole* and places it at the top of the Decision Requirements Diagram. That might sound obvious, but actually the concept or term "business decision as a whole" is never mentioned in the DMN specification. Nor is it mentioned or used in the methodologies of Alan Fish's *Knowledge Automation*,[12] the source of the DRD idea, or *The Decision Model*. Instead, all of those sources describe the business decision as a whole as a *business process* defined by *a companion BPMN model*. In fact, the DMN spec explicitly describes the DRD as the link between decisions in a decision model and activities in a business process model.

But that interpretation actually sells the DRD short, because DRD is able to capture, in a single diagram, a high-level view of the entire end-to-end decision logic, even when that logic is executed in multiple steps separated in time. In addition to decision services that execute model-defined decision logic, the DRD may include human decisions and external decisions, in which the decision logic is not defined in the model. *In the Method, the DRD describes, on its own, the decision logic of the business decision as a whole.*

This use of DRD is consistent with DMN concepts and rules, but it leads to a different model structure and a different methodology than one that relies on a BPMN process model to communicate the end-to-end decision logic. The DMN Method starts with the business decision as a whole and the available input data elements. The top decision node in the DRD represents the end-to-end business decision: *Is the insurance application accepted, and what is the price?* The Method then guides the modeler in the *top-down decomposition* of that decision

---

[9] http://www.brcommunity.com/b618.php

[10] http://www.brsolutions.com/downloads/TableSpeak%20Primer.pdf

[11] von Halle and Goldberg, *The Decision Model*

[12] Alan Fish, *Knowledge Automation: How to Implement Decision Management in Business Processes* (Wiley Corporate F&A, Kindle Edition, 2012)

node into a hierarchy of supporting decisions, and ultimately down to the input data. To aid in that decomposition, the Method also provides a set of *common decision logic patterns* useful for modeling specific scenarios.

Objectives

The goals of this book, then, are threefold:

1. To clarify for modelers the concepts, formats, and standard expression language of DMN, as defined in the DMN 1.1 specification.

2. To define the characteristics of "good DMN" – models that succeed in fulfilling that essential mission of precise, clear, and complete communication of the decision logic – along with a methodology and modeling style elements designed to achieve them. Method and Style is layered on top of the DMN spec but is not the official specification. The book will be careful to distinguish the requirements of the specification from those of Method and Style.

3. To explain to implementers the technical aspects of the standard: the metamodel and schema, FEEL, and the boxed expression format, with the goal of encouraging tool providers to incorporate *all* the major features of the standard, not just a few.

Just as there are for BPMN, there will be a wide assortment of DMN books available, and I expect this one will include more technical detail than most. But, like DMN itself, the book is primarily intended for business users, not developers. And just as with BPMN, there may be some who say that by venturing beyond DRDs and simple decision tables, I am making DMN "too hard for business people." But after nine years of BPMN Method and Style training for thousands of business people and business analysts, I know this is not the case. Non-technical practitioners of decision modeling can learn DMN, even the advanced Level 3 patterns, and apply it well in their daily work.

Let me say it again: DMN was created for business users not programmers. But like BPMN, using it well requires a disciplined approach, lots of examples, and a clear methodology. Presenting that is the real objective of the book.

Organization of the Book

The book is organized into three parts, covering Business Decision Management, the DMN Standard, and DMN Method and Style.

Chapter 1 explains the concepts and objectives of Business Decision Management, the background and business value of decision modeling, and its application to risk and compliance, predictive analytics, and the Internet of Things.

Chapters 2-7 explain the DMN 1.1 standard, as described in the specification.

- Chapter 2 presents basic decision modeling concepts, the origins of the DMN standard, and an overview of DMN's five key components.

- Chapter 3 explains the elements of the Decision Requirements Diagram. DRDs provide a high-level view of end-to-end decision logic understandable to any business user.

- Chapter 4 discusses decision logic at Conformance Levels 1 and 2, with a focus on DMN decision tables. Conformance Level 2 is DMN's baseline for executable decision logic, based on a simple business-oriented expression language called S-FEEL.

- Chapter 5 discusses decision logic at Conformance Level 3, including a comprehensive explanation of the FEEL language and boxed expressions.

- Chapter 6 presents a step-by-step walkthrough of the Lending decision example from the DMN specification, illustrating the various decision table formats and the linkage between the DRD and detailed decision logic. DMN is best learned by studying examples, and this one shows how all the pieces fit together in a basic end-to-end decision model. Chapter 12 later presents an alternative model for the same decision logic, but following Method and Style.

- Chapter 7, aimed at DMN implementers, explains the DMN 1.1 metamodel and schema, significantly changed from DMN 1.0.

Chapters 8-17 explain DMN Method and Style.

- Chapter 8 summarizes the literature on what makes a good decision table, as background to DMN Style.

- Chapter 9 presents DMN Style, a set of recommendations for modelers, with emphasis on element naming and decision tables.

- Chapter 10 reviews the literature on decision modeling methodology, and then presents an overview of the DMN Method.

- Chapter 11 discusses common patterns used in DMN decision logic, including arithmetic computation, classification patterns, iteration patterns, table lookup and query patterns, sorting and optimization patterns, action subtable patterns, and validation patterns.

- Chapter 12 explains top-down decomposition of the DRD using the DMN Method, illustrated by restructuring the Lending decision discussed in Chapter 6.

- Chapter 13 discusses data modeling for DMN and elements of a Business Glossary.

- Chapters 14 and 15 present detailed examples of advanced decision logic modeled using DMN Method and Style and the patterns of Chapter 12. The first determines approval and annual premium for auto insurance, requiring iteration over cars and drivers on the application. The second is a mortgage product recommendation, involving iteration and table query patterns. While the logic of these examples may seem daunting at first glance, taking the time to work through them in detail lets you appreciate the expressive power of DMN. You don't need to be a programmer to understand them. If you can use the Formulas menu of Excel, you can learn to create DMN models like these.

- Chapter 16 discusses decision analysis and testing, a capability of decision modeling tools that is not part of the DMN specification but is a critical element of any decision modeling project. The chapter discusses completeness checking, consistency checking, decision simulation and analysis, using examples from the Signavio tool.

- Chapter 17 summarizes what is important about DMN, what to look for in a DMN tool, and the path to improving the standard.

- Appendix A is a very brief tutorial on BPMN.

- Appendix B provides a real-world example of business decision management in global banking today.

Acknowledgments

In the course of preparing this book, I have requested and received a great wealth of explanation, background information, opinion, encouragement, and reviewer comments from many people, and I would like here to thank those who gave it so generously.

Larry Goldberg of KPI (now Sapiens DECISION) first introduced me to decision modeling and encouraged me to think more seriously about the relationship between decisions and process modeling. His book *The Decision Model* announced to the BDM community the message I have long preached in the BPMN world: *Business users, you can do disciplined modeling yourselves!*

Gary Hallmark of Oracle not only invited me to join the DMN 1.1 RTF but took extra time to help me understand FEEL, boxed expressions, and other "hidden gems" of DMN. It's why the book I ended up writing is so different from the book I started out to write. We battled at times over the metamodel and schema, but in the end, together we made it a lot better!

James Taylor of Decision Management Solutions, author of the Decision Management Manifesto and the original evangelist of BDM, has helped me understand the decision management market and its forerunners, and has provided valuable comments and advice.

Alan Fish of FICO, inventor of the DRD, also helped me with valuable clarifications, a great methodological starting point, and a well-written book, *Knowledge Automation*. His comments on an early draft of the book have been extremely valuable.

Gil Ronen of Sapiens DECISION provided not only the basics of the Mortgage Recommender example of Chapter 15 but many valuable comments on the draft.

Amid all the conflicting opinions about what makes a decision table "good," Jan Vanthienen of KU Leuven was the one who convinced me why *Unique* decision tables are the right way to go, even when they are not the most compact. He also provided me many examples from the academic literature that demonstrate that while the DMN standard may be new, many of its ideas are not.

Gero Decker and Bastian Steinert of Signavio not only offered me use of their DMN tool for examples in the book but added features in the tool to assist my purpose. Now *that* is a responsive partner! Also, Gero was the one who suggested using *patterns* as an organizing principle for decision logic, and that became a cornerstone of the Method.

Jacob Feldman of Open Rules not only provided detailed comments on the draft, but as overseer of the DMCommunity website,[13] he continues to provide the most interesting publicly available examples of decision models.

Aaron Sayles, a Senior Financial Implementation Consultant with extensive implementation experience in risk and regulatory reporting, contributed Appendix B, a compelling here-and-now example of the need for business decision management in the new regulatory compliance regime affecting banks around the world.

I also would like to acknowledge most helpful interactions with Nick Broom, Falko Menge, Will Thomas, Ron Ross, Denis Gagne, and Carol Leyba. Thanks to all of you.

A Final Word

Finally, let me say that many of the reviewer comments took issue with certain details of the DMN standard itself. I myself do not agree with everything in the spec, nor, I am quite sure, does anyone else on the drafting committee. The standard is based on compromise, give and take among many intelligent and strong-willed individuals. But I have tried in the book to present DMN as it actually is specified, not as I wish it were specified. Even the Method and Style recommendations are intended to be layered on top of the rules of the specification, not calls to disregard or rewrite parts of the spec. DMN will surely evolve, and OMG provides an open process for all to participate in that evolution.

Bruce Silver
Pasadena, CA, January, 2016

---

[13] https://dmcommunity.wordpress.com/

PART I:
BUSINESS DECISION MANAGEMENT

CHAPTER 1

What Is Business Decision Management?

Like business process management, business intelligence, and similar categories straddling the business-IT divide, *business decision management* (BDM) signifies both a *management discipline* – a particular approach to defining, maintaining, and improving business logic – and a *technology stack* that supports that discipline. The term is relatively new, just a few years old. It was created to signify a new approach to managing the business logic executed on *Business Rule Engines*: more agile and focused, starting from the *key operational decisions* driving business metrics rather than laboriously *discovering business rules*. And just as new standards like BPMN once transformed the landscape of proprietary workflow, application integration, and business process analysis tools into the integrated, standards-based BPM we know today, BDM is now receiving a similar jump-start from the new Decision Modeling and Notation (DMN) standard.

James Taylor, the prime mover of BDM and its most effective evangelist, summarizes it well in his Decision Management Manifesto:

> "Decision Management is an approach that improves day to day business operations. It increases an organization's business agility and adaptability by making its systems easier to monitor and change. It puts Big Data to work improving the effectiveness and profitability of every action. It is a proven framework for effectively applying innovative technologies such as business rules, predictive analytics, and optimization." [14]

---

[14] James Taylor, "The Decision Management Manifesto" (2014), http://www.decisionmanagementsolutions.com/wp-content/uploads/2014/11/Manifesto-White-Paper-October-7.pdf.

A hallmark of the BDM approach is "working top-down." That means starting by thinking about the *decisions* required to meet business objectives, and working down from there to the *business rules* required to make those decisions.

> "Projects go wrong when they focus on details first rather than working top-down. When business rules projects focus on collecting and document business rules first, the result is a 'big bucket of rules' that are hard to manage or implement and often too diffuse to be useful.... A top-down focus on the decisions involved provides structure, context, and business awareness for improved results."[15]

This is meant to contrast with the traditional discipline of *business rules management*, as advocated by Ron Ross and others, which asks practitioners to start by cataloguing all the business rules buried in the company's various policies, application systems, and the heads of subject matter experts. BDM instead adopts a "decisions-first" approach: First, define the *decisions*, then determine the *decision rules* they require. There are many types of business rules. Decision rules are just one of them.

A second fundamental pillar of BDM is that decision logic should be described not by unstructured text but by *models* composed of diagrams and tables with defined structure, syntax, and semantics. That all sounds very technical, but BDM intends these models to be *created and maintained by business people*, not programmers. This intention is a critical underpinning of the DMN standard.

Decisions Drive Business

Decisions are pervasive in business and vary widely in complexity and degree of business impact. *Operational decisions* are those that occur every day, typically affecting a single transaction or customer. For a seller on the Internet, simple operational decisions include things like:

- Is the order information complete?
- Is the requested discount applicable to this order?
- What delivery options are available for this order?

More complex operational decisions include things like:

- Is this mortgage application approved?
- What premium should be charged to this life insurance applicant?
- Which add-on or related products should be offered at checkout?
- What credit terms should we offer to this customer?
- What offer should we make to retain this dissatisfied customer?

---

[15] Taylor, DM Manifesto.

- Which employees should receive a bonus this year?

Strategic decisions, on the other hand, occur infrequently and affect management and control of the overall business. They include things like:

- Should we acquire Company X?
- How many customer service reps should we hire this year?

DMN is intended for *operational decisions.*[16] These cover a wide spectrum. For some, the answer is a *single value* – *yes* or *no,* a number, or a particular selected option. For others, the answer is a *list of values.* Some decisions depend only on information relating to the particular order, customer, or product in question. Others, like the bonus list example above, require some kind of scoring or ranking decision applied to *all* eligible employees before selecting the lucky few.

But these decisions all have something in common. They all can be framed as *questions* for which *the answers can be selected from a domain of possible values,* such as a list of possible text values or a number within a defined range. Although DMN does not use the term, the BDM literature often calls such a data item with a defined domain of allowed values a *fact.* In DMN, decision inputs are also facts, so a decision can be said to *determine an output fact value from a given set of input fact values.* Not all business decisions can be framed in this way, but the ones modeled using DMN all share this trait.

The Business Value of Model-Based BDM

If you work in a decision-intensive industry such as financial services, you might be asking why you should be taking on this new burden of decision modeling and management, instead of the traditional practice of harvesting business rules and handing them off to IT. What is the business value?

A white paper from BDM vendor Signavio[17] provides an excellent summary of how standards-based business decision management addresses today's challenges in decision-intensive industries like financial services, in ways that the traditional business rules approach cannot:

1. Time pressure. Ever-changing regulations impose heavy demands on institutional infrastructure, made more acute by short deadlines for compliance. BDM offloads the burden of defining new decision logic to the business, so IT can focus on adapting

---

[16] According to Alan Fish, "The line [between strategic and operational decisions] is being eroded as capabilities of BDM move toward the strategic end. For example, FICO intend to be able to call optimization models from a DRD within the year, so [these] examples strategic decisions might soon be within the scope of an executable DMN model." Private communication, December 2015.

[17] http://www.signavio.com/resources/white-paper/meeting-8-challenges-financial-compliance-bdm/

the infrastructure. BDM tools allow business users to specify and test even complex decision logic against real and synthetic data and identify at an early stage data quality issues and inconsistencies, avoiding last-minute surprises.

2. Decision complexity. In a global business environment, local variations in rules and regulations can make the decision logic almost overwhelmingly complex. BDM allows the most complex decision logic to be broken down into maintainable units and reusable modules.

3. Lossy translation of requirements. Correct implementation of complex decision logic requires that what is executed is what subject matter experts in the business intend. BDM, using a methodology such as DMN Method and Style, unifies business-oriented decision modeling with automated execution. It is not necessary to translate the decision model to another rule language, so there is no translation loss. What you model is what you get.

4. Faulty requirements. Text-based decision requirements documents are notoriously inconsistent and error-prone. BDM's model-based approach allows gaps and inconsistencies to be rapidly identified, tested, and fixed *before* implementation in the infrastructure.

5. Continual change. Compliance rules often change on a quarterly basis, sometimes even more frequently. Because the decision logic is model-driven and business-transparent, BDM accommodates continual change more easily than a traditional business rules approach.

6. Consistency across the enterprise. Compliance must be applied consistently across a wide range of products and services across the enterprise, managed through a diverse set of business processes. BDM separates decision logic from process logic and organizes it for consistent reuse.

7. Auditability. It's not enough simply to *be* compliant with regulations. You need to be able to *prove* compliance, to demonstrate the business logic that enforces it. With model-based decision logic, every clause of a regulation can be linked to a specific rule or other decision model element, making the decision logic auditable and traceable.

8. Data quality. BDM helps detect data quality problems by checking the datatype and values of input data against their specification in the decision model. Also, while it is not part of the DMN standard, most BDM tools also provide some kind of *business glossary* that both standardizes the business vocabulary and helps screen out bad data.

9. Testability and Execution. BDM provides the ability to test/execute decision logic before it is incorporated into the IT infrastructure. The same business people who create a model also create, execute, and maintain test cases for this model.

BDM, Big Data, and Predictive Analytics

While the list of challenges and BDM benefits above emphasizes regulatory compliance, the issues and BDM advantages apply equally well to maximizing operational performance while minimizing risk. In recent years, the importance of BDM has accelerated sharply with the rise of *Big Data* and the widespread adoption of *predictive analytics*. It used to be that selected customer transaction data, captured in data warehouses, had to be carefully organized in advance to allow analytical reporting. Today, Big Data technology allows essentially all transaction data to be captured and analyzed without knowing in advance the specifics of the analytics of interest.

Predictive analytics looks at past customer transactions in order to predict future ones. As explained by James Taylor,

> "Analytics predict risk: How risky is this customer's application for service, and how should we price it?
>
> Analytics predict fraud: How likely is this claim to be fraudulent, and what should we do about it?
>
> Analytics predict opportunity: What represents the best opportunity to maximize loyalty, and revenue? And when should we promote it?"[18]

The goal of predictive analytics is *insight*: What characteristics of a customer, taken in combination, predict future behavior, such as likelihood to purchase or likelihood to default on a loan? But that insight has little value unless it can be turned into *action*, and that is where BDM comes in. The characteristics of past customer transactions that are the best predictors of risk, fraud, or opportunity in future transactions provide the input data and decision rules needed to answer questions like, *Do we approve or reject the loan? What is the insurance premium for this customer? What promotional offer should we extend to this prospect?*

Figure 2 illustrates the relationship of BDM to analytics. Customer transactions generate information, which is evaluated by *analytical models*. Those models seek correlations between attributes known in advance and resulting transaction outcomes, both good and bad. These modelsare statistical, averaging the transactions of thousands of customers, looking for the best predictors of future outcomes. The analytical models are continually refined, as new "Challenger" predictors are compared against the current "Champions."

The best analytical models determine the *decision rules* applied to new customer transactions to take some *action*: accept or reject the loan application, set the price of the premium, or raise a fraud alert. If you set the rules too tightly – deny credit to too many applicants, or set the price too high – you may lower your risk but at the same time drive away too much business. This is the customer *reaction* to the action of the decision. It's always a balancing act.

---

[18] James Taylor, "Predictive analytics in decision management systems," http://www.slideshare.net/jamet123/predictive-analytics-in-decision-management-systems

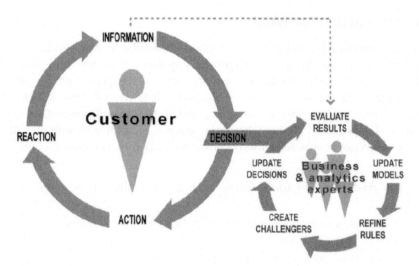

Figure 2. How BDM relates to analytics. Source: James Taylor

That is why BDM is a closed loop, with the decision logic continually changing. A given decision model is intended to produce some optimum combination of opportunity, risk, and compliance. But the business environment is continually changing, and what is optimum today may not be so tomorrow. This is another reason why BDM's *model-driven approach*, which *assumes continual change*, is the right one.

BDM and BPM

For many years, practitioners of business process management and practitioners of business rules management seldom crossed paths. Each discipline barely acknowledged the existence of the other. With the rise of business decision management, that has changed completely. Now, decision models make explicit reference to process models, and process models explicitly reference decisions. Many BPMN tool vendors are now adding DMN editors to their product suite. Why has this come about?

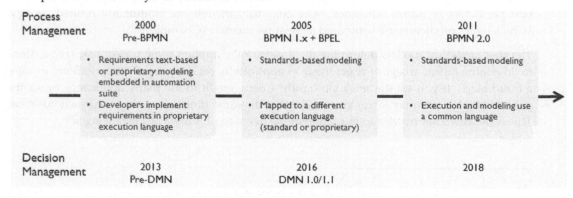

Figure 3. Evolution toward model-driven business-empowered implementation

A lot can be explained by the market evolution diagram discussed in the Preface, and reproduced here (Figure 3). The traditional "business rules market" represents the Pre-DMN phase, emphasizing text-based decision requirements handed off to programmers for interpretation and implementation.

DMN represents a new paradigm: decision requirements based on *models* with defined semantics and formats, empowering business users to more directly specify their decision logic. This objective and mindset has been the underpinning of BPM for a decade, so BDM feels to BPM practitioners and tool vendors like a natural extension.

Moreover, identification of BDM as a distinct but related discipline allows BPM vendors the opportunity to correct a common source of "bad BPMN," *modeling decision logic as process logic*. The fundamental distinction between *decision logic* – determining an output data value based on some combination of input values – and *process logic* – specifying a sequence of actions performed to achieve a desired result – is lost on some process modelers, who like to embed complex decision logic as a flowchart within their BPMN diagrams.

Figure 4 provides an example. The top BPMN diagram depicts an insurance claim process with decision logic embedded as a chain of gateways, the diamond shapes. Both BPM and BDM consider this bad practice, for several reasons:

- It unnecessarily complicates the process logic. The entire network of gateways is really a single decision. It should be modeled as a single decision task (Figure 4, inset).

- It makes the process logic more "brittle." The BPMN model must be revised whenever the decision logic changes.

- It makes the decision logic *procedural*, meaning a fixed order of evaluation. That sequence may not be the most efficient or even the one actually followed in execution. Decision logic definition should be *declarative*, meaning the order of evaluation does not affect the outcome.

- It hides the logic of supporting decisions. A gateway in BPMN tests the value of some data available to the process. In this case, that data is only what is contained in the *claim* (the start message) and *policy data* obtained in the first activity. The determination of the first two gateways – *State of Policy* and *Coverage Available?* – is almost certainly more than simple Boolean (i.e., true/false) test of claim and policy data. The details of those determinations can be described within a decision model, but not by a simple BPMN gateway.

It is better to extract the decision logic, remove it from the business process model, and detail it instead in a separate decision model. This improves the quality, clarity, and agility of both the DMN and BPMN models. The resulting BPMN model (Figure 4, inset) is much simpler. The fact that DMN, the decision modeling standard, and BPMN, the process modeling standard, are managed by the same organization, the Object Management Group (OMG), has helped clarify and harmonize the relationship between the disciplines. In fact, BPMN and DMN provide explicit connection points between the two types of models. Today we are beginning to see tools for business analysts and business users that include both DMN and BPMN editors and a shared model repository.

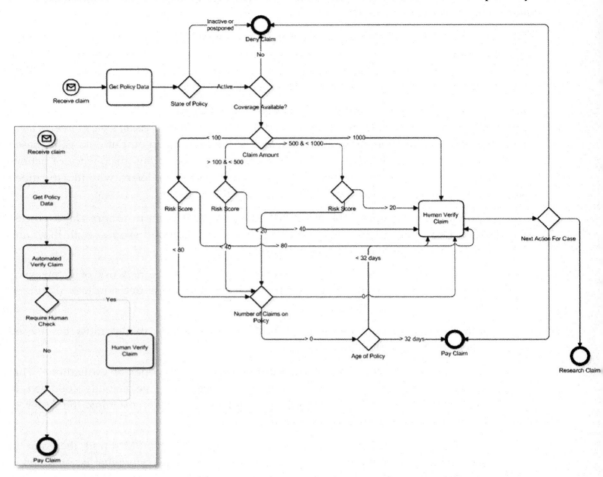

Figure 4. Decision logic modeled as chain of gateways (top) vs a single decision task (inset). Source: Decision Management Solutions[19]

BDM, Event Processing, and Internet of Things

The focus of the DMN specification is on decisions executed by a business process task, but that is by no means the only way DMN can be used. Another application of DMN that ultimately may prove important is event processing, including the Internet of Things.

---

[19] James Taylor, "Decision Management 101," http://www.slideshare.net/Decision-CAMP/decision-camp-2014-james-taylor-decision-management-101

An *event* is a signal that "something happened." Business *systems* can issue events: *a new order has been placed in the ERP system.* Business *processes* can issue events, as well: *Task XYZ is overdue.* Decision logic may be triggered by these common business events. But the real buzz today about event processing concerns the *Internet of Things. Devices* of all sorts, from your car's engine to the Fitbit on your wrist, are continuously spewing events reporting some aspect of their internal state. Each event signal identifies the issuer of the signal, a timestamp, and some relevant payload data.

Some event processing system or infrastructure continuously listens for these events, filters and correlates them with other related events, such as those previously issued by the same device or system, interprets the payload data, and then triggers some action. The filtering, correlating, and interpreting constitute decision logic. Filtering and correlating require a time dimension in the decision logic that is not part of DMN today; the rest could, in principle, use DMN.

To date, DMN has not been widely adopted in event processing or Internet of Things. In these systems, technical details still matter more than business user empowerment. However, once the technical infrastructure for it matures, we could see a need for business to define its own model-driven event decision logic.

PART II:
THE DMN STANDARD

CHAPTER 2

What Is DMN?

What Is a Decision?

The DMN specification defines a *decision* as "the act of determining an output value... from a number of input values, using logic defining how the output is determined from the inputs." In other words, the decision is not the specific outcome value chosen but the application of *business logic,* modeled as a set of *decision rules,* employed to select an output value given some combination of input values. A DMN *decision model* specifies the output value for *any* allowed combination of input values.

A common business decision is approving or rejecting some request, such as an application for insurance. In that case, *approved* and *rejected* would be possible output values of the decision, which might be named *ApprovalStatus*. The inputs to that decision might be things like the applicant's age, gender, medical history, and various risk factors. The *decision logic* means the rules that determine the output value, *approved* or *rejected*, based on the applicant's particular input values.

In DMN, a decision does not specify an *action* to be performed based on the result. It simply determines the value of the decision output, a data item. Any action resulting from a determination of *approved* or *rejected* is outside the scope of the decision model. Typically it would be modeled as an *activity* in an associated *business process model*. Also outside the scope of the decision are any actions required to obtain the input values, such as querying a business system or requesting information from an external service provider. Those actions would also be activities performed in a business process that executes the decision.

Decision Tables

The most familiar form of decision logic in DMN is the *decision table*. Decision tables have been around in various forms for over thirty years, but DMN defines specific formats and syntax for them.

In a decision table, the decision logic is equivalent to a list of *if..then* expressions...

```
If [input condition 1] then [output value 1]
If [input condition 2] then [output value 2]
...
```

... displayed in one of several tabular formats. Each *If-then* expression is called a *decision rule*. An example might be:

```
If AccountStatus = "Delinquent" then MaxCredit = 0;
If AccountStatus = "OK" and CreditScore < 600 then MaxCredit = 0;
If AccountStatus = "OK" and 600<=CreditScore<=720 then MaxCredit =
500;
If AccountStatus = "OK" and CreditScore > 720 then MaxCredit =
1000;
```

As a decision table, it would look like this:

U		Account Status		CreditScore	MaxCredit
		(OK,Delinquent)		[0..900]	Currency ($)
1	■	Delinquent		-	$ 0
2	■	OK	<	600	$ 0
3	■	OK	∈	[600..720]	$ 250
4	■	OK	>	720	$ 1000

Figure 5. A decision table

Here *AccountStatus* is an input to the *MaxCredit* decision. Its value, either *OK* or *Delinquent*, is possibly not retrieved directly from a business system but instead is another decision! It is quite common that one decision depends on such *supporting decisions*, which may depend in turn on their own supporting decisions. These chains of supporting decisions can be quite long. The output of a supporting decision becomes an input to the *dependent decision*. In fact, complex decision logic is almost always modeled that way, and a goal of this book is to show you how to decompose the logic of a complex decision into a network of simple decisions that can be easily understood and maintained by business users.

In DMN, each *decision* defines a *variable* with the same name that holds its output value.[20] The variable representing a supporting decision is then referenced by the *value expression* of the dependent decision. For example, here the decision *MaxCredit* uses the result of the supporting decision *AccountStatus* by referencing the variable *AccountStatus* in its decision logic.

---

[20] This is new in DMN 1.1. In DMN 1.0, variables were defined in *information requirements* not in decisions. The outward appearance of the decision table is unchanged, however.

No ORs or Parentheses

In a decision table, the input conditions of any decision rule must be ANDed together. Combining them with logical OR is not allowed because the order of operations is *ambiguous without parentheses*. For example,

```
InputX = "a" AND InputY = "b" OR InputZ = "c"
```

is ambiguous, because

```
(InputX = "a" AND InputY = "b") OR InputZ = "c"
```

does not mean the same thing as

```
InputX = "a" AND (InputY = "b" OR InputZ = "c").
```

In the default decision table format, the inputs are columns and can't be grouped with parentheses, so DMN avoids the ambiguity by forbidding ORed input conditions in a decision table. It's part of the *declarative principle*, which says that the order of evaluating decision inputs does not affect the outcome. This only works if their input conditions are ANDed together.

In DMN, *OR'ed conditions are indicated by additional rules*. For example, instead of

```
If (InputX = "a" AND InputY = "b") OR InputZ = "c"
  then output value = 1,
```

DMN requires you to model it this way:

```
If InputX = "a" AND InputY = "b" then output value = 1
If InputZ = "c" then output value = 1
```

Each IF statement is a separate decision rule. In this case, both rules select *output value = 1*, so that if *either* rule is true, the output value 1 is selected. In Figure 5, we see that the first two rules together are equivalent to

```
If AccountStatus="Delinquent" or (AccountStatus="OK" and
CreditScore<600) then MaxCredit=0;
```

By modeling ORs as additional rules, even complex decision logic can be handled by decision tables, even though any individual rule contains only ANDed conditions. It is possible, however, for a rule to OR possible values of a *single input*, for example:

```
If InputX = ("a" or "b") then output value = 1.
```

Decision table logic is detailed in Chapter 4.

Logic Transparency

The great thing about decision tables is the decision logic is *transparent*. The rules that determine the decision result are *visible and understandable to a business user*. The condition expressions in each rule are simple and unambiguous. The condition expression for any column and row concatenates the *input expression* shown in the column heading with the *input entry* for that table cell. Each row of the table is a *decision rule*. A decision rule for which all condition expressions are true is said to *match* and its *output entry* value is selected as the decision table outcome.

Notice in Figure 5 that below each input expression is displayed its *domain of allowed values*. Decision tables are not required to define these, but it is a good idea, since they allow the modeler to verify by visual inspection that the decision logic is *complete*, meaning all combinations of input values are accounted for.

Those things make a critical difference. These three characteristics of DMN decision tables...

1. Rules visible and understandable to business users

2. Input conditions visually verifiable for completeness

3. Rules visually verifiable for self-consistency

... are the very things that empower "the business" – business analysts, business architects, and line of business end users – to *take charge of their decisions*! You might ask, why worry about visual verification when a decision modeling tool can validate the decision logic anyway? In reality, the days of paper-and-pencil decision modeling are probably over, and most DMN tools should be able to verify completeness and consistency automatically. Nevertheless, the ability to visually inspect decision tables adds confidence in and maintainability of the decision logic, particularly with business users.

Modeling decisions without this kind of transparency to business users harkens back to the dark ages of hundred-page "business requirements" documents handed off to a programmer. That method can work if properly managed, but putting the business in charge of its own decisions gets to the desired end state more quickly, is more likely to be correct on the first pass, and results in higher likelihood of end user acceptance.

Origins of the Standard

In 2008-2009, around the same time it was developing BPMN 2.0, the Object Management Group (OMG) began discussions around the idea of standardizing a decision modeling notation. While numerous decision modeling tools existed at that time, complaints such as this one from Wells Fargo reflected a growing problem:

> "Due to a lack of common standards in the marketplace for modeling, execution and interchange of business rules, Wells Fargo is faced with an abundance of disparate languages, skill sets, approaches and support models, resulting in increased costs and time to market for the combined company. The core value propositions driving the company's interest in Decision Model and Notation (DMN) are lower costs and improved time to market by standardizing on common languages, skill sets, training providers and support models for business rule management initiatives across the enterprise." [21]

---

[21] "Introducing a proposal to standardize a Decision Model and Notation," http://www.omg.org/ news/meetings/tc/agendas/va/DMN_pdf/Vincent_SainteMarie_vanThienen.pdf

Accordingly, an RFP for DMN was issued in March 2011. Two teams submitted proposals, which were eventually merged. As noted on the DMN RFP wiki page,

> "The goal of DMN is to standardise notations (and associated metamodel for) decision modelling. This is a business modelling challenge that touches on:
>
> 1. entities like decision tables
>
> 2. decisions in process models
>
> 3. business vocabularies and policy-type business rules (guidance and constraints)
>
> 4. "Business Rule Management Systems" providing decision table model and automation capabilities
>
> 5. methodologies such as KPI Decision Model (TM) and Business Rule Solutions Q-Charts (TM), and their associated notations for decision models" [22]

The scope of the proposed new standard would target three primary goals:

1. A common *metamodel* providing a foundation for a variety of decision modeling notations and methodologies. A metamodel is a feature of all standards managed by the Object Management Group. It is a set of UML class diagrams that formally describe the relationships between the various semantic elements that comprise the model. Besides standardizing the meaning of each model element, the metamodel is used to generate the *XML Schema* used to interchange decision models between the tools of different vendors.

2. Standardization of *at least one type* of decision logic, a *decision table*. DMN would allow for a wide variety of decision logic formats, but would detail the structure of the most commonly used one, the decision table.

3. Diagrammatic representation of a complex business decision, the *Decision Requirements Diagram (DRD)*, in which individual decision nodes could be linked to an associated business process. DMN would support not only decisions executed as a decision task in a process but those driven by events, data mining, and other use cases.

The DMN 1.0 specification was finalized in November 2014 but not published officially until September 2015. In the end, DMN 1.0 did not wind up covering business vocabularies and policy-type rules, nor methodologies of any kind. The broader the scope of any standard, the more difficult it is to get consensus within the standards body.

By the spring of 2015, after finalization but before official publication of DMN 1.0, it was realized that the metamodel and schema contained technical errors that would prevent their use in executable models. Fixing this became the primary focus of the DMN 1.1 Revision Task Force (RTF), which completed its work in November 2015, with official publication scheduled

---

[22] http://www.omgwiki.org/dmn-rfp/doku.php

for mid-2016. The outward appearance of DRDs and decision tables, as well as the details of the FEEL language, changed little in DMN 1.1, but the internal object model, critical to implementers, changed significantly from DMN 1.0. *This book is based on the final DMN 1.1 specification.*[23]

DMN Overview

The acronym DMN stands for Decision Model *and* Notation. The *and* emphasizes the distinction between the *metamodel* – the formal definition of the model elements and their relationships – and the *notation*, the graphical depiction of both *Decision Requirements Diagrams* and the *decision logic*, including decision tables and other forms of *boxed expressions*. The metamodel, specified as a set of UML class diagrams, is the basis of the *XML Schema* (XSD), defining the standard *XML interchange format* for DMN models.

The DMN standard includes five key elements. Two of them are virtually unknown and certainly unappreciated, but the full impact of DMN as a standard will hinge on adoption of *all five elements*. They are:

1. *Decision Requirements Diagram (DRD)*

A *decision requirements diagram*, or DRD (Figure 6), depicts a decision's information dependencies, or "requirements," in the form of supporting decisions and input data. Technically, the DRD is a possibly truncated or filtered view of a *decision requirements graph* (DRG), a complete list of the decision's dependencies. DRDs are intended to be created by business people and business analysts, not by technical architects or developers.

Each rectangle shape in the DRD is a *decision* node. Each solid arrow into a decision represents one of the decision's *information requirements*, either a *supporting decision* (another rectangle) or an *input data* element (oval shape). Input data signifies external information, typically stored in a database or business system. The rectangles with clipped corners are called *business knowledge models* (BKM), representing reusable bits of decision logic. A dashed arrow from a BKM to a decision, called a *knowledge requirement*, signifies that the decision *invokes* the BKM. The shapes with curved bottom are called *knowledge sources*. They are optional annotations of the diagram representing policies, analytics models, or human experts that serve as authority for the decision logic.

What makes a DRD so interesting and valuable is that it can describe, in a single diagram, the business decision as a whole, even when it must be executed in multiple steps separated in

---

[23] The latest publicly released version of DMN can be obtained from
http://www.omg.org/spec/DMN/Current. As of this writing, this is DMN 1.0; DMN 1.1 should be released publicly in mid-2016. In the meantime, DMN 1.1 is available to OMG members at http://www.omg.org/cgi-bin/doc?dtc/15-11-51. Implementers are strongly urged to work from the DMN 1.1 specification, not DMN 1.0.

time. Also, a DRD may contain human decisions and external decisions, for which the decision logic is opaque – unknown to the decision model.

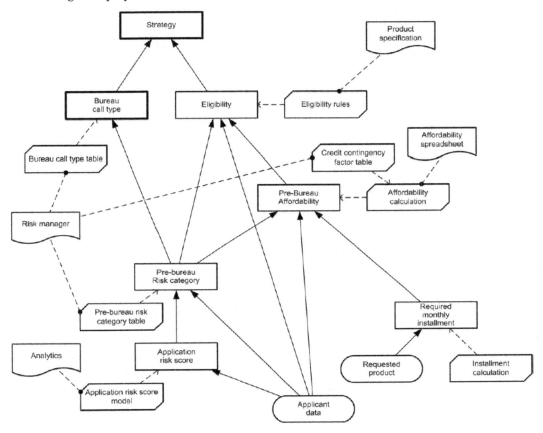

Figure 6. DRD of the *Strategy* decision

DRDs are discussed in more detail in Chapter 3.

2. *Decision Table*

Within each decision or BKM node in a DRD, determination of the output value from the set of input values is called *decision logic*. The most common decision logic format is the *decision table* (Figure 7). DMN supports a variety of decision table layouts. The one shown in Figure 7, called *Rules-as-rows*, is the default. In that layout, decision inputs and outputs are shown in columns, and the *decision rules* are the rows. Input and output columns are separated by a double line. The combination of an input column heading, called the *input expression*, and a cell in that column, called an *input entry*, defines a Boolean (true/false) condition, for example *OrderSize<10*. If all the input conditions for a particular decision rule are true, the rule is said to *match* and the rule's value in the output column, called *output entry*, is selected as the decision table output value.

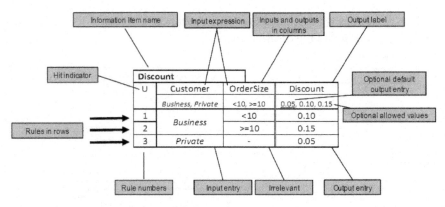

Figure 7. Decision table elements

Decision tables are discussed in more detail in Chapter 4.

3. FEEL

DMN aspires to be more than a way to generate requirements translated into another rule language for execution. *DMN models can actually be executed on a decision engine.* Executability requires a *formal expression language,* and DMN defines a new one called *FEEL,* which stands for *Friendly Enough Expression Language.* FEEL is used both in decision table output entries and DMN *literal expressions.* The latter can describe decision logic patterns, including iteration and table queries, that you cannot describe with simple decision tables.

FEEL is intended for use by business analysts and advanced business users. I would say that someone comfortable using the Formulas menu in Excel can learn and use FEEL. So far, first-generation DMN tools seem to be ignoring FEEL in favor of their own proprietary expression languages, partly because they don't want to rewrite their existing implementations, and partly because the FEEL chapter of the DMN spec is hard to understand. But a tool-specific rule modeling language – especially if it has to be mapped to a different rule execution language – really defeats the purpose of a standard, so I am hopeful that the explanations and examples in this book will help stimulate greater FEEL adoption by DMN tools.

FEEL is discussed in more detail in Chapter 5.

4. Boxed Expression

DMN defines a tabular notation for data and decision logic called *boxed expressions* (Figure 8). Decision tables are one form of boxed expression but all other forms of DMN decision logic also have boxed expression representations.

In boxed expressions other than decision tables, the left (shaded) column defines a *name* (a variable or component of a variable) and the right column (unshaded) is an *expression* providing the value for that name. A multi-row boxed expression with a name/expression pair in each row, called a *context,* can model complex decision logic within a single decision node. In a boxed expression, the right column may possibly contain another context, a *nested list* of name/expression pairs, so the boxed expression format can describe arbitrarily complex data or decision logic.

Applicant Data		
Age	51	
MaritalStatus	"M"	
EmploymentStatus	"EMPLOYED"	
ExistingCustomer	false	
Monthly	Income	10000.00
	Repayments	2500.00
	Expenses	3000.00

Eligibility	
Age	Applicant. Age
Monthly Income	Applicant. Monthly. Income
Pre-Bureau Risk Category	Affordability. Pre-Bureau Risk Category
Installment Affordable	Affordability. Installment Affordable

if Pre-Bureau Risk Category = "DECLINE" or
    Installment Affordable = false or
    Age < 18 or
    Monthly Income < 100
 then "INELIGIBLE"
 else "ELIGIBLE"	

Figure 8. Boxed expressions for input data (left) and decision logic (right).

Boxed expressions are used to model both data and decision logic. For example, the left diagram in Figure 8 uses a boxed expression to describe the input data element *Applicant Data*, a data structure. It has five components, *Age, MaritalStatus, EmploymentStatus, ExistingCustomer,* and *Monthly,* but *Monthly's* expression is a nested context with three components, *Income, Repayments,* and *Expenses.* In FEEL, these component elements are referenced by *qualified name,* for example, *ApplicantData.Monthly.Income.*

The right diagram in Figure 8 is a boxed expression for the decision *Eligibility,* which contains a *context* as its value expression. The rows of name/expression pairs called *context entries.* The first four context entries define *local variables* used in the decision logic and their mappings from the decision's information requirements. The final row, unshaded, with no name, just an expression, is the *final result box,* here a FEEL literal expression.

Boxed expressions provide a uniform business-friendly tabular format for all types of DMN data and decision logic. They are illustrated by many examples throughout the book.

5. *Metamodel and Schema*

Like BPMN and other OMG standards, the names and relationships of elements are defined in a formal *metamodel,* specified as a set of UML diagrams and an XML serialization called XMI. Figure 9, for example, shows the metamodel for *definitions,* the top-level element in a decision model.

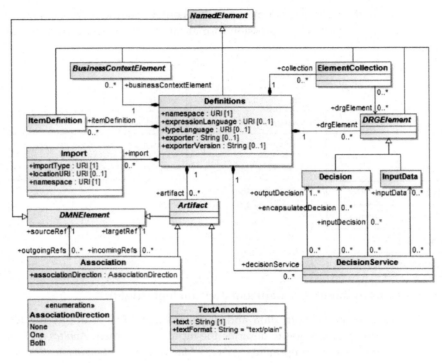

Figure 9. *Definitions* **metamodel**

The metamodel is also the basis of the DMN XSD, or *XML Schema*, which specifies the XML interchange format for DMN models. As mentioned earlier, the metamodel and schema underwent significant change in DMN 1.1. They are described in detail in Chapter 7.

What's Not in the Standard

It is also important to understand what is *not* in the DMN standard, including:

1. A boxed expression format or other user interface for data modeling

2. Business glossary

3. Link to the Structured Business Vocabulary and Rules (SBVR) standard

4. Policy/constraint-oriented rules (except as "knowledge sources")

5. Anything to do with methodology (although a bit of methodology sneaked in the back door with the Lending decision example)

6. Anything to do with decision model testing, including consistency and completeness checking, test case generation, and simulation

7. Details of decision execution, including:

    • Actions to obtain input data

- Access to physical data or systems

- Actions triggered by the decision result

- Fault handling

- Performance optimization

- Rule maintenance applications

8. Anything to do with decision model maintenance, including:

- Model repositories, versioning, and access control

- Model governance and change control

Items 1-3 on this list may be reconsidered in a future version of the standard, but the others, for the most part, are areas that OMG usually tries to avoid. They are aspects of decision modeling where practitioners and tool vendors are free to provide their own "value-add."

Relating DRD to Decision Tables and BPMN

Figure 10, a loan approval decision clipped from the spec, illustrates the relationship between DRDs, decision tables, and BPMN. The DRD for the decision called *Routing* indicates that its decision logic depends on two supporting decisions, *Application risk* and *Eligibility*, and the input data element *Application*. The *names* of these supporting decisions and input data elements are the names of *variables* used in *Routing's* decision logic.

In Figure 10, the *Routing* decision is visually linked to the *decision task*[24] named *Decide routing* in an associated BPMN business process model. (The dotted oval and connector are not DMN, just PowerPoint to show the linkage.) An attribute of *Routing* can point to the BPMN task *Decide Routing*, but it is not displayed as part of the DRD. The possible values of *Routing*, *ACCEPT* or *DECLINE*, become the *gate conditions* in BPMN.

The lower part of the DMN box is the *decision table* for the BKM *Eligibility rules*. (Again, the dotted oval and connector linking the decision table to the DRD are not part of DMN, just PowerPoint to show the linkage.) The columns to the left of the double line are the *inputs*, here *Employment status, Country,* and *Age*; the column to the right, *Eligibility*, is the *output*. The column header indicates the *allowed values* of the output, *INELIGIBLE* and *ELIGIBLE*. The four rows of the table are the *decision rules* that collectively determine the output value from the input values.

The BKM *Eligibility rules* represents decision logic *invoked* by the decision *Eligibility*. It is not required that every decision must invoke a BKM, and, to be honest, BKMs are used far more often than necessary in the DMN spec examples. Not shown in this diagram is the mapping of the input data *Application* to the decision table inputs.

---

[24] BPMN 2.0 technically calls it a *businessRule task*, but decision task is a better name for it.

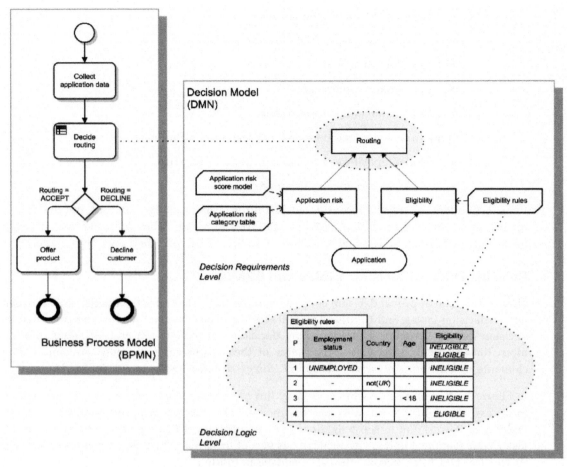

Figure 10. DRD, Decision Table, and associated BPMN process. Source: OMG

Declarative Decision Logic

One of the guiding principles of decision management has always been that decision logic should be *declarative*, meaning the order of evaluation does not change the outcome, as opposed to *procedural*, specifying a particular order of evaluation. The non-declarative nature of the logic is one of the problems with modeling decision logic as a business process.

A decision table such as Figure 11 is explicitly declarative. The order of input columns does not matter, and the order in which the rules are listed does not matter. A given set of input values always results in the same output values.

Applicant Risk Rating			
U	Applicant Age	Medical History	Applicant Risk Rating
1	>60	good	Medium
2		bad	High
3	[25..60]	-	Medium
4	<25	good	Low
5		bad	Medium

Figure 11. *Applicant Risk Rating* **decision table. Source: OMG**

The meaning of Figure 11 is as follows:

1. If *Age*>60 and *Medical History* is "*good*", then *Risk* is "*Medium*"
2. If *Age* >60 and *Medical History* is "*bad*", then *Risk* is "*High*"
3. If *Age* in range 25-60, then *Risk* is "*Medium*". (The "-" means the value of *Medical History* is irrelevant to the rule.)
4. If *Age* <25 and *Medical History* is "*good*", then *Risk* is "*Low*"
5. If *Age* <25 and *Medical History* is "*bad*", then *Risk* is "*Medium*"

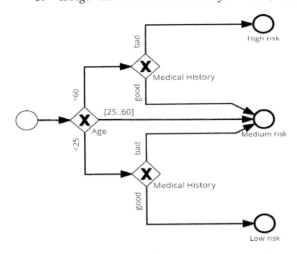

Figure 12. *Applicant Risk Rating* **as** *decision tree* **(not supported by DMN)**

Contrast this format with the *decision tree* (Figure 12), an alternative decision logic representation not supported by DMN. A *decision tree* is a graphical representation of a *sequence* of decisions. In a decision tree, the logic is drawn as a tree of choices. The "root" of the tree does not signify the top level decision but simply the first of a sequence of decisions. A decision tree thus describes a particular *procedure* or order of evaluation to arrive at the final result.

A Hierarchy of Decisions

The decision table of Figure 11 alone does not *completely* describe the decision logic of *Applicant Risk Rating*, since one of its inputs, *Medical History*, seems to be itself a decision. We see that it has possible values *good* and *bad*. But these values, *good* and *bad*, are almost certainly not provided as input data from the applicant's medical record. They are actually determined by a decision that weighs various details in the applicant's medical record. Thus *Medical History* is a *supporting decision* of *Applicant Risk Rating*. Its *output* – with value *good* or *bad* – serves as an *input* to the *Applicant Risk Rating* decision. In DMN, the *name* of the supporting decision, *Medical History*, is also the name of its output and provides an input of the *dependent decision, Applicant Risk Rating*.

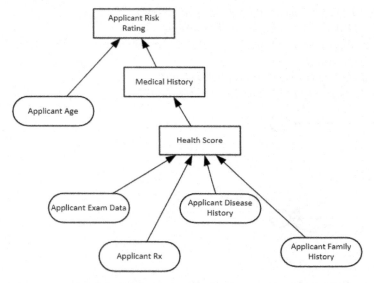

Figure 13. Decision Requirements Diagram for *Applicant Risk Rating*

Thus, in addition to a decision table for *Applicant Risk Rating*, which represents the logic of that decision node, a full description of the decision logic requires its DRD, along with the logic of each supporting decision. In Figure 13 we see that *Applicant Risk Rating* has two inputs, *Applicant Age* and *Medical History*, and *Medical History* has one input, *Health Score*. The arrow from *Medical History* to *Applicant Risk Rating*, called an *information requirement*, means that *Medical History* is a *supporting decision* to *Application Risk Rating*, supplying one of its inputs. Alternatively, we can say that *Application Risk Rating* depends on *Medical History*.

The Value of Hierarchical Decision Structure

There is considerable value in organizing complex decision logic as a hierarchy of supporting decisions, as opposed to a single giant decision table in which all of the input expressions reference only input data. Imagine the decision table required to determine *Applicant Risk Rating* value of High, Medium, or Low from rules directly referencing the applicant's age, exam data (body mass index, blood pressure, lipid panel), record of past diseases, hospitalizations, and prescriptions, and family history. It would be immense and essentially unmanageable – nearly impossible to analyze, test, or modify.

The interposition of a single decision, *Health Score*, between *Medical History* and the input data, while still vastly oversimplified, illustrates how the hierarchy adds flexibility and manageability to the decision logic. The name *Health Score* implies decision logic that computes a numeric score by summing risk values based on each input data element. In other words, instead of selecting a *Health Score* value, each satisfied rule in the decision table contributes an incremental score, and these are summed to compute the *Health Score* output. (DMN supports such a decision table.) This allows a medical expert to appropriately weight the medical risks by assigning an incremental risk score contribution to conditions on each input data element.

Mapping from that aggregate score to a *Medical History* rating of *good* or *bad* is then a separate classification decision with logic modeled by an insurance underwriting expert. That mapping, affecting the *Applicant Risk Rating* and ultimately the premium charged, could change based on the insurer's accumulated claims experience even when the medically-based *Health Score* algorithm is unchanged.

Moreover, the same set of applicant input data could be used to separately rate his or her risk profile for health, long-term disability, and life insurance. Details of the *Health Score* decision logic would change based on the type of insurance, as would the mapping from *Health Score* to *Medical History*, but many aspects of the decision would be reusable.

Risk rating decisions in home mortgage lending involve a more diverse set of considerations, ranging from the borrower's ability to pay, credit history, and employment stability to the loan-to-value ratio, risk of fire or flood, applicable laws and regulations, market liquidity, and other factors. By separately rating or scoring each of these considerations in a separate supporting decision, the hierarchical decision structure allows separation of expertise specialized for each supporting decision, and facilitates adjustment of the relative weighting of each consideration in the final lending decision.

DRD and the Business Decision as a Whole

We will be discussing both DRDs and decision tables in great detail throughout the book, but for now I want to call attention to the relationship between elements in the DRD and elements in the associated BPMN. Fundamentally, BPMN describes *process logic*, a sequence of *actions*, while DMN describes *decision logic*, inferential relationships between elements of data. They are not the same thing. Decision logic simply determines an outcome, or set of output data values, for a given set of input data values. The actions of obtaining the input data, executing the decision, and doing whatever is required by the decision outcome are not part of DMN. They are part of a business process, as is the action of executing a *decision service*, a fragment of the DRD that is evaluated all at once.. So yes, it is appropriate to define a relationship between a BPMN model and a DMN model, but one must always keep in mind that they describe different things.

The DMN spec makes the linkage between the DRD and BPMN explicit but, I believe, distorts their true relationship. The DRD, it says, is intended to create…

"… a bridge between business process models and decision logic models:

- Business process models will define tasks within business processes where decision-making is required to occur

- Decision Requirements Diagrams will define the decisions to be made in those tasks, their interrelationships, and their requirements for decision logic

- Decision logic will define the required decisions in sufficient detail to allow validation and/or automation."[25]

The distortion comes from the fact that primary purpose of DRD is *not* to suggest the procedural aspects of executing the end-to-end decision logic. *Its primary purpose is to describe the decision logic of the business decision as a whole.* The DRD structure may be influenced by the steps in its execution, but the DRD is able to describe the end-to-end decision logic entirely on its own.

In a business decision evaluated as a single stateless action – i.e., implemented as a single decision service – there is no distortion. The problem arises in business decisions evaluated in *multiple steps separated in time,* corresponding to multiple tasks in the BPMN model. This could occur for many reasons:

- The DRD includes human decisions.

- The DRD includes external decisions.

- It may be faster or more cost-efficient not to obtain in advance, for every instance of the decision, *all* of the input data elements in the DRD. The Lending decision detailed in the DMN specification is an example of this, and we will come back to it in connection with this issue repeatedly in the book.

The DRD is really a fabulous innovation. It is able to describe, in a single diagram, the logic of the "business decision as a whole" – *What is the annual premium (or is the application declined)?* – in a purely declarative manner, independently of any BPMN model… even when it may be executed in multiple steps separated in time! This capability is unique to DMN: TDM doesn't have it, for instance. DMN *allows* it, but the spec fails to exploit it. Instead it assigns DRD the far more pedestrian role of linking fragments of the end-to-end logic to a *process* representing the decision as a whole.

What Is the Business Decision as a Whole?

The concept of the *business decision as a whole,* or what I sometimes call the end-to-end decision logic, never appears in the DMN spec, nor in TDM, not even in Fish's *Knowledge Automation*

---

[25] DMN 1.1 spec, section 5.1.

book, where DRD originated in the first place! All of these basically rely on BPMN to describe the business decision as a whole. I don't agree with that. Even though its *implementation* may require a multistep process, the business decision as a whole does represent some end-to-end *decision logic*, which is not the same as process logic. Properly structured, a DRD can describe that decision logic, independently of BPMN, and doing so forms the basis of the DMN Method. In the Method, the DRD for the business decision as a whole has a single top-level decision node representing the ultimate outcome, such as *approved* or *declined*.

It should be no surprise that both Larry Goldberg (TDM) and Alan Fish question this. They still argue that the end-to-end decision logic is better understood as a business process than as a DRD. Since each of them has many years of practical experience with decision modeling and implementation, their points must be taken seriously.

Goldberg's main argument[26] is that the business decision as a whole may be *too big and complex* for its logic to be represented effectively as a single DRD. Once the DRD contains over 30 decisions, it becomes too difficult for stakeholders to understand, much less to rely on for maintaining the decision logic.

A second argument is that the final outcome from the customer's standpoint may not be the principal focus of the decision-making organization. For example, the logic determining whether an application for a new bank account is approved or denied may be of less interest to the bank than the Know Your Customer decision logic, which is just one component of that "end-to-end" decision.

A third argument is that the decision *process may change the decision logic*, either by requiring some variant of a decision or possibly different input data.

Where Goldberg's concern is that the end-to-end logic is too big, Fish considers the other extreme:[27] Not all processes that contain decisions, he says, are fundamentally about making the decision. The decision logic is often incidental to the end-to-end process. For example, he says, a loan origination process is more about actions like contract signing and disbursement of funds than the decision logic to approve the loan:

> "You could focus just on processes which do nothing but decision-making but I think that would greatly limit the usefulness of the approach."

Finally, he questions whether the "end-to-end" determination is always a single decision:

> "I think a good methodological principle would be that if you need the words 'and' or 'or' to express the question, it is not a single decision."

End-to-End Decision Too Big

The concern that the end-to-end DRD may be too large and complicated to be useful is a valid one. It is related, I believe, to a flaw in the DMN standard, in which the DRD is a single-level,

---

[26] L. Goldberg, Private communication, December 2015.

[27] A. Fish, Private communication, December 2015.

i.e., "flat," structure, instead of a multi-level one like a BPMN model, which supports both high-level and detailed views of the logic within the context of a single end-to-end definition. We discuss this more in Chapter 17, and maybe we can get a solution for it into DMN 1.2, but in the meantime I take Goldberg at his word, and accept that DRDs with over 30 decision nodes become unmanageable, and end-to-end decisions larger than that should not attempt to define their logic in a single DRD.

Process May Change the Decision Logic

This argument, to me, is not persuasive. If the nature of the change is known in advance, this is just another way of saying that the end-to-end decision logic is too big, discussed above. The other possibility is that some bit of decision logic is determined or modified on an ad hoc basis when some exception occurs in the decision process. Like BPMN, DMN is not well equipped to handle ad hoc changes.

The Business Process Is Not a Decision Process

This objection is a misunderstanding. In the DMN Method, the "decision process" is merely a description of the steps that obtain the input data and execute pieces of the decision logic. It determines the *decision points* of some *implementation* of the decision logic, and has no value other than that. It certainly is not the same as the real business process that implements loan origination or an insurance claim.

End-to-End Decision Not the Primary Focus

In BPMN Method and Style, the end-to-end process normally means the process encompassing a *customer-facing transaction*. There can be legitimate debate about when that process ends: Is it when the invoice is sent or when payment is received? But the point is to get the modeler to think beyond the limits of a single departmental or system function.

In DMN Method and Style, my original notion basically followed this "customer-facing" idea. In loan origination, that means, "Is the loan application approved or rejected?" In an insurance claim that means, "Is the claim approved or denied, and how much is paid?" These are things that the customer cares about, but admittedly, the bank or insurance company making those determinations may want to focus their decision modeling and implementation on just some part of that. So, to Goldberg's second argument, I would say that if, to the bank, the Know Your Customer decision is more important than the larger account opening decision that includes it, then the Know Your Customer decision effectively becomes the business decision as a whole.

It is true that often an important bit of decision logic is completely invisible to the customer and almost incidental to the customer-facing process. For example, consider a customer service request in a global organization. The logic that determines who should handle the request, based on the particular product or service involved, geography, time of day, requestor's native language, and customer status could be extremely complicated, but it is nothing one would normally term "end-to-end." So let's be clear. By the business decision as a whole, I simply mean "the question this decision is supposed to answer," be that large or small.

End-to-End Is More Than One Decision

To me, this objection is mostly stylistic. When a customer applies for insurance, he or she is asking a single question: *What is my monthly payment (assuming I am approved)?* So approval of the application for insurance and determination of the premium are, to me, both part of one end-to-end decision, not two separate decisions. The result of a single decision node in DMN is always captured in a single variable, even if that variable has multiple components, such as *isApproved* and *PremiumAmt*. So it is not unreasonable to insist that a DRD describing an end-to-end decision must have a single top-level decision node.

End-to-End Decision Logic and the DMN Method

In DMN Method and Style, the business decision as a whole – the question this decision is supposed to answer, be that large or small – should be represented by a DRD with a single top-level decision node representing the ultimate outcome. That is, the output values of the top-level decision node are the possible output values for the business decision as a whole. Moreover, this DRD describes the end-to-end decision logic on its own. When *execution* of that logic – and obtaining the required input data – occurs in multiple steps separated in time, the *process* describing those steps may influence the DRD structure, but the DRD should be able to describe the end-to-end decision logic on its own, without reference to a BPMN model.

Your first reaction might be that's impossible in business decisions where not all of the input data is available at the start, as in the Lending example in the spec. We'll discuss that one in detail later, but here is a stripped-down preview.

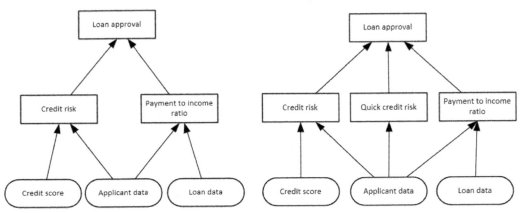

Figure 14. *LoanApproval* **DRD**

In the first diagram in Figure 14, *Loan approval,* including its supporting decisions *Credit risk* and *Payment to income ratio,* can be executed as a single decision service, modeled in BPMN as a single decision task... *if* all three input data elements are available at the start. But let's say there is a cost to obtaining the credit score from a service bureau, and we don't want to do that if we can make the *Loan approval* decision without it. That leads to the DRD in the second diagram, which adds a third supporting decision, *Quick credit risk*, that does not require the credit score.

From this DRD alone, it is difficult to tell whether the business decision as a whole is executed all at once or in multiple steps separated in time. The way to understand the implementation is by consulting a BPMN diagram for the process that executes it. For example, the process may indicate that the task that obtains the credit score executed only if the *Quick credit risk* is not *High* and the *Payment to income ratio* is between 10% and 30%, inclusive.

Another way is to overlay an implementation, in the form of *decision services*, on the DRD. For example, Figure 15 indicates *Loan approval* is executed in two distinct steps.

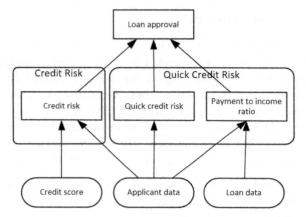

Figure 15. *Loan Approval*, with overlaid decision services

U		Quick credit risk ⓘ		Credit risk ⓘ		Payment to Income ratio ⓘ	**Loan Approval**
		{High,Medium,Low}		{High,Medium,Low,null}		Percentage	**{Approved,Declined}**
1	=	High		-		-	Declined
2	∈	{Medium, Low}		-	>	30.00 %	Declined
3	∈	{Medium, Low}	=	High	∈	[10 %..30 %]	Declined
4	∈	{Medium, Low}	=	Medium	∈	(15 %..30 %]	Declined
5	∈	{Medium, Low}	=	Low	∈	(20 %..30 %]	Declined
6	∈	{Medium, Low}		-	<	10.00 %	Approved
7	∈	{Medium, Low}	=	Medium	∈	[10 %..15 %]	Approved
8	∈	{Medium, Low}	=	Low	∈	[10 %..20 %]	Approved

Figure 16. *LoanApproval* decision table

Either way, even though the input data *Credit score* is not available at the start for all instances of this business decision, we can still represent the end-to-end decision logic as a single DRD with a single top decision node, *Loan approval*, providing the final outcome, *Approved* or *Declined*. Figure 16 shows the decision table for *Loan Approval*.

Note that in the *Credit risk* column, three rules have a *hyphen*, meaning that input is irrelevant to the rule. Hyphen includes the value *null* – no value – for this supporting decision, which allows the rule to match when a required input of *Credit risk*, the *Credit score*, is unavailable. Other rules specify non-*null* values for *Credit risk*, where *Quick credit risk* is not *High* and the *Payment to income ratio* is between 10% and 30%. Those are the conditions under which we want to obtain the *Credit score*.

Figure 16 accurately describes the decision logic if we are absolutely sure that the credit score is available *only* when *Quick credit risk* is not *High* and the *Payment to income ratio* is between 10% and 30%. Those might be the conditions under which we want to spend the effort and cost of obtaining the credit score, but suppose we already have it for this applicant. Wouldn't we want to use it? Certainly *Credit risk*, which includes the credit score, is a better predictor than *Quick credit risk*, which does not. In that case, does Figure 16 give the best decision result?

U	Quick credit risk ⓘ		Credit risk ⓘ		Payment to Income ratio ⓘ		Loan Approval
	{High,Medium,Low}		{High,Medium,Low,null}		Percentage		{Approved,Declined}
1	=	High		-		-	Declined
2	∈	{Medium, Low}	=	High		-	Declined
3	∈	{Medium, Low}	=	Medium	>	15.00 %	Declined
4	∈	{Medium, Low}	=	Low	>	20.00 %	Declined
5	∈	{Medium, Low}	=	null	>	30.00 %	Declined
6	∈	{Medium, Low}	=	Low	≤	20.00 %	Approved
7	∈	{Medium, Low}	=	Medium	≤	15.00 %	Approved
8	∈	{Medium, Low}	=	null	<	10.00 %	Approved

Figure 17. A better *LoanApproval* decision table

In particular, what if *Credit risk*, based on this unusually available credit score data, is *High*, but *Payment to income ratio* is less than 10%? The decision table of Figure 16 gives the outcome *Approved*, because it ignores the *Credit risk* value, assumed to be *null*. But in this case it is not *null*. So if you want your decision logic to include this possibly rare possibility, the decision table must be modified a bit. Figure 17 better represents the top level *decision logic*, even though it is less suggestive of the normal *process logic* than is Figure 16. Note that both versions of this decision table could be considered *incomplete*, since no rule matches when *Credit risk* is null, *Quick credit risk* is not *High*, and *Payment to income ratio* is between 10% and 30%. These are the conditions where we expect to have non-*null Credit risk*. Completeness in the case of *null* inputs is not well defined in the spec.

BPMN Describes Decision Implementation

I believe this example better illustrates the relationship between DMN and BPMN. *DMN describes decision logic; BPMN describes implementation of that logic.* They are not the same thing. DMN Method and Style says that DRD on its own describes the compositional structure of the decision logic, but (without overlaying decision services) not its implementation. The DRD must be *consistent* with the implementation but does not define it.

As we just saw, the *normal* decision process – say, the one initially captured in a decision discovery workshop with the stakeholders – may not be the process followed in all instances. Also, the normal process might change over time. Decision implementation is often a matter of cost and speed, factors that can and do change. Suppose it no longer costs significant time and money to obtain the credit score. Suppose we can get it instantly for all applicants, for free. In that case we likely would change the process and execute the end-to-end decision as a single decision service. It's simpler, faster, and probably costs less.

The DMN spec never speaks of the business decision as a whole. There is no semantic element in the DMN metamodel to represent it, nor is there any standard meaning assigned to a top-level decision node in a DRD. These are purely matters of Method and Style.

Does DRD Prescribe an Order of Execution?

We have already established that unlike a decision tree, a DMN decision table is *declarative*, meaning the order of evaluating columns in a rule or evaluating rows in the table does not matter; the resulting decision output value is always the same.[28] You might think, of course a DRD implies an order of evaluation. You have to process the tree starting at the leaves, the input data, followed by the decisions with no supporting decisions, and incrementally progress toward ultimately evaluating the top-level decision at the root of the hierarchy. That procedure seems intuitive, but it is not the only possible one, and often not the most efficient one. It is called *forward chaining*, or data-driven reasoning. As explained by Goldberg and von Halle in *The Decision Model*,

> "Forward-chaining begins with facts that are true and assesses conditions about those facts, thus leading to the corresponding conclusions that are true. Each true conclusion is added to a virtual list of true facts. This process continues until no further true facts lead to a conclusion."[29]

But it is also possible, and sometimes more efficient, to start at the other end, called *backward chaining*, or goal-directed reasoning:

---

[28] Technically, DMN does define two types of non-declarative decision table, with a hit policy of either *First* or *Rule order*, meaning the *first* matching rule selects the output value. But the spec goes on to deprecate their use (because of this non-declarative behavior). DMN Method and Style does not allow a hit policy of *First* or *Rule order*. Hit Policy is described further in Chapter 4.

[29] von Halle and Goldberg, *The Decision Model*, 225

"Backward-chaining starts with a conclusion value and finds those conditions that lead to the conclusion value. Backward-chaining continues by starting again with those condition values as conclusions and finds the next set of condition values that lead to the conclusion values. This process continues until a set of condition values is found that is based on known facts, in which case, the original conclusion value is now known to be true."[30]

Applicant Risk Rating			
U	Applicant Age	Medical History	Applicant Risk Rating
1	>60	good	Medium
2		bad	High
3	[25..60]	-	Medium
4	<25	good	Low
5		bad	Medium

Figure 18. To select *Applicant Risk Rating* of *Low*, backward chaining is faster.

If a particular decision output value of interest can be selected by a rule testing only input data while other output values might depend on a long chain of supporting decisions, backward chaining will get you the answer faster, on average, than forward chaining. For example (Figure 18), if you are looking for an *Applicant Risk Rating* of *Low*, only possible for *Age <25*, you only need to evaluate *Applicant Age*, simple input data, not *Driving Record Category*, a complex decision. That is backward chaining. The most efficient order of evaluation depends on the decision logic in detail and the nature of the input data. Commercial decision engines implement algorithms that determine, based on the details of the data and decision logic, the most efficient order of evaluation, forward chaining, backward chaining, or something in between. What's important is that *you always get the same answer*, regardless.

Declarative decision logic allows you to evaluate the decision outcome without regard to the order of evaluation. That just affects the speed or efficiency of execution. It does not change the decision outcome. That is not to say it is unimportant in the implementation. Decision engines may be either *sequential*, executing their rule language in modeler-specified order, or *inferential*, in which the engine determines the order of execution. Most commercial BREs are in fact sequential.

So here is a question: *Does a DRD prescribe an order of execution of the end-to-end decision logic?* Whatever execution algorithm is employed, the DRD should be executable, and we know that the end-to-end logic may require execution in multiple steps separated in time. This suggests that DRD represents procedural logic. But that is not the case. Unlike a decision tree, a DRD does not specify a particular order of evaluation.

---

[30] von Halle and Goldberg, *The Decision Model,* 225

Admittedly, the order of evaluation is not as free as it is in a decision table. The logic of the top-level decision node implies, by backward chaining, which supporting decisions and input data elements are required to produce any particular outcome value, but other than that the DRD allows flexibility in the order of evaluation.

Perhaps a better question is whether end-to-end decision logic executed in multiple steps can be described by a DRD with a single top-level decision node. DMN Method and Style insists that it can. Other methodologies, such as those described in TDM and Fish's *Knowledge Automation*, suggest the opposite. Instead they focus on the logic of individual *decision service*s independently, rather than the business decision as a whole. To describe the business decision as a whole, they rely on BPMN, a process model.

But that is not necessary. There *is* decision logic to the business decision as a whole, and DMN can describe it. A DRD should not require an associated BPMN model any more than a decision table should require specification of forward vs backward chaining.

Three Meanings of "Decision"

It is important to note that the term "decision" is used to mean different things in different contexts, so we always need to keep in mind exactly which meaning we are talking about:

1. The *business decision as a whole*, or "end-to-end decision". This is a business concept important to the DMN Method, but is never mentioned in the DMN specification. Method and Style allows end-to-end business decisions be modeled as a DRD with a single top-level decision node representing the ultimate outcome.

2. A *decision service*, a *unit of decision execution* as a single stateless action. In DMN, decision service typically encapsulates multiple decision nodes. A decision service may be represented in the DRD by a rounded rectangle overlay enclosing decision nodes encapsulated in the service.

3. A single *decision node* in a DRD, the rectangle shape, corresponding to the semantic element *Decision* in the metamodel. This is the fundamental unit of decision logic in DMN, modeled as a *single value expression*.

Value Expressions

The DRD describes only the overall structure of an end-to-end business decision, the relationship of each decision node to its supporting decisions and input data. What computes the *value* of each decision node or BKM is called its *decision logic* or *value expression*.

DMN defines several types of value expressions:

- **Literal expression**. In a *literal expression*, the value expression is a text string in some *expression language*. The default expression language is one defined in the DMN specification, called *FEEL*. Models may specify alternative expression languages, such as Java, javascript, or a tool-specific language. In basic decision models, literal expressions are limited to a small subset of FEEL elements called S-FEEL. FEEL is described in more detail in Chapter 5.

- **Decision table**. In a *decision table*, the value expression is displayed as a grid. In the most common layout, columns represent inputs and outputs, and rows represent decision rules. Cells in the input columns define conditional tests on the input. If the tests for all cells in a rule evaluate to true, that rule is said to *match* and the value in that row's output columns are selected as the decision table's output value. S-FEEL is the default expression language for decision tables. Decision tables are described in more detail in Chapter 4.

- **Invocation**. An *invocation* represents a call to a reusable *function definition*, usually contained in a business knowledge model, or BKM. The invocation names the called function and maps decision inputs to function *parameters*. Execution of an invocation returns the value of the called function back to the invoking decision or BKM.

- **Context**. A *context* is a form of "advanced" decision logic. It is composed of a list of *context entries*, each comprising a *local variable* (local to the context) and its *value expression*, which may be any of the value expression types listed here. Contexts allow a single decision node to have an arbitrarily complex value expression.

- **Function definition**. A *function definition* is a reusable bit of decision logic, typically the value expression of a BKM or context entry. A function definition specifies a list of parameters and a value expression referencing those parameters.

- **Relation**. A *relation* is DMN's analogue to a relational table in a database. Each row represents an item in the table, and each column represents an attribute of that item. Relations are normally used to represent tables of data, but technically the table cells may be expressions.

It is important to remember that a value expression does not normally have a *name*. Its name is taken from the name of the decision (or BKM) that "owns" it. For example, the name of a function is the name of the BKM or context entry that has the function definition as its value expression.

In the DMN 1.1 specification, every decision defines a corresponding *variable* with the same *name* as the decision and the value of the decision's *value expression*.

DMN Conformance Levels

Because DMN is intended to serve a wide spectrum of users, OMG expects that many tools may support only part of the specification. To that end, DMN specifies three *conformance levels* that help to segment the DMN tool landscape. The specification of the levels is too fuzzy to define strict rules about what is conformant and what is not, but the levels are valuable in defining three general classes of DMN tools.

- Conformance Level 1 (CL1) tools support DRDs and non-executable decision logic. CL1 decision tables and literal expressions are not based on any formal expression language. The variables and expressions they contain are descriptive only.

- Conformance Level 2 (CL2) tools support DRDs and simple executable decision logic (decision tables and literal expressions) based on S-FEEL or equivalent. CL2 tools, for example, could possibly check decision table completeness and consistency and simulate decision execution, but would not typically support execution in production.

- Conformance Level 3 (CL3) tools support DRDs and directly executable decision logic. In the standard, CL3 conformance is specified in terms of FEEL support, but it is likely that a significant fraction of CL3 tools will use some other executable expression language.

In practice, CL1 tools most likely will be used to create decision models that serve as business requirements for programmers in some BRE rule language. CL2 tools also will most likely be used as business-friendly "front ends" for models executed in a BRE rule language, and may provide direct export from expressions in the model to the executable rule language. CL3 tools represent modeling and execution in a single unified language, FEEL or equivalent.

CHAPTER 3

Decision Requirements

Decision Requirements Diagram (DRD)

The notion that a piece of decision logic, such as a decision table, depends on the output of other supporting decisions is not new with DMN. It goes back decades. Vanthienen[31] points to the cover of the 1982 CODASYL report on decision tables (Figure 19), which shows links between a decision table and its supporting decisions.

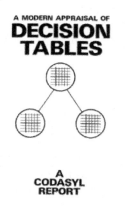

Figure 19. Hierarchy of supporting decisions is nothing new. Source: CODASYL[32]

DMN carries this idea forward in the form of *decision requirements*. A *Decision Requirements Graph* (DRG) and its visual representation, the *Decision Requirements Diagram* (DRD), describe a decision's dependencies on supporting decisions and input data. Those dependencies are

---

[31] Jan Vanthienen, "History of Modeling Decisions using Tables (Part 1)," http://www.brcommunity.com/pb637.php

[32] Codasyl, "A Modern Appraisal of Decision Tables," Report of the Decision Table Task Group, ACM, New York, 322 pp., 1982.

described in the form of *information requirements,* solid arrow connectors linking a decision to the output of a supporting decision or input data element. Every decision or input data element contains a *variable* having the same name, and the value expression of a decision may reference only variables corresponding to that decision's information requirements.

The details of DMN decision requirements borrow heavily from *Decision Requirements Analysis* (DRA), a decision management project methodology described by Alan Fish of FICO in his excellent book, *Knowledge Automation.* One of DRA's defining principles (also in Taylor's *Decision Management Manifesto*) is *Decisions require information*:

> "You can discover the requirements of a decision by asking *what information is required* to make the decision. Information is of three kinds:
>
> 1. Business knowledge (in all its forms: business rules and their metaphors, algorithms, and analytic models)
> 2. Data describing the case to be decided on
> 3. The results of other decisions
>
> The last point is the key: Decisions depend on subdecisions. This allows decision-making to be decomposed into a network that can be drawn in a Decision Requirements Diagram (DRD)."[33]

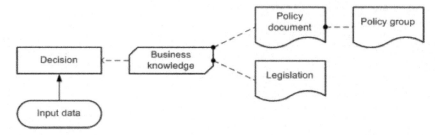

Figure 20. Decision Requirements Diagram elements. Source: OMG

In DMN, a DRD is a diagram that captures the relationships between a decision and its supporting decisions, business knowledge models, and input data, as well as the knowledge sources (also called authorities) behind the decision logic. The basic DRD element types are shown in Figure 20.

- A *decision* (rectangle) represents the decision logic for a particular set of inputs. It may either directly contain the decision logic or invoke the decision logic specified in an attached business knowledge model.

- *Input data* (oval shape) represents literal data values received from a database, business system, or other external source. Input data has no value expression.

---

[33] Fish, *Knowledge Automation,* Chapter 4.

- A *business knowledge model* (rectangle with two clipped corners) represents a reusable bit of decision logic. Its value expression is a *function definition*, an expression of its *parameters*. A decision *invokes* a BKM by mapping its own information requirements to the BKM parameters; the BKM output value is then passed back to the invoking decision. The spec says that the names of any DRD element – decision, business knowledge model, or knowledge source – must be unique in the model, so a BKM and a decision may not share the same name.

- A *knowledge source* (rectangle with wavy bottom) represents the *authority* for some bit of decision logic. It could be a document, such as a published policy; an external model, such as predictive analytics; or a person, such as a domain expert.

The dependencies between decisions, business knowledge models, input data, and knowledge sources are shown graphically as *connectors* called *requirements*:

- The *information requirement* connector, solid arrow, represents the dependency of a decision on a supporting decision or input data.

- The *knowledge requirement* connector, dashed arrow, represents the invocation of a business knowledge model by a decision or another business knowledge model.

- The *authority requirement* connector, dashed line with dot, represents the dependency of a decision, business knowledge model, or knowledge source on a knowledge source.

The semantic model of *all* a decision's requirements is called *a Decision Requirements Graph* (DRG). Its diagrammatic representation, the DRD, may reflect just a partial view of the DRG, omitting certain details. The spec says the DRG is "self-contained in the sense that all the modeled requirements for any Decision in the DRG (its immediate sources of information, knowledge and authority) are present in the same DRG."

Also, the DRG must be "acyclic," meaning if Decision A depends on Decision B (directly or indirectly), then Decision B may not depend on Decision A. Another way of saying it is there should be no chain of information requirements leading from Decision A and cycling back to Decision A.

Of the connectors in a DRD, we focus mainly on the *information requirements*, the solid arrows linking a decision to its dependencies. In the simple DRD of Figure 21, we note several things:

- The label of a decision in the DRD, a noun, is both the name of the *decision* and the name of the *variable* that holds its output value. Best practice is to name the decision in a way that suggests the data type. Thus *Applicant Risk Rating* suggests an enumerated rating type; *Health Score* suggests a numerical value. *Medical History* is not a good name; a better one might be *Medical History Rating*.

- Each of a decision's incoming information requirements represents makes the *variable* corresponding to the node at its tail end available for use in the decision's value expression. Only variables represented by information requirements may be referenced in the value expression.

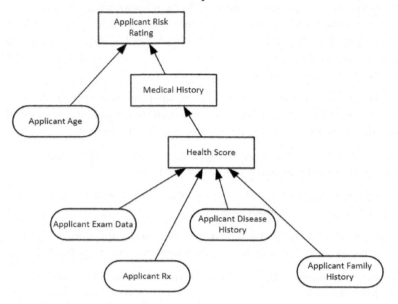

Figure 21. A simple DRD

- The oval shapes, called *input data*, represent values determined outside of the decision model and passed to it upon execution. Like a decision, each input data element defines a variable with the same name. This variable may represent either a complex business object, such as *Applicant*, or a simple attribute, such as *Applicant Age*. When a separate input data element is drawn for each individual attribute, as in Figure 21, the specific inputs to a decision are visible in the DRD. That can lead to extremely cluttered diagrams. For this reason, it is more often best practice to consolidate such details in a single input data element like *Applicant*, representing the entire business object or source document. This reduces visual clutter, but it means the specific attributes of the input data used in the decision logic are not visible in the DRD.

As discussed in the previous chapter, the DMN spec positions DRD as the link between the logic of each decision node and a process model that describes the business decision as a whole. Here we can see how that linkage works. Figure 22 shows the DRD for the Lending decision example from the DMN spec, discussed at length in Chapter 6. Like any DRD, it describes the input elements required, but not the decision logic. In that sense it provides a "big picture" view of a complex business decision.

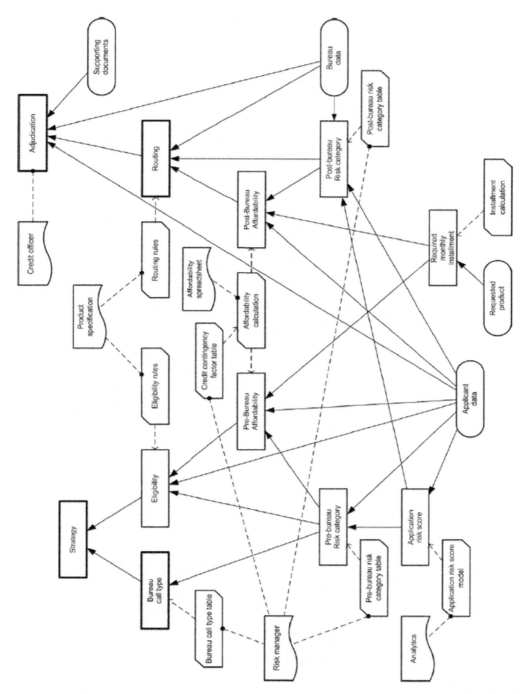

Figure 22. Decision Requirements Diagram, Lending example in DMN spec. Source: OMG

Figure 23 is a companion business process diagram, modeled in BPMN, describing the *decision points* in the decision process, the activities that execute various decisions in the DRD. The BPMN also shows the activities that obtain or develop the input data elements used in the decision.

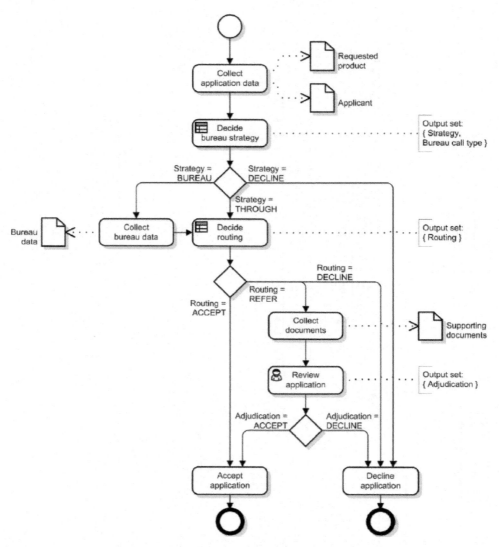

Figure 23. Business process diagram, DMN spec example. Source: OMG

Figure 22 and Figure 23 provide a number of cues that visually link DRD elements to their counterparts in the business process model. These visual cues are not required by either DMN or BPMN, but they illustrate good practice.

- In BPMN, the DMN *input data* elements are depicted as *data objects* (the dog-eared page shape) connected to the process *activities* that obtain the data. The name of the data object corresponds to the name of the input data element. Thus the BPMN task *Collect application data* is the source of the DMN input data elements *Requested product* and *Applicant*.

- BPMN *decision tasks* (also called *business rule tasks*, with the decision table icon) represent execution of an atomic *decision service*. Here a BPMN *text annotation* (square bracket) names the DMN *decision* nodes that comprise the *output decisions* of the decision service. Thus the decision task *Decide bureau strategy* executes the decision service whose output decisions are *Strategy* and *Bureau call type*. Similarly, the decision task *Decide routing* executes the decision service with the output decision *Routing*.

- BPMN *user tasks* (with the head and shoulders icon) and defined output set represent *human decisions*. A DRD may include these as well, even though their decision logic is opaque, unknown to the decision model. The text annotation for *Review application* links this user task to the DMN decision *Adjudication*.

Visual cues such as these linking the DRD to an associated BPMN diagram are helpful in creating a big picture view of the business decision as a whole.

Decision Services

Because implementation of the business decision as a whole may require multiple decision points separated in time, the DRD for the end-to-end decision can be said to describe "stateful" decision logic. But not every decision node in the DRD requires a separate decision point. Certain fragments of the DRD encompassing multiple decision nodes may be evaluated all at once in an *atomic stateless action*. Such a fragment may be encapsulated as a *decision service*.

At the very last minute, DMN 1.1 adopted a proposal to define a decision service as a "normative," i.e., official, part of the standard. (In DMN 1.0 it was described in Annex B, which was "non-normative.") We need to remember that a decision service describes an *implementation* of decision logic, not the decision logic itself. It effectively *overlays* the DRD to show the decision nodes encapsulated in each decision service, the service's output decisions, and its information requirements.

Figure 24 illustrates the decision service notation in the DRD. It is a rounded rectangle that surrounds all of the encapsulated decisions in the service. The inputs to the service are defined by all of the information requirements leading into the rounded rectangle. The outputs of the service are the decisions shown above the straight line bisecting the rounded rectangle. If there is no such line, all encapsulated decisions are exposed in the service output.

A decision service represents an implementation of the decision logic described by the DRD. A single decision node in the DRD may belong to more than one decision service, or none at all.

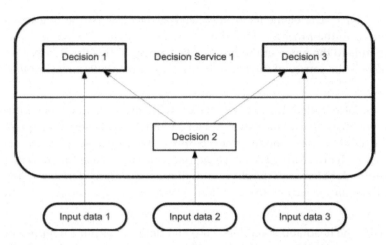

Figure 24. Decision service notation in DRD. Source: OMG

Business Knowledge Models

Business knowledge models (BKMs) are an interesting and somewhat controversial component of DMN. There are actually two different interpretations of what they signify and how they should be used. One interpretation and usage is agreed by all: A BKM represents *reusable* decision logic, exposed as a *function definition* that may be invoked by any decision, even one defined in a different decision model. In contrast, a *decision* node represents a particular instance of that logic. If the decision table that details some decision logic is contained in a DRD decision node, the logic is embedded in that particular decision; it is not reusable.

By "reusable" we mean the decision logic is defined once and then simply called – or in DMN terminology, "invoked" – by any decision that requires it. To do that, the reusable decision logic is defined as a BKM, a *function* with defined *parameters*. The decision that uses it is modeled as an *invocation* that calls the BKM, supplying values for the parameters. In the DRD, the invocation is depicted as a *knowledge requirement* connector, which represents a *mapping* between the variables corresponding to the decision's *information requirements* and the *parameters* of the BKM. An information requirements connector must not connect to a BKM.

The second, more controversial interpretation of BKM is a logical partition of "knowledge" used to make a decision. In this interpretation, which derives from *Knowledge Automation* by Alan Fish, most decisions have one or more BKMs. For example, the Lending decision example in the DMN spec uses a BKM – sometimes two – for almost every decision in the model, even when no reuse of the logic is apparent. The problem with this interpretation is that it both clutters the DRD with additional shapes and adds extra invocation logic to the normal value expression. So it results in unnecessary complexity, in both the diagram and the decision logic.[34]

The spec does say that this interpretation is *optional*, but its use in the spec examples makes DMN appear much more complicated than it needs to be. DMN Method and Style limits use of BKMs to situations where reuse of the decision logic is needed. Actually, it comes up more than you might think!

Like a decision, a BKM defines a variable with the same name to hold its result.[35] When the BKM is invoked by a decision, the value of this variable populates the decision's output variable. The reason for a separate BKM output variable is to allow reusable decision logic to be maintained independently of the decision models that use it, for example, in a DMN *function library*. Upon importing the function library model, another decision model may invoke the reusable function by the BKM variable name. We will discuss this further in Chapter 5.

Figure 22 shows the relationship between decisions and BKMs depicted in the DRD for the Lending example. The BKM *Affordability calculation* involves real reuse. It is invoked by two separate decisions in the same decision model, *Pre-Bureau Affordability* and *Post-Bureau Affordability*. The invocations are depicted as *knowledge requirements*, the dashed arrow connectors. Note there are no *information requirements* (solid arrow connectors) into the BKM. Instead, those connect to the decisions that invoke the BKM, supplying values to the BKM parameters. Note, however, that a BKM can invoke another BKM. In Figure 22, *Affordability calculation* invokes the BKM *Credit contingency factor table*.

Most of the other BKMs in this diagram involve no apparent reuse. Since the decision logic they contain could have been put directly inside the decisions that invoke them, some would say these BKMs just clutter up the diagram. You be the judge!

Business Context and Motivation

Even though there is no defined notation for them in the DRD, DMN also specifies a number of optional business context and motivation attributes for each decision node in the model:

- *Question and answer.* This comes straight from the Decision Management Manifesto, which says "The best way to define a Decision is with a question and a set of known possible answers." In DMN, the question and allowed answers are each a simple text string.

---

[34] One man's "clutter" is another's essential component. In correspondence with the author, Fish maintains that use of BKM's "is not primarily representational but methodological. In fact, it should be central to the 'top-down method' prescribed in your book." Actually, I agree with his methodological argument, but not the visual clutter. More to say about this in Chapter 17.

[35] This is new in DMN 1.1; it was not the case in DMN 1.0.

- *Supported objective.* This is a pointer to an *Objective* defined in an external Business Motivation Model.

- *Impacted performance indicator.* This is a pointer to a *Performance Indicator* defined in a DMN model.

- *Decision maker* and *Decision owner.* These are pointers to an *Organization Unit* defined in a DMN model.

- *Using process* and *Using task.* These are pointers to a *process* and *task* element in an external BPMN model.

CHAPTER 4

Decision Logic
at Conformance Levels 1 and 2

Decision logic at Conformance Level 1 is not considered executable and thus DMN places no constraints on its content, format, or completeness. CL1 models may express the decision logic in ordinary natural language or in some basic tool-defined modeling language. CL1 decision models typically serve as either documentation or *business requirements for developers* creating an automated implementation in a proprietary rule language. A CL1 tool may be able to export its DRD to a BRMS.

Conformance Level 2 is intended as DMN's baseline for executable decision models. Decision logic in a CL2 model must be consistent with the DMN metamodel and thus semantically precise. For example, although it is not a stated requirement in the spec, a CL2 tool should be able to validate the decision logic described in the model for completeness and consistency. While CL2 models are executable, they also will frequently serve as business requirements for developers of implementations in another rule language. Unlike CL1 tools, some CL2 tools are able to export its decision logic to a commercial BRE rule language.

The DMN specification defines CL2 decision logic in terms of a limited subset of the FEEL expression language called S-FEEL. S-FEEL expressions are limited to arithmetic formulas and simple comparisons (equals, not equals, in an enumerated list, in a numeric range, etc.), with a specific syntax and grammar defined by the DMN spec. Although the examples in this chapter are based on S-FEEL, it is reasonable to apply the CL2 label (and the information in this chapter) to any tool that supports executable decision logic using DMN graphical notation in combination with a simple business-friendly expression language equivalent to S-FEEL.

This chapter describes what is allowed by the DMN 1.1 specification, without regard to methodology or best practice. Where appropriate, we will indicate changes from DMN 1.0. In Part III, we will discuss what makes a "good" decision table and the additional recommendations of Method and Style.

The Big Picture

All executable decisions in DMN follow the same basic pattern:

- Each *decision* defines a *variable* with the same name as the decision. Upon execution, the decision's *value expression*, whether defined as a decision table or literal expression, populates the variable with a *value*.

- Each of the decision's *information requirement* connectors references either a *supporting decision* or *input data* element, the DRD node at the tail of the connector. Only variables associated with an information requirement may be used in the decision's value expression.

- An *input data* element has no value expression, just a value, which is passed to the element when the decision is executed, for example, by a BPMN decision task.

- If a decision has a *knowledge requirement* – a dashed arrow connector from a *business knowledge model* (BKM) – the decision's value expression *invokes* the BKM. The invocation maps variables from the decision's information requirements to the *parameters* of the BKM, and the BKM's value then populates the output variable of both the BKM and the invoking decision.

With this big picture in mind, let's look at the decision table for *Applicant Risk Rating* (Figure 25) and its associated DRD (Figure 26).

Applicant Risk Rating			
U	Applicant Age	Medical History	Applicant Risk Rating
1	>60	good	Medium
2		bad	High
3	[25..60]	-	Medium
4	<25	good	Low
5		bad	Medium

Figure 25. Decision logic for *Applicant Risk Rating*. Source: OMG

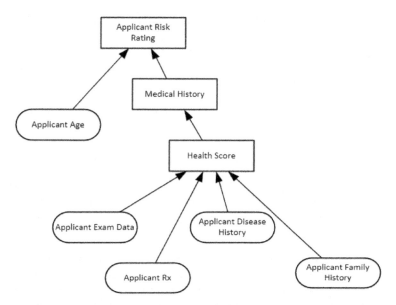

Figure 26. Requirement subgraph (DRD) of *Applicant Risk Rating*

Variables

Here input data *Applicant Age* and decision *Medical History* both define *variables* that hold their value. The *information requirements* (solid arrows) linking those nodes to *Applicant Risk Rating* allow those variables to be used in *Applicant Risk Rating's* value expression. Those variables are said to be "in scope" in the decision logic for *Applicant Risk Rating*.

CL2 can describe reasonably complex decision logic, even though each decision node in the DRD is limited to relatively simple logic. In CL2 models, complex decision logic requires complex DRDs, typically involving a great number of decision nodes. At Conformance Level 3, DMN allows an alternative modeling style that requires fewer decision nodes in the DRD, each implementing more complex decision logic using *contexts*. We will discuss this in Chapter 5.

The choice between DRDs containing a large number of simple decisions and those containing a smaller number of more complex decisions is strictly a matter of style, and should be based on the preferences and skills of the modeler and other stakeholders.

Datatypes

Besides a *name*, each variable specifies its *datatype* via the attribute *typeRef*. Every expression language has a corresponding *type language* defining a list of base datatypes. In DMN, the default *type language* is FEEL, but modelers may specify an alternative type language such as XSD, typically used for data defined externally and *imported* into the DMN model.

Base types in the FEEL type language include *string* (text), *number*, *Boolean*, and a few date/time and duration types. A variable specifying a *typeRef* of *string* says that the variable can take any string value. But it is generally better to say that the variable is a string with enumerated *allowed values* such as "High", "Medium", and "Low". In that case, the *typeRef* indicates a *custom type*.

In DMN a custom type, called an *item definition*, is specified as a base type restricted by a list of allowed values. For example, a variable named *DefaultRisk* with *typeRef* indicating the item definition *tDefaultRisk*, a string with allowed values "High", "Medium", and "Low," means that *DefaultRisk* can only take those three possible values.

Allowed values are not limited to enumerated text values. For number, date/time, and duration types, the allowed values may also be a *range*, such as >2 or [1..100), or a *comma-separated list* of ranges. (The notation [1..100) is shorthand for *greater than or equal to 1 and less than 100*. More on this later in this chapter.)

In addition to defining simple types restricted to allowed values, item definitions are also used to define *complex types* composed of structured data. In that case, the item definition specifies a list of *item components*. Each item component is itself an item definition, which could include a nested list of item components. In this way, item definition can define arbitrarily complex data structures.

As an alternative to specifying item definitions in DMN, datatypes may be created externally in some other type language, such as XSD, and imported into the DMN model. For example, suppose *CustomerType*, a complex type, is defined in an XML Schema Document (XSD) with target namespace *methodandstyle.com/myDMNTypes*. In the DMN model, an *Import* element must be specified that identifies the XSD file containing *CustomerType* with that namespace. Then DMN elements of type *CustomerType* can reference the type simply by standard *typeRef*, which is a *namespace-qualified name* (QName). Child elements and attributes of *CustomerType*, defined as XSD types, are automatically mapped to their FEEL equivalents upon import, so they can be directly referenced in FEEL value expressions.

Since item definitions are referenced by name, their (possibly namespace-qualified) names must be unique in the decision model.[36]

S-FEEL

As we've discussed, a decision's value expression maps its input variables into some output value. To communicate that decision logic, it is possible to describe it in words, possibly in combination with a tabular format, so that business people can understand it easily. But in order to make that value expression *executable*, those words and table cells must use a *formal expression language*, with precise semantics, grammar, and rules. S-FEEL is DMN's solution

---

[36] This is also new in DMN 1.1. DMN 1.0 had a more complicated way to reference datatypes.

for a business-friendly execution language for use in decision tables and simple literal expressions.

Names

One "business-friendly" aspect of S-FEEL (and FEEL) is that the names of variables and built-in functions may contain *spaces*. A business-oriented diagram, such as a DRD (Figure 26), often may use spaces in the names of decisions and input data. In fact, FEEL's creator Gary Hallmark maintains that expression languages like XPATH, in which variable names must start with a special character like $ and may not contain spaces, are inherently business-unfriendly.

However, variable names that include spaces make parsing expressions for execution much more difficult for tool vendors. For that reason most other expression languages do not allow spaces in the names of variables or functions. And possibly for that reason, it is already clear that many first-generation DMN tool vendors are substituting their own FEEL-ish expression languages, easier for their own engines to parse and execute. However, in this book we'll focus on FEEL and S-FEEL as they are presented in the spec. DMN will ultimately be much more useful if FEEL is widely adopted.

Of course, even in FEEL, modelers are not obligated to use spaces in element names. They can always replace spaces with underscores (e.g., *Applicant_Risk_Rating*) or "camel case" (*ApplicantRiskRating*). And when a variable is used in a literal expression, a tool may elect to prefix its name with a symbol like # or $, again to simplify parsing the expression for execution. Alternatively, a tool may elect to display the decision's *label* attribute, including spaces, in the DRD, and generate from that label a corresponding *variable name* (used in expressions) without spaces.

In Figure 26, all of the input data elements and decisions – and the variables that hold their values – represent *simple datatypes:* a string (i.e., text), a number, a Boolean value, etc. But a single variable could also represent *structured data*, sometimes called a *business object*. This is quite often the case for input data. For example, instead of separate input data elements *Applicant Age, Applicant Disease History, Applicant Rx*, etc., we would more typically have a single input data element *Applicant*, a data structure containing all this information in its attributes or sub-elements. In that case the DRD would look like Figure 27.

Using structured data elements like *Applicant* for input data simplifies the DRD and is generally best practice. When you do that, individual elements of the structured data are referenced in expressions by their *qualified names*. For example, in order to reference a particular element of *Applicant*, such as *Age*, you use the qualified name *Applicant.Age*. Qualified names in FEEL use a "dot notation," with a *period* separating parent and child elements in a data structure. Some modelers may see restricting input data to simple types (Figure 26) as more "business-friendly" than structured types (Figure 27), but when modeling real-world decision logic for execution, it's hard to avoid structured data, and in DMN it's best not to try.

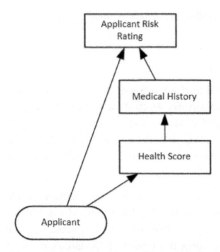

Figure 27. DRD of *Applicant Risk Rating* with structured input data, *Applicant*

Literals

In a decision table, the combination of an input column heading (*input expression*) and table cell in that column (*input entry*) defines a Boolean condition used in a decision rule. If an input expression is *Risk Rating*, then the input entry High does not test whether *Risk Rating* has the string value "High". It actually tests whether the value of *Risk Rating* matches the value of a *variable* named High. If you mean the literal string "High", you need to enclose it in quotation marks. Without the quotation marks, the input entry High means the *variable* named High; the input entry "High" means the *string literal* "High". In a decision table, you can indicate a literal string value without the quotation marks by putting the string in *italics*: In a decision table, "High" and *High* mean exactly the same thing, a literal value. Figure 28 provides another example.

Input expression	Input entry	Meaning
Customer.name	"John"	True if Customer's name is "John"
Customer.name	*John*	True if Customer's name is "John"
Customer.name	John	True if Customer's name equals the value of the variable named John

Figure 28. Names vs. literal strings in FEEL expressions

Dates take the format YYYY-MM-DD, where YYYY is the 4-digit year, MM is the 2-digit month, and DD is the 2-digit day of the month. But if you write the expression 2015-01-01, S-FEEL does not see January 1, 2015. It sees the number 2013, subtracting 01 twice from the number 2015. And if you write "2015-01-01", it sees the string "2015-01-01", not the date. So how do you write January 1, 2015?

In S-FEEL, you need to use the *date()* constructor function operating on a literal string value in the required date format: *date("2015-01-01")*. You probably didn't see that one coming! That's a mouthful for a decision table, so in a decision table (or in any *boxed expression*), you can write the date string without the constructor and quoted date string but formatting the date in **bold italics**, and it means the same thing:

Jan. 1, 2015 = date("2015-01-01") = ***2015-01-01***

Time and *duration* datatypes follow the same pattern. The time format is HH:MM:SS.SSS(Z). The optional suffix Z (without the parentheses) means the time referenced to GMT (also called UTC). Without the Z it means local time. (The local time zone is not specified. Unlike xsd, FEEL/S-FEEL does not allow you to indicate the local time zone.) For example,

2:30pm (local time) = time("14:30:00") = ***14:30:00***

Because a month is not a fixed duration, there are two separate duration types, *days and time duration* and *years and months duration*. *Days and time duration* has the format P*n1*DT*n2*H*n3*M*n4*S, where *n1* is the number of days, *n2* is the number of hours, *n3* the number of minutes, and *n4* the number of seconds. For example, the days and time duration one day, two and a half hours would be

duration("P1DT2H30M") = ***P1DT2H30M***.

Following the same pattern, the *years and months duration* 2 years, 1 day would be

duration("P2Y0M1D") = ***P2Y0M1D***.

Ranges

Input entries and allowed values of number, date, time, and duration types may specify one or more *ranges* of values. The S-FEEL range syntax is *[endpoint1..endpoint2]*, where the endpoints may be either literal values or names. Closed intervals are denoted by square brackets, open intervals by parentheses. Thus the range *[1..100)* means greater than or equal to 1 and less than 100.

Expressions

In S-FEEL, expressions are limited to *simple expressions*, meaning arithmetic operations and comparison tests. All other FEEL operators and functions, including logical *and* and *or*, *if..then..else*, and string concatenation, are not allowed in S-FEEL expressions.

Arithmetic Expressions

S-FEEL arithmetic operations – addition, subtraction, multiplication, division, exponentiation, and negation – are allowed only for number types, with the following exceptions:

- A *date* may be subtracted from a *date*, resulting in a *days and time duration* or *a years and months duration*.

- A *time* may be subtracted from a *time*, resulting in a *days and time duration*.

- A *days and time duration* may be added to or subtracted from a *time*, resulting in a *time*.

- A *years and months duration* may be added to or subtracted from another *years and months duration*, and *days and time duration* may be added to or subtracted from another *days and time duration*, yielding a duration of the same type.

- A *duration* may be multiplied or divided by a *number*, yielding another *duration*.

- A *duration* may be added to or subtracted from a *date*, resulting in a *date*.

Comparison Expressions

In Level 2 decision tables, S-FEEL comparison operators are used in input entries and input expressions.[37] They are defined only for operands of the same type.

- Arithmetic comparison operators >, >=, <, and <= apply to number, date, time, and duration types.

- String and Boolean types can only be compared for equality.

- Officially, there is no = operator in an input entry. The input entry just includes a literal value, list, or range. For example, if the input expression is *Age*, a number, and the test is *Age=25*, the input entry should simply be 25, not =25. Some tools may include the = sign, but this is technically incorrect.

- If the input entry is a list of values or a range, the cell evaluates to true if the input expression is a member of the list or range. Again, officially the input entry should not include the = or a symbol to indicate membership in a set, although some tools may display those.

- Logical negation is represented by the *not()* operator. Not-equals symbols used in other expression languages, such as <> or !=, are not part of S-FEEL syntax, although FEEL does allow != in literal expressions. For example, if the input expression is *Age*, a number, and the test is *Age not equal to 25*, the input entry should be *not(25)*.

Literal Expressions

A *literal expression* is an expression in text form. In CL2 models, literal expressions are most often used as value expressions for a decision or BKM, or as output entries in a decision table. In both of those cases, the only variables that may be referenced in the expression are those corresponding to one of the decision's *information requirements* (or for BKM, its *parameters*).

Recall that literal expressions in S-FEEL are limited to *simple expressions*, meaning either simple values (literal values or names), arithmetic expressions, or comparison expressions.

---

[37] Comparison in input expressions was added in DMN 1.1.

Notably absent from that list is *if..then* logic. For that reason, CL2 decisions modeled as literal expressions are typically *unconditional computations*.

For example, consider the DRD shown in Figure 29. The input data *Loan* includes the sub-elements *principal, rate,* and *term*. The decision *Monthly payment* calculates payment amount based on as the literal expression,

```
(Loan.principal *Loan.rate/12) / (1 - (1 + Loan.rate/12)**-Loan.term)
```

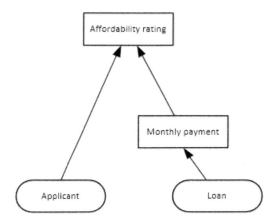

Figure 29. Decision *Monthly payment* is a literal expression.

Note that all arguments of this expression reference the input variable *Loan*, defined in the information requirement connector linking *Monthly payment* to the input data *Loan*.

A CL2 decision modeled as a literal expression can also be used to define *a named constant*. For example, if we wanted to define a duration constant *oneHour*, we could use a decision named *oneHour* with the literal expression, *duration("PT1H")*. Then, for example, another decision with an information requirement to *oneHour* could use the variable *one hour* in an input entry, e.g., > *oneHour*, to test the value of a duration-type input expression.

Decision Tables

Figure 30 illustrates the basic structure of a DMN decision table displayed in the most common orientation, called *rules-as-rows*.

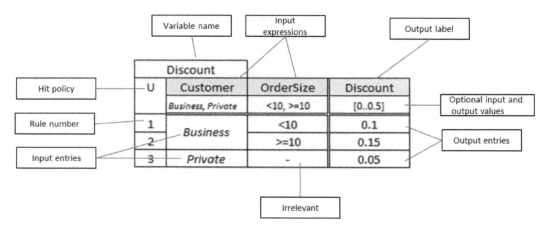

Figure 30. A decision table. Source: OMG

Variable Name and Output Label

In CL2 decision tables, the *variable name* is displayed in a tab at the top, in Figure 30 called *Discount*. When the table is the direct value expression of a *decision*, the variable name is identical to the *decision name*.[38] When the table is the value expression of a BKM, the variable name shown in the tab at the top is the *BKM name*.

Note in Figure 30 that the same value is also shown at the head of the decision table output column. This is called the *output label*. Technically, the DMN 1.1 spec says the output label can be anything you like. Normally, when the table is the direct value expression of a decision, output label should match the variable name, but when the table is the value expression of a BKM, this cell may be left empty or use the BKM name.

In a decision with *compound output* – more than one output column – the table output is a data structure in which each output column represents an *output component*. Below the optional *output label* spanning the output columns, the *output component name* should be displayed at the top of each output column.

Input Expression

At the top of each input column, the header row displays the *input expression*. Normally this is a *qualified name* referencing an *input variable*, such as *ApplicantData.Income*. Technically it is allowed to be a *simple expression*, meaning an arithmetic expression, such as *ApplicantData.Income / 1000*, or a comparison, such as *ApplicantData.Age>18*, but best to stick to a simple name. Note: When the decision table is the value expression of a BKM, the input expression may ONLY be a name, not an expression. This is because a BKM represents a

---

[38] Once again, this is how it works in DMN 1.1, a change from DMN 1.0.

function definition, and the inputs of a BKM decision table name its *parameters.* We'll say more about BKMs later in this chapter.

An input expression may reference only variables *in scope.* When the decision table is directly contained in a decision, the variables in scope are limited to the variables referenced by the decision's *information requirements.* When the decision table is directly contained in a BKM, the variables in scope are limited to the BKM *parameters.*

Figure 31 illustrates what is allowed and not allowed as an input expression in a CL2 decision table for a decision that has inputs *Applicant* and *Loan.*

Input expression	Allowed?
Applicant.annual income	Yes (qualified name)
Applicant.annual income / 12	Yes (arithmetic expression)
2015-01-01 – Applicant.Date of Birth	Yes (arithmetic expression with date-time literal)
Applicant.monthly expenses + Loan.monthly payment	Yes (arithmetic expression involving two qualified names)
Loan.monthly payment / Applicant.monthly income	Yes (arithmetic expression involving two qualified names)
Applicant.age > 18	Yes (comparison expression)[39].
Applicant.first name + " " + Applicant.last name	No (string concatenation not allowed in S-FEEL.)
max(Applicant[1].income, Applicant[2].income)	No (FEEL List expressions like Applicant[1] and built-in functions like max() are not allowed in S-FEEL).

Figure 31. Input expressions allowed or not allowed in CL2 decision tables

Input and Output Values

A decision table header row may also display optional lists of *input values* and *output values* defining the domain of possible values for the input expression or output entry. In Figure 30, the input expression *Customer* has input values *Business* and *Private.* As mentioned earlier, the use of italics in Figure 30 for these values indicates they are *literal strings,* not variable names. The input expression *OrderSize* here has enumerated range values *<10* and *>=10,* implying *OrderSize* is a number type. Input or output values for a numeric expression may be a list of numbers or *numeric ranges,* as it is here. In Figure 30, output values of the output *Discount* must be in the range from 0 to 0.5, inclusive.

---

[39] Added in DMN 1.1.

You may recall that a variable's *typeRef* may point to an *item definition* that also contains a list of *allowed values*, so there seems to be some duplication here. No doubt there may be some duplication of effort in populating both item definition allowed values and decision table input values and output values, but keep the following in mind:

- A variable's item definition allowed values are reused with any DMN expression referencing the variable. Decision table input and output values are specific to that decision table.

- Decision table input values refer specifically to an *input expression*, which may have a different datatype from the *input variable* it references.

- The decision table column headings display the input and output values, not item definition allowed values. Populating the input values allows verification that the decision table is *complete*, meaning all possible combinations of input values are matched by some rule in the table. If input values are not specified for a decision table, it is a good idea to at least specify the datatype. Even though the spec does not mention this, it is not uncommon for a DMN tool to display the datatype for input and output columns in a decision table.

When a decision table's *hit policy* is *Priority*, the listed order of output values determines their priority. Hit policy will be discussed later in this chapter.

Input Entry

The cells of the input columns are called *input entries*. S-FEEL requires an input entry to be list of *simple unary tests*. (Usually the list has only a single member, but technically in the spec it is a list.) In CL2 decision tables, an input entry can be a *literal value* or *list* of values, or a variable *name* or list of names, or a *range* of numeric or date/time values or list of ranges. Technically, an input entry is just a fragment of an expression. In combination with the input expression, the input entry defines a complete Boolean expression, with value either true or false.

If the input entry is just a literal value, the condition tests whether the value of the input expression is equal to that value, either true or false. Tools are not supposed to put the = sign in the input entry, although some first-generation tools ignore this; *equals* is implied by simply entering the value. If the input entry is a list of values, it tests whether the input expression value is a member of that list, true or false. Again, no operator symbol such as = is required; the input entry should just be the list. (Signavio, for example, uses the symbol ε to mean "element in the list.")

If the same input entry applies to adjacent rows of the table, it is allowed to merge the input entry cells, as with the entry *Business* in Figure 30. This can make complex tables more easily readable, but so far few DMN tools support this.

For example, if the input expression is *Applicant.MonthlyIncome* and the input entry is a range like *>5000*, the cell tests the condition, *Applicant.MonthlyIncome >5000*, either true or false. If the input entry is a comma-separated list of values or ranges, such as *(0, >5000)*, the cell tests the condition *(Applicant.MonthlyIncome = 0 or Applicant.MonthlyIncome > 5000),* either true or false.

A range can also be specified as an *interval* written as [x..y] or (x..y). The square bracket means the interval includes the adjacent endpoint, while parenthesis means the interval excludes the adjacent endpoint. Thus (0..1] means *greater than 0 and less than or equal to 1.* [40]

Input expression	Input entry	Meaning
Customer.name	*John*	Allowed. True if Customer's name is "John"
Customer.name	John	Allowed. True if Customer's name is the same as the variable John. Usually this is not what you mean.
Applicant.age	<18, >=65	Allowed. True if Applicant's age is either under 18 or greater than or equal to 65
Applicant.age	[18..65)	Allowed. True if Applicant's age is greater than or equal to 18 or under 65.
Applicant.age	not([18..65])	Allowed. True if Applicant's age is less than 18 or greater than 65. The not() operator, if used, must apply to the whole list, not selected elements.
Applicant.age	<18 or >=65	Not allowed. Conjunctions "and", "or" are not allowed in input entries. Use comma-separated values instead of "or". Use separate input clauses instead of "and".
Borrower.income	>Co-borrower.income	Allowed. True if Borrower's income is greater than Co-borrower's income.
Borrower.income	>3.3*MonthlyPayment	Not allowed. Simple expressions are not allowed in an input entry. Value must be a literal or qualified name only.
Borrower.income	>max(Co-borrower1.income, Co-borrower2.income)	Not allowed. FEEL functions like max() are not allowed in S-FEEL input entry.

Figure 32. Examples of input entries allowed and not allowed

Figure 32 provides examples of input entries allowed and not allowed in CL2 decision tables.

An input entry of *hyphen* (-) means the input *is irrelevant* to the rule; effectively it is the same as the rule condition automatically evaluating to true. For example, in Figure 30, if *Customer* is "Private" the *Discount* is .05; the input *OrderSize* is irrelevant, so its input entry is hyphen.

---

[40] An open interval may also be indicated by a reversed square bracket. For example,]0..1] means the same as (0..1], greater than zero but less than or equal to one. Parentheses are more familiar and are recommended over reversed square brackets.

In some first-generation DMN tools, the cell is left blank, but this is incorrect. Input entries should never be blank.

Output Entry

The cells of the output column are called *output entries*, either a literal value or an expression conforming to the output data type and (if present) the listed allowed values. In CL2 decision tables, an output entry may be either:

- a literal value, such as *.10* or *"Approved"*;
- a simple expression of decision inputs that evaluates to a literal value, such as *Total Cost * .095*. Here *Total Cost* must be a variable in scope, meaning its value is provided by an information requirement in the DRD; or
- a list of the items above.

Decision Rules

Each row of the table below the header row represents a *decision rule*, logic determining the output value from the combination of input values. Here is how it works. For any rule, if the condition expressions for *all* input columns evaluate to true, the rule is said to *match*. The *all* part is critical; the columns of the decision table are always ANDed together.

If a single rule matches, the decision table output is assigned the value shown in the output entry for that rule. (In a compound table, if the rule matches, the corresponding output entry for each output component is assigned.) If more than one rule matches, determination of the output depends on the table's *hit policy*, discussed later.

If no rule matches, the output is determined by the table's *default output entry*, if one is provided. (In the diagram, the default output entry is denoted by an underlined value in the list of output values.) If no rule matches and no default output entry is provided, the decision table returns an error.

For example, rule 1 of Figure 30 is a match if *Customer* is "Business" and *OrderSize* <10.

The interpretation of the decision logic in Figure 30 is as follows:
- If *Customer* is "Business" AND *OrderSize* is <10, then *Discount* is .10.
- If *Customer* is "Business" AND *OrderSize* is >=10, then *Discount* is .15.
- If *Customer* is "Private", then *Discount* is .05. *OrderSize* is irrelevant in this case.

Note that this decision table is *complete*, meaning there is no possible combination of *Customer* and *OrderSize* within the domain of allowed input values for which there is no matching rule.

Compound Output

A decision table with more than one output column is said to have a *compound output*. Any rule that matches selects its output entry for *each* of the output columns. For example, in

---

Figure 33 both the *Discount* and *Shipping* method are determined in a single decision. DMN considers this compound output a single structured data output, *Adjustments*.

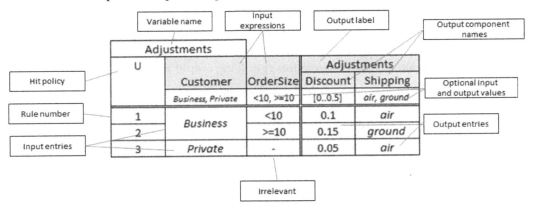

Figure 33. Compound decision table. Source: OMG

Hit Policy

In any single rule the input columns are always ANDed together. Assuming *Customer* can be either *Business* or *Private*, not both simultaneously, only one of these rules can be satisfied. However, this is not always the case. A decision in which more than one rule may be satisfied is said to have *overlapping rules*, and requires specification of a *hit policy*.

- A decision table without overlap has a hit policy of *Unique*, code *U*. This is the default.

- A decision table with overlap but in which all overlapping rules generate the same output value has a hit policy of *Any*, code *A*.

- A decision table in which overlapping rules generate different output values uses the hit policy to select the correct one.

  o A hit policy of *Priority*, code *P*, means select the output of the rule with the highest priority, as determined by the listed order of output values. Remember, decision table output values are optional, but they must be provided with hit policy *P*.

  o A hit policy of *First*, code *F*, means evaluate the rules in the order listed in the table, and select the first one to match. This hit policy is explicitly non-declarative, and the spec deprecates its use.

Hit policy codes *U, A, P,* and *F* signify *single-hit policies,* meaning the decision returns the value of one output only.[41] However, DMN also supports *multiple-hit policies,* in which the outputs of all satisfied rules are collected and possibly aggregated.

- A hit policy of *Output order* (code *O*) means collect and list the output values in decreasing order of output priority, based on the order of listed allowed output values. Again, hit policy *O* requires specifying output values.

- A hit policy of *Rule order* (code *R*) means collect and list the output values in order of the rules in the decision table.

- A hit policy of *Collect* (code *C*) with no appended *collect operator* returns all hit outputs in arbitrary order. If appended with a collect operator, a single aggregated value is returned:

  - Sum (+) sums the output values.

  - Min (<) returns the minimum output value.

  - Max (>) returns the maximum output value.

  - Count (#) returns the number of distinct output values.

Completeness Indicator

In DMN 1.0, the table cell containing the hit policy code also contained a *Completeness indicator* code, either *C* (complete) or *I* (incomplete). The metamodel *isComplete* attribute and the Completeness indicator code, however, were eliminated in DMN 1.1, for several reasons:

- The intended meaning of completeness – that all possible combinations of input values are matched by at least one rule – is ambiguous in practice, when default output entries and table restrictions and exclusions are considered.

- The Completeness indicator code *C,* optional in the hit policy cell of the table, conflicts with the hit policy *Collect,* also code *C.*

- When the Completeness indicator code *C* was omitted, the intended meaning was *complete,* but when the *isComplete* attribute in the schema was omitted, the intended meaning was *incomplete.*

While DMN no longer has a Completeness Indicator, it is not uncommon to see examples of it in diagrams created in first-generation tools. Typically you might see a code of *UC – Unique, Complete –* where technically DMN 1.1 says it should simply say *U.*

---

[41] Some pre-DMN writings on decision tables use the term *single-hit* to mean only what DMN calls Unique, and refer to equivalents of *Any, Priority,* or *First* as *multi-hit.*

Table Orientation

Figure 34 illustrates the most common table orientation, called "rules-as-rows." In the *rules-as-rows* orientation, columns represent inputs and outputs, while each row represents a rule. DMN also supports two other orientations, "rules-as-columns" and "crosstab."

Discount				
U	Customer	OrderSize	Delivery	Discount
	Business, Private, Government	<10, >=10	sameday, slow	0, 0.05, 0.10, 0.15
1	Business	<10	-	0.05
2		>=10	-	0.10
3	Private	-	sameday	0
4			slow	0.05
5	Government	-	-	0.15

Figure 34. Decision table, rules-as-rows orientation. Source: OMG

Figure 35 shows the same decision table in the *rules-as-columns* orientation. Here, the header column is at the left, and rows represent inputs and outputs. Columns in the table represent rules.

Discount					
Customer	Business, Private, Government	Business		Private	Government
Ordersize	<10, >=10	<10	>=10	-	-
Delivery	sameday, slow	-	-	sameday	slow	-
Discount	0, 0.05, 0.10, 0.15	0.05	0.10	0	0.05	0.15
U		1	2	3	4	5

Figure 35. Decision table, rules-as-columns orientation. Source: OMG

For rules-as-columns, also called *vertical tables*, DMN also allows a *shorthand notation*, a style used in the early days of decision tables (Figure 36). Here each *output value* has a separate row, indicated by selected (x) or not selected (-).

Discount						
Customer	Business, Private, Government	Business		Private		Government
Ordersize	<10, >=10	<10	>=10	-		-
Delivery	sameday, slow	-	-	sameday	slow	-
0.00		-	-	x	-	-
0.05		x	-	-	x	-
0.10		-	x	-	-	-
0.15		-	-	-	-	x
U		1	2	3	4	5

Figure 36. Vertical table shorthand notation

Figure 37 presents the decision table in yet another orientation, called *crosstab*. The crosstab format is generally more compact but it is limited to decision tables with a *Unique* hit policy. In this format, both the header row and header column headings represent *input expressions*. The second row and second column (white) represent distinct *input entries*. The cells represent the *output entries* for the intersecting input values.

Discount					
Discount		Customer, Delivery			
		Business	Private		Government
		-	sameday	slow	-
Ordersize	<10	0.05	0	0.05	0.15
	>=10	0.10	0	0.05	0.15

Figure 37. Decision table, crosstab orientation. Source: OMG

Crosstab works best when there are only two inputs. In this decision table there are three. This is allowed by combining inputs, as seen in Figure 37, where *Customer* and *Delivery* are both listed in the input expression area. In that case, each combination of allowed values of the combined inputs creates a separate column, so with more than two inputs, the complexity of crosstabs can get easily out of hand. It is manageable in this particular case because the *Delivery* input is irrelevant except for *Customer ="Private"*.

Business Knowledge Models

Suppose you have some bit of decision logic, whether modeled as a decision table or literal expression, that is going to be used in multiple decision models. No doubt you have many of those in your organization. You don't want to have to enter that decision logic, or even copy and paste it, into every decision model that uses it. You would rather define it once as a *reusable function* and allow any decision that uses that logic to simply call it. In DMN, the most common form of a reusable decision function is called a *business knowledge model*, or BKM.

A BKM body is an example of a *function definition*. The BKM's *parameters* are the variables referenced by the function's value expression. In CL2, a BKM's value expression can be either a decision table or a simple literal expression. In general, you should assume that the BKM may be defined in a separate imported model, and that the BKM parameters do not have the same name as the variables of the calling decision. The variables of the calling decision must be *mapped* to the BKM parameters in an *invocation*.

In a DRD, the invocation is indicated graphically as a *knowledge requirement* connector, a dashed arrow leading from the BKM to the decision that invokes it. *A BKM has no information requirements*, those incoming solid arrows in the DRD. Any input data or supporting decisions required by the BKM logic must be provided by *the calling decision via invocation*.

If the BKM's value expression is a decision table, the input expressions of that table must be the named parameters, not expressions of those parameters, as they could be if the decision table were directly contained in a decision.

When a BKM is *invoked* by a decision, the decision maps its inputs to the BKM parameters, and the resulting BKM output value is returned to the decision output. While various tools may define their own way of defining this parameter mapping, the DMN spec defines it graphically as a *boxed expression* (Figure 38). The tab above the top line names the invoking decision, *Application risk score*. The top line in the box names the BKM, here *Application risk score model*. (According to the spec, the decision name and its BKM name must be different.) Below that are rows with two columns. The first column, shown shaded, names a *parameter* of the BKM. The second column, unshaded, is a *binding expression*, a mapping of the decision variables to the parameter in the first column. Here the decision has a single variable, *Applicant data*, and the mapping for each parameter is a simple qualified name. At CL2, the binding expression must be an S-FEEL simple expression.

Application risk score	
Application risk score model	
Age	Applicant data.Age
Marital Status	Applicant data. MaritalStatus
Employment Status	Applicant data. EmploymentStatus

Figure 38. Boxed invocation maps variables of the calling decision to BKM parameters

As shown in Figure 39, it is possible for a decision to directly invoke more than one BKM, but this requires Conformance Level 3. At CL2, a decision may directly invoke at most one BKM. Also, a BKM may invoke another BKM, but this also requires CL3. For example, in Figure 39, *Decision* would not be an *invocation* expression but instead a *literal expression* containing two *function invocations*, such as

```
Business knowledge 1(param1, param2) + Business knowledge 2(param3).
```

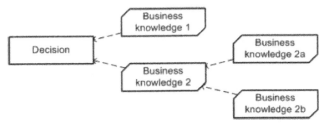

Figure 39. A decision may invoke multiple BKMs, and a BKM may invoke a BKM, but either of these requires Conformance Level 3. Source: OMG

CHAPTER 5

Decision Logic at Conformance Level 3

A wide range of expressions important in real-world decision logic cannot be described by the decision table and literal expression formats allowed by Conformance Level 2. Conformance Level 3 provides additional modeling elements and formats and a more powerful expression language to handle those. Key features of CL3 models include:

- The full *FEEL language*, including built-in functions, filter expressions, operators, and sorting.

- *Contexts*, lists of intermediate (local) variables and their associated value expressions, used to construct complex logic for a single decision.

- *Function definitions*, reusable fragments of decision logic that can be invoked directly from literal expressions.

- *Relations*, lists of similar contexts that look and act like relational database tables.

As noted previously, it is likely that some tools conforming to the DMN metamodel and schema will elect to create executable decision models using an expression language other than FEEL. While the DMN specification describes CL3 conformance only in terms of FEEL, it is useful here to classify as CL3 any DMN tool in which the graphical notation is unified with an executable expression language functionally equivalent to FEEL. The examples in this chapter, based on FEEL, along with the *decision logic patterns* described in Chapter 11, will illustrate what is meant by functional equivalence.

Boxed Expressions

An important but often overlooked aspect of the DMN notation is the use of *boxed expressions* to specify decision logic. A boxed expression is a table of element *names* and their corresponding *value expressions*. Besides decision tables, which DMN calls a type of boxed expression, CL2's only use of boxed expressions is to define parameter mappings in an invocation.

A boxed expression is not limited to a single variable/literal expression pair, but can be a *context*, a list of rows called *context entries*, each representing a variable/expression pair. The expression cell may contain another *nested boxed expression*, such as an invocation, a decision table, or another nested context. The combination of contexts and nested boxed expressions allows boxed expressions to represent even complicated decision logic in a common tabular format, easing understanding by business users. That decision logic includes all of the patterns discussed in Chapter 11, including iteration, table query, and more.

Boxed expressions play a significant role in DMN at CL3. They are in fact DMN's *standard graphical representation for decision logic*. Rather than define their own proprietary formats for defining such decision logic, tool vendors should adopt the boxed expression format as an aspect of the DMN notation just as important as the decision table.

Context

The spec defines a *context* is a list of key-value pairs. The *key* is the element *name*, and the *value* is an *expression*. The *boxed context* format (Figure 40) is, in its simplest form, a two-column table drawn with the left (key) column shaded and the right (expression) column unshaded. Each row, or *context entry*, defines a *variable* and its *value expression*. The scope of the variable is limited to the context, so its name must be unique only within the context. The value expression may be a literal value or list, a literal expression, an invocation, or even another context, nesting another list of context entries.

Applicant Data		
Age	51	
MaritalStatus	"M"	
EmploymentStatus	"EMPLOYED"	
ExistingCustomer	false	
Monthly	Income	10000.00
	Repayments	2500.00
	Expenses	3000.00

Figure 40. Boxed context describing data. Source: OMG

A context may be used to describe both data, such as an input data element (Figure 40), and decision logic (Figure 41). In Figure 40, *Applicant Data.Monthly* is itself a context, with entries *Income, Repayments,* and *Expenses.* In a boxed context there is no limit to the possible levels of nesting. The tab at the top of the boxed context identifies the *variable* for which the context acts as the value expression.

Figure 41 shows how decision logic can be defined as a boxed context, in which the value expression for a context entry is typically a literal expression. Here the decision *PolicyOptionsPremium* is defined as a context. Context entries *Uninsured* and *Medical* define local variables used in the context's last row, called the *final result box*. The value expressions of the context entries and the final result box are literal expressions. The *if..then..else* syntax in the literal expressions represents a FEEL construct unavailable in S-FEEL.

PolicyOptionsPremium	
UninsuredPremium	if PolicyOptions.UninsuredMotorist=true then $300 else 0
MedicalPremium	if PolicyOptions.Medical=true then $600 else 0
UninsuredPremium + MedicalPremium	

Figure 41. Boxed context describing decision logic

Figure 42 provides another example, from the Lending decision in the DMN spec. The final result box may reference both inputs to the decision and local variables defined in context entries.

Eligibility	
Age	Applicant.Age
Monthly Income	Applicant.Monthly Income
Pre-bureau Risk category	Affordability.Pre-bureau Risk category
Installment Affordable	Affordability.Installment Affordable

If Pre-bureau Risk category = "DECLINE" or
   Installment Affordable = false or
   Age < 18 or
   Monthly Income < 100
then "INELIGIBLE"
else "ELIGIBLE"	

Figure 42. Boxed context with final result box.

Function Definitions

A *function definition* is a reusable bit of decision logic, an expression of *parameters*. The most common use of function definition is as a value expression of a BKM, but it can also be the value expression of a context entry. The *name* of the BKM or context entry – which is also the name of its *output variable* – effectively names the function.

The boxed expression for a function definition displays the list of parameters enclosed in parentheses in the top row. *The order of parameters in this list is significant.* While the expression type *invocation* maps values to parameters *by name*, a function invocation in a *literal expression* maps values to parameters *by position*.

Installment calculation	
(Product Type, Rate, Term, Amount)	
Monthly Fee	if Product Type = "STANDARD LOAN" then 20.00 else if Product Type = "SPECIAL LOAN" then 25.00 else null
Monthly Repayment	PMT(Rate, Term, Amount)
Monthly Repayment + Monthly Fee	

Figure 43. Boxed function. Source: OMG

Figure 43 shows the function definition for the BKM *Installment calculation*. The function parameters are *Product Type, Rate, Term,* and *Amount*. The value expression for a function definition is often a *context*, as it is here. Note that the final result depends on the local variables *Monthly Fee* and *Monthly Repayment*, which are context entries.

In this example, taken from the DMN spec, the value expression for the context entry *Monthly Repayment* is a literal expression that includes a *function invocation*. The list of arguments enclosed in parentheses in the literal expression for *Monthly Repayment* indicates that *PMT* is the name of a function, defined by another BKM. As mentioned earlier, function invocations pass parameter values by position. Here *Monthly Repayment* passes values in the order *Rate, Term, Amount*. If the function definition of *PMT* does not list its parameters in that exact order, the wrong result will be returned.

Lists

In a *boxed expression*, including a decision table, a *list* is a single cell containing comma-separated elements. In a *text expression*, comma-separated elements enclosed in square brackets also signifies a list. For example, ["a","b","c"] is a list. A variable whose datatype is a *collection* is also a list, and the output of a decision with hit policy *Collect* is a list, as well.

In a literal expression, specific items may be selected from the list by a *filter expression*, an integer or Boolean expression enclosed in square brackets, called a *predicate*.

- When the predicate is an *integer*, it selects a list item by *position*, a 1-based index. For example, if list *L* = ["a","b","c"], *L*[2] = "b". A position value of -1 selects the *last* item in the list: *L*[-1] = "c".

- When the predicate is a *Boolean expression*, it acts as a *filter*, selecting one or more items from a collection. For example, if *Order.Items* is a collection, then *Order.Items[price>10]* selects instances of *Order.Items* for which the price is greater than 10. This is used extensively in the *table query patterns* discussed in Chapter 11.

Relations

A *relation* is a FEEL expression representing a relational table. In Figure 44, *car models* is a context entry whose value expression is a relation. Like all expressions, the relation takes its *name* from the decision/BKM (indicated by a tab at the top of the table) or context entry (indicated by shaded box to the left of the table) that it defines. The boxed expression for a relation is a grid in which each row represents an instance of the repeating table element, and each column represents an attribute of that element. The shaded box at the top of each column names the attribute.

car models	group	manufacturer	model	number of occupants
	compact	Ford	Focus	4
	compact	VW	Beetle	5
	mid-sized	Toyota	Camry	5
	mid-sized	Chevrolet	Malibu	6

Figure 44. Relation. Source: Gary Hallmark

A small but important technical note: The variable representing the relation is not the table containing the rows, just the *collection of rows*, an array.

As with lists, a *filter expression* is used to select elements from the relation, typically a Boolean expression enclosed in square brackets. For example, the FEEL expression

```
car models[group="compact" and number of occupants > 4]
```

applied to the relation shown Figure 44 selects the row shown in Figure 45.

group	manufacturer	model	number of occupants
compact	VW	Beetle	5

Figure 45. Selected context. Source: Gary Hallmark

An individual attribute (column value) can be selected by combining the filter expression with a path expression. For example,

```
car models[group="compact" and number of occupants > 4].manufacturer
```

gives the string value "VW".

FEEL

The problem confronting DMN's creators was that the rule languages used in popular Business Rule Engines and standard expression languages like XPATH were designed for developers not business people. Before DMN, decision modeling was viewed as a way to generate *business requirements* that would then be interpreted by developers and coded for execution in a technical rule language. But DMN was seeking a more direct mapping from decision modeling to execution. Like BPMN, DMN seeks to break down the barriers between modeling and execution. Business users should be able to define decision logic that is not only clear from a set of diagrams but directly executable on a decision engine! In order to achieve that, the DMN spec had to specify an expression language both powerful enough to handle real-world decision logic and accessible to business users. The result is *FEEL*, which stands for *Friendly Enough Expression Language*.

I once asked Gary Hallmark, DMN task force chair and the inventor of FEEL, what was the reason for basing DMN on an entirely new expression language for which no commercial execution engine already existed? The answer was not really surprising: Existing expression languages were designed for use by developers, not business people. Also, most BRE rule languages are based on protected intellectual property, not royalty-free, and are procedural, not declarative.

Inventing a new language avoided those problems. In particular, Hallmark told me, it skirted "the tedious 'my language is friendlier than yours' war which is unhelpful to most users."[42] FEEL enables modeling of a wide range of decision logic with precisely defined execution semantics. It is a functional language similar to XPATH 2.0, and contains built-in functions similar to those available in that language.

On the other hand, FEEL runs the very real risk of being ignored by many, possibly most, executable DMN tools. If that should occur, DRD structures would be interchangeable but not the executable decision logic. It is analogous to the BPM market in the days when BPMN 1.x models had to be mapped to BPEL and proprietary process execution languages. It worked for a while, but ultimately it gave way to BPMN 2.0, which unified modeling and execution in a single language. Similarly, DMN will be much stronger as a standard if FEEL is ultimately adopted by tool vendors.

What Is FEEL?

FEEL is a true *expression language*, not a programming language. That means it can *reference variables* to compute a value, but it *cannot define variables*. (The variables used in FEEL expressions are defined instead by decisions, BKMs, input data, and context entries.) FEEL's distinguishing features include:

- *Side-effect free.* This is another way to say that FEEL logic is *declarative*. When a decision can be decomposed into multiple FEEL expressions, the order of evaluating those expressions does not affect the result.

- *Simple syntax designed for a wide audience.* In particular, FEEL variable names have no special start character like $, and can include spaces and other characters not normally allowed in expression languages. Whether or not this really makes the language "business friendly" is subject to debate.

- *Strongly typed variables and expressions.* FEEL base types include string, number, Boolean, and a few date, time, and duration types, but custom types specifying allowed values and complex data structures can be defined as well.

---

[42] Hallmark, private communication, September 2015

- *Three-valued logic (true, false, null), following SQL.*

In many ways, FEEL resembles XPATH, an expression language embedded within XSLT and XQuery, except that FEEL data is not based on XML. The FEEL data model is intended to be similar to JSON, a data representation widely used in REST services:

> "A FEEL object is a number, a string, a date, a time, a duration, a function, a context, or a list of FEEL objects (including nested lists).... A JSON object is a number, a string, a context (JSON calls them maps) or a list of JSON objects. So FEEL is an extension of JSON in this regard. In addition, FEEL provides friendlier syntax for literal values, and does not require context keys to be quoted."[43]

In DMN, FEEL is the default expression language for literal expressions, function parameter mappings, and decision table input expressions and output entries.

Chapter 10 of the DMN spec is the official FEEL specification. While FEEL is the *default* expression language in DMN, its use is not required. A DMN model may specify some other expression language for the whole model or for individual elements of it. In fact, many first-generation DMN tools do not support FEEL as defined by the DMN spec, but instead rely on a FEEL-like syntax and function library using their own expression language.

FEEL Names

An important difference between FEEL and most other expression languages is that FEEL element names may contain spaces, apostrophes, and other characters that are usually forbidden in element names. They may not contain commas, colons, or parentheses, which serve as delimiters in the language. As admitted in the spec,

> "This naming freedom makes FEEL's syntax ambiguous. Ambiguity is resolved using the scope. Names are matched from left to right against the names in-scope, and the longest match is preferred. In the case where the longest match is not desired, parenthesis or other punctuation (that is not allowed in a name) can be used to disambiguate a FEEL expression."[44]

Notwithstanding this guidance, allowing variable names – not to mention the names of built-in functions – to contain spaces presents an obstacle to adoption by tool vendors. Very few other expression languages allow the names of variables or functions to contain spaces. It is difficult enough for a tool to implement FEEL without having to figure out, when parsing a FEEL expression, what is a variable, what is a built-in function, and what is something else.

Like XML, FEEL supports structured data, referencing their attributes and components through *qualified names*, also called a *path expression*, using a "dot notation" such as

---

[43] DMN Spec, section 10.2.2

[44] DMN Spec, section 10.3.1.5.

Customer.age or *Customer.maritalStatus.* The dot (.) plays the same role in FEEL as slash (/) does in XPATH expressions.

A FEEL expression can reference a variable imported from another DMN model through its *namespace-qualified name*, again using dot notation. Every DMN model defines a *namespace,* a globally unique string usually specified as a URI, e.g. *methodandstyle.com/ns/functionLib.* In that case, to reference the function *payment()* imported from that namespace, the FEEL syntax would be

```
methodandstyle.com/ns/functionLib.payment(principal, rate, term)
```

Datatypes

Variables and certain expressions contain a *typeRef* attribute specifying the datatype. FEEL supports the following *base types*:

- *string*, i.e., text. Equivalent to xsd:string in XML Schema.

- *Boolean*, i.e., true or false. Equivalent to xsd:Boolean in XML Schema.

- *number*, a numeric value. Equivalent to xsd:decimal in XML Schema.

- date, time, and duration types:

  o *time*, equivalent to xsd:time in XML Schema without the optional time zone indicator.

  o *date*, equivalent to xsd:date in XML Schema.

  o *days and time duration*, equivalent to xsd:dayTimeDuration.

  o *years and months duration*, equivalent to xsd:yearMonthDuration.

Modelers may also define *custom types* in the form of *item definitions.* An item definition may be as simple as a base type with enumerated values, or it can be a data structure based on *item components.*

Ternary Logic

Like SQL, FEEL uses the value *null* to represent either the empty set or an error condition. In value comparison expressions, the values must be of the same type to obtain a non-*null* result. For example:

- The expression FEEL ("1" = 1) is *null*, because the string "1" cannot be compared to the number 1.

- The expression "A" * 3 is *null*, because you cannot multiply a string by a number.

- There is no value for *notANumber, positiveInfintity,* or *negativeInfinity,* special values used in other expression languages. Use *null* instead.

- When any FEEL built-in function encounters input outside its defined domain, the function returns *null*.

If the value of a decision's required input data or supporting decision is missing, it is considered *null* in the decision's value expression, and the decision logic may test for a value of *null*. For example, in a decision table with input expression *CreditScore*, an input entry of *null* means "if no credit score value is available."

Path Expressions

The same dot notation used in qualified names can be used in more complex path expressions that select one or more instances of a complex type from a collection, and then reference an attribute of that instance or list of instances.

Path expressions also allow reference to components of date, time, and duration values.

Example 1:

```
sum(credit delinquency[record date > date("2011-01-01")].amount)
```

Here *credit delinquency* is a relation, a list of items containing a *record date* and an *amount*. The filter expression

```
record date > date("2011-01-01")
```

selects only those items for which the *record date* is after January 1, 2011. The path expression *credit delinquency.amount* selects the *amount* attribute for those items, creating a list of *amount* values. The *sum* function sums that list.

Example 2:

```
date("2011-01-01").year
```

results in the value *2011*.

Built-In Functions

FEEL's built-in functions closely mirror those in XPATH 2.0.

Arithmetic Functions

1) Addition

For number, date/time, and duration operands, the + operator signifies *addition*. Number can be added to number; duration can be added to duration, date, or time.

For string operands, + signifies *concatenation*, e.g., String1 + String2. Any other combination of operands returns *null*.

2) Subtraction

The - operator signifies subtraction. Number can be subtracted from number. Date and time can be subtracted from date and time, giving duration. Any other combination of operands returns *null*.

3) Multiplication

The * operator signifies multiplication. Number or duration can be multiplied by number. Any other combination of operands returns *null*.

4) Division

The / operator signifies division. Number or duration can be divided by number. Any other combination of operand returns *null*. Division by zero returns *null*.

5) Exponentiation

The ** operator signifies exponentiation. Only number operands are supported.

String Functions

6) +

string1 + string2 returns a single concatenated string.

7) substring

substring(myString, startPos, length?) returns string of [*length*] characters from *myString*, beginning with character *startPos* (1-based index). If *length* is omitted, return all characters beginning with *startPos*.

8) string length

string length(myString) returns the number of characters in *myString*.

9) upper case

upper case(myString) converts all lower case to upper case.

10) lower case

lower case(myString) converts all upper case to lower case.

11) substring before

substring before(myString, matchString) returns fragment of *myString* occurring before *matchString*. Returns empty string "" if no match.

---

12) substring after

substring after(myString, matchString) returns fragment of *myString* occurring after *matchString*. Returns empty string "" if no match.

13) replace

replace(myString, pattern, replacementString, flags?) performs regular expression pattern matching and replacement. Pattern matching follows XPATH 2.0 except error results are mapped to *null*. [45]

14) contains

contains(myString, matchString) returns true if *myString* contains *matchString*, otherwise false.

15) starts with

starts with(myString, matchString) returns true if *myString* starts with *matchString*, otherwise false.

16) ends with

ends with(myString, matchString) returns true if *myString* ends with *matchString*, otherwise false.

17) matches

matches(myString, pattern, flags?) returns true if *myString* matches regular expression, otherwise false. Pattern matching follows XPATH 2.0 except error results are mapped to *null*.

List Functions

18) list contains

list contains(myList, myVal) returns true if *myList* contains the value *myVal*, otherwise false.

19) count

count(myList) returns number of items in the list.

20) min, max, sum, mean

min, max, sum, and *mean (myList)* return the minimum, maximum, sum, and mean values, respectively, from a list of number values. *Min* and *max* also work on date and time values.

---

[45] A good reference for *matches* and *replace* functions, including use of patterns, regular expressions, and flags, is Michael Kay, *XSLT 2.0 and XPATH 2.0 Programmer's Reference*, 4th edition (Indianapolis: Wiley, 2008)

21) and

and(myList) returns false if any item in list of Boolean values is false, returns true if all items are true, else *null*.

22) or

or(myList) returns true if any item in list of Boolean values is true, returns false if all items are false, else *null*.

23) sublist

sublist(myList, startPos, length?) returns a list of length (or all) elements of *myList*, starting with *myList[startPos]*.

24) append

append(myList, addList) returns a new list with items appended.

25) insert before

insert before(myList, position, newItem) returns a new list with *newItem* inserted at *position*.

26) remove

remove(myList, position) returns a new list with item at *position* removed.

27) reverse

reverse(myList) returns a new list with items in reverse order.

28) index of

index of(myList, matchValue) returns a list of positions (index values, i.e., numbers) of list items matching *matchValue*.

29) union

union(myList, list2,…, listN) concatenates the list and removes duplicates.

30) distinct values

distinct values(myList) returns a new list with duplicates removed.

31) concatenate

concatenate(list1, list2,…) returns a concatenated list of lists.

32) flatten

flatten(list1, list2,…, listN) returns a single list of individual elements.

Numeric Functions

33) decimal

decimal(numExpression, scale) returns the value of *numExpression* with *scale* digits following the decimal point.

34) floor

floor(numExpression) returns the largest integer less than or equal to *numExpression*.

35) ceiling

ceiling(numExpression) returns the smallest integer greater than or equal to *numExpression*.

FEEL Operators

Many FEEL operators closely parallel those in XPATH 2.0.[46]

If..then..else

The *if* operator is the workhorse of conditional logic in literal expressions. The syntax is:

```
if [Boolean expression] then [expression1] else [expression2]
```

In FEEL, the *else* clause is required. The *else* expression may include another *if..then..else* clause.

Example:

DiscountPct		
AirbagDiscountPct	if hasDriverAirbags=true and hasPassengerAirbags=false and hasSideAirbags=false then .12 else if hasDriverAirbags=true and hasPassengerAirbags=true and hasSideAirbags=false then .15 else if hasDriverAirbags=true and hasPassengerAirbags=true and hasSideAirbags=true then .18 else 0	
AlarmDiscountPct	if PotentialTheftCategory="High" and hasAlarm=true then .10 else 0	
AirbagDiscountPct + AlarmDiscountPct		

for..return

for is an iterator across a list or relation. The syntax is:

```
for [item] in [list or relation] return [expression(item)],
```

where *item* is a dummy variable that signifies an item in the list or a row in the relation. The value returned is a list or relation. The *for..return* construct is featured in the *iteration patterns* of Chapter 11 and the examples in Chapters 14 and 15.

---

[46] Kay, *XSLT 2.0 and XPATH 2.0 Programmer's Reference*

Example:

TotalAutoPremium	
AutoPremiumList	for car in Application.Cars return AutoPremium(car)
sum(AutoPremiumList)	

every, some..satisfies

every applies a test condition to a list or relation, returning true if *every* item in the list or relation satisfies a Boolean function of the item. The syntax is:

```
every [item] in [list or context] satisfies [Boolean expression(item)]
```

where [item] is a dummy variable that signifies an item in the list or a row in the relation.

some applies a test condition to a list or relation, returning true if *any* item in the list or relation satisfies a Boolean function of the item. The syntax is:

```
some [item] in [list or context] satisfies [Boolean expression(item)]
```

where [item] is a dummy variable that signifies an item in the list or a row in the relation.

Example:

```
some ch in credit history satisfies ch.event = "bankruptcy"
```

Here *ch* is a dummy variable representing a row in the relation *credit history*. *ch.event* selects the event column for that row. If no row satisfies the condition, the expression returns false.

instance of

instance of checks the datatype of an expression, returning true if the expression matches the specified type, else false. The syntax is:

```
[expression1] instance of [type]
```

The *validation patterns* of Chapter 11 make use of *instance of*.

in

in followed by a list of values or ranges is used in literal expressions, returning true if the input expression value is contained in any of the values or ranges specified. The syntax is:

```
[input expression] in [range1, range2, …]
```

Example:

```
if applicant.maritalStatus in ("M","S") then "valid" else "not valid"
```

If *applicant.maritalStatus* has the value "M," the result is "valid". The *validation patterns* of Chapter 11 make use of *in*.

sort

sort(myList, precedesFunction(x,y) [expression]) sorts *myList* into a new list ordered by the *precedesFunction expression*, a comparison expression applied to any pair (x,y) of *myList* elements. For normal ascending numerical sort, the syntax is *precedesFunction*(x,y) x<y. To sort the rows of a relation by ascending values of its *cost* column, you would write,

```
sort(myRelation, precedesFunction(x,y) x.cost<y.cost
```

Example:

This example is taken from the *Mortgage Recommender* decision detailed in Chapter 15.

RankedProducts		
FinancialMetrics	(product, Requested)	
	LenderName	product.LenderName
	MortgageType	product.MortgageType
	ConformanceType	product.ConformanceType
	LoanAmt	Requested.LoanAmt * (1 + product.Points/100) + product.FeesAmt
	DownPct	max(product.MinDown, Requested.DownPct)
	DownAmt	LoanAmt * DownPct
	Rate	product.Rate
	Points	product.Points
	FeesAmt	product.FeesAmt
	r	product.Rate/12
	Payment	LoanAmt * r / (1 - (1 + r)**-product.Term)
	P36	LoanAmt * (1+r)**36 - Payment * ((1+r)**36 - 1) / r
	V	Requested.LoanAmt / (1 - DownPct)
	EquityPct	1 - P36/V
ProductMetrics	for m in MatchingProducts return FinancialMetrics(m, Requested.LoanAmt)	
RankByRate	sort(ProductMetrics, precedesFunction(x,y) x.Rate<y.Rate)	
RankByPayment	sort(ProductMetrics, precedesFunction(x,y) x.Payment<y.Payment)	
RankByEquity	sort(ProductMetrics, precedesFunction(x,y) x.EquityPct>y.EquityPct)	
RankByDown	sort(ProductMetrics, precedesFunction(x,y) x.DownAmt<y.DownAmt)	
if Requested.Objective="Rate" then RankByRate else if Requested.Objective="Payment" then RankByPayment else if Requested.Objective="Equity" then RankByEquity else if Requested.Objective="Down" then RankByDown else null		

Imports

A DMN model is able to reference decisions, BKMs, and datatypes defined *externally* and *imported* into the model. Technically, import functionality is not limited to CL3, but simple CL2 tools probably won't support it. Common examples of imports are:

- Decisions, function definitions (BKMs), and item definitions defined in other DMN models, to support modularity or reuse
- Datatypes defined in an XML Schema Document (XSD)
- Data tables defined in an XML document.
- Functions defined in Java or some other language

Each *import* must be declared in the model, specifying the type of import (e.g., DMN, XSD, or XML), the file location, and a *namespace* used to prevent name collisions between the importing and imported models.

DMN Import

Each DMN model specifies a *namespace*, a string that should be unique to the model, used to distinguish its variable and type names from those defined in another DMN model that might import it. The namespace-qualified name of an imported variable or type will not "collide" with a name in the importing document.

In the importing model, an *import* element specifies both the file location and namespace of the imported model. Many DMN elements, such as *information requirement* or *knowledge requirement*, support *remote DMN references*, meaning they can point to a node defined in the imported model. This allows modular development of complex decision projects in separate DMN documents that are linked together by these remote references. It also lets you create a *library of commonly used functions* in a DMN document that is imported for use by other models.

Most remote DMN references are attributes of type *tDMNElementReference*, which points to the remote element by a combination of *filename* and *id*. While a *knowledge requirement*, the DRD element that links a decision to a BKM, uses this type of reference, *invocation* references the called function by *namespace-qualified name*. *Literal expressions* referencing an imported variable or function reference it by namespace-qualified name, as well.

In the DMN schema, following standard XSD practice, the model namespace is defined as type *anyURI*. Outside of DMN, you normally see such namespaces specified as a proper URL, such as *http://methodandstyle.com/ns/LoanApproval/*. But this is not actually required. In reality, the namespace can be *any string* that uniquely identifies it. Because colon (:) is a character NOT allowed in a FEEL name, DMN recommends not using it in the namespace. The reason is that when an imported decision, BKM, or input data is referenced in a FEEL expression, it must use the FEEL syntax for qualified names.

So instead of using *methodandstyle.com/ns/LoanApproval/* as the namespace, a shorter string without colons, like *msLoanApproval*, might be more practical. Then a FEEL expression in a model that imports this one could invoke the imported *Prequalification* function as

```
msLoanApproval.Prequalification(Customer, Loan)
```

where *Customer* and *Loan* are values passed to the function from the invoking decision.

XSD Import

Instead of defining a custom datatype as a DMN item definition, it may be more convenient to define it outside of the DMN model using a standard data modeling language such as XSD. The XSD document defines a *targetNamespace*, a URI that should be unique, and the importing

DMN model declares a *prefix* that stands for this namespace. In the DMN model, a *typeRef* pointing to this datatype is a *QName*, its *namespace-qualified XML name* (not FEEL name).

For example, suppose *CustomerType* is defined as a complex type in an imported XSD with namespace *http://methodandstyle.com/ns/LoanTypes/*, and the importing DMN model assigns the prefix *n1* to this namespace. Then input data element *Customer* can specify its *typeRef* as *n1:CustomerType*. All of the child elements of *n1:CustomerType* are automatically mapped to their FEEL equivalents and can be referenced by FEEL path expressions. For example, the XPATH element *n1:Customer/n1:name* is automatically mapped to *Customer.name* in FEEL.

XML Import

Instead of defining a relational data table as a DMN *relation*, it is often more convenient to define it externally as an *imported XML element*. In the DMN model, a variable representing this table is modeled as a *literal expression* with *imported values*. Such an expression specifies an *expression language* for selecting the referenced elements. For XML imports, that language is typically XPATH.

Here is an example. Suppose we have a large XML table, *InternationalShippingRates*, with two columns, *CountryCode* and *ShippingRate*. Each row represents a *Country*:

```
<InternationalShippingRates>
        <Country>
                <CountryCode>AF</CountryCode>
                <ShippingRate>1.05</ShippingRate>
        </Country>
        <Country>
                <CountryCode>AL</CountryCode>
                <ShippingRate>0.85</ShippingRate>
        </Country>
        <Country>
                <CountryCode>AU</CountryCode>
                <ShippingRate>1.05</ShippingRate>
        </Country>
        . . .
</InternationalShippingRates>
```

Technically, the relation is not the table *InternationalShippingRates* but the list of rows (*Country* elements) in the table, so in the DMN model, a context entry *RateList* references this imported relation as a literal XPATH expression *n2:InternationalShippingRates/n2:Country*, where *n2* is the namespace prefix for the imported XML document. We can then use this to determine the *ShippingRate* for our order in a FEEL filter expression like

```
RateList[CountryCode = Order.ShipToAddress.CountryCode].ShippingRate
```

where *Order* is an information requirement of this decision.

Example: *Collections of Cars* Challenge

The combination of boxed expressions with FEEL's built-in functions and operators gives DMN remarkable expressive power, the ability to describe complex decision logic in just a few rows of a table. This example, a modified version of Gary Hallmark's FEEL solution to the *Collections of Cars Challenge* on DMCommunity,[47] illustrates it well.

Given an arbitrary table of cars arranged in groups (Figure 46), the challenge was to find the set of make-model combinations common to all groups, and the set belonging to only one group. The DMN solution combines *table query patterns* using filter expressions, *iteration patterns* using *for..return*, and the *distinct values* built-in function. These and other patterns are discussed in more detail in Chapter 11.

Group	Make	Model
G1	Ford	Pickup
G1	Ford	T
G1	Ford	Taurus
G1	Austin	Mini
G1	Hyundai	Santa Fe
G2	Ford	Pickup
G2	Ford	T
G2	Ford	Taurus
G2	Hyundai	Tucson
G2	Hyundai	Santa Fe

Difference	
Make	Model
Hyundai	Tucson
Austin	Mini

Intersection	
Make	Model
Ford	Pickup
Ford	T
Ford	Taurus
Hyundai	Santa Fe

Figure 46. DMCommunity *Collections of Cars* challenge. The table on left is the input data element *cars*

groups	distinct values (cars.Group)	
carType	(car)	
	make	car.Make
	model	car.Model
	groupCnt	count(distinct values(cars[Make=car.Make and Model=car.Model].Group))
commonList	distinct values(for car in cars return carType(car)[groupCnt=count(groups)])	
uniqueList	distinct values(for car in cars return carType(car)[groupCnt=1])	

Figure 47. DMN solution to the *Collection of Cars* challenge.

The relation shown in Figure 46 represents the input data element *cars*. The DMN solution is shown in Figure 47:

- Local variable *groups* is a list of the distinct values of element *Group* in the input data *cars*. Here it is a list of two values, "G1" and "G2".

- *carType* is a function definition with one parameter, *car*, representing a single row in the relation, *cars*. The output of the function has three components, *make*, *model*, and *groupCnt*. *Make* and *Model* are attributes of the parameter *car*, implying *car* is a data

---

[47] https://dmcommunity.files.wordpress.com/2015/09/garyhallmarkcars.pdf

structure. The *groupCnt* value expression starts with the list of rows in the *cars* table for which the *Make* and *Model* attributes match the parameter *car*'s *Make* and *Model* attributes, and then counts the number of distinct values of *Group* in that list.

- *commonList* uses a *for..return* expression to *iteratively invoke* the function *carType* for each row of the input data table *cars*, and *filter that list* to include only rows for which the component *groupCnt* matches the count of *groups*, which is 2. The *distinct values* function applied to that filtered list removes the duplicates.

- *uniqueList* works similarly, except the filter expression includes only rows for which the component *groupCnt* is 1, meaning cars in a single group only.

The solution is very compact, with a lot of functionality packed into only 4 context entries! Fortunately, most DMN decision logic is not this dense.

* *

Through the combination of DRDs, FEEL functions and operators, contexts, reusable functions, and boxed expressions, DMN provides non-programmers the tools to model executable decision logic, no matter how complex. The past three chapters describe the catalogue of modeling elements available. The trick is learning to use them effectively.

The next chapter illustrates how they are combined in a basic end-to-end decision model, the Lending decision example presented in the DMN spec. It shows the mechanics of linking decisions, input data, and BKMs, but not a methodology for modeling *your* end-to-end business decision. That is the subject of Part III, DMN Method and Style.

CHAPTER 6

Lending Example Walkthrough

Chapter 11 of the DMN specification presents a detailed example of a Lending decision that shows how the various features of the standard work together. We are now ready to walk through that example. It illustrates many aspects of DMN, including the link between DRD and the decision process, the various decision table hit policies and aggregation, and BKM invocation. In this chapter, we examine that example in detail.

Before we start, it is important to acknowledge up front that in certain respects, the Lending example in the spec omits some important DMN features. For example, because every decision except one invokes a BKM, every decision table input expression in the example is simply a variable name (as required in a BKM), not an expression. Also, in every decision table, all of the input entries and output entries reference only literal values, never variables. A casual reader of the spec might justifiably assume that a decision table input expression may *only* be a variable name, not an expression, or that an input entry or output entry may reference *only* literal values, not variables. *Those conclusions would be incorrect!*

Thus, while detailed, the spec example illustrates only a narrow slice of the decision logic possible in DMN. Moreover, the decision logic of the business decision as a whole – *is the loan approved or declined?* – is not defined in DMN at all. Instead it requires reference to a companion BPMN model. In Chapter 12 we will present an alternative model of the same end-to-end decision following Method and Style.

Overall Decision Flow

The scenario is a Lending decision: Depending on various attributes of the applicant and the requested loan product, the end-to-end business decision can either approve or decline the loan application. In some cases, the decision to approve or decline can be made automatically based on the input data collected at the start of the process. In other cases, additional input must be collected from a credit bureau. And in some of those cases, human adjudication is required.

The overall flow of the decision logic is described by the BPMN process model depicted earlier, reproduced here as Figure 48.

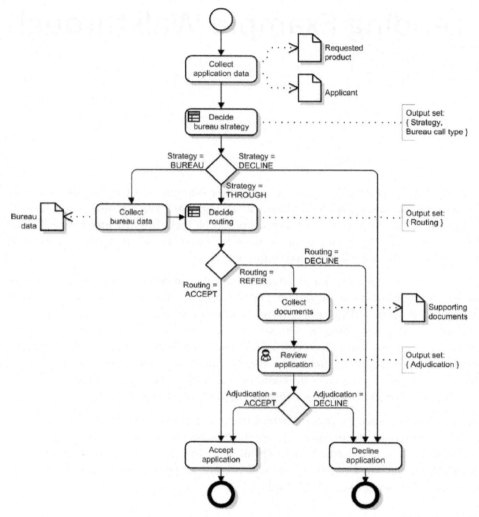

Figure 48. End-to-end process for the Lending decision example. Source: OMG

1.   Some work is performed to collect information about the applicant and the requested loan product. That information is shown as data objects in the BPMN, corresponding to input data in the DMN model. Matching the names of the data objects and input data elements is not required by DMN but good practice.

2.   The collected information is used as input data in the decision called *Strategy*, represented in the BPMN as a *decision task* (also called *business rule task)*. A BPMN

decision task signifies execution of a *decision service,* typically on a Business Rule Engine. The decision output has three possible output values:

a. *Bureau,* meaning additional information is required from the credit bureau. There are two types of requests to the credit bureau, *Full* and *Mini.* The type required is specified by the decision *Bureau call type,* a supporting decision of *Strategy.* A third output value is *None,* meaning no credit bureau call is required.

b. *Through,* meaning continue immediately to the next decision task, which executes the *Routing* decision without need for the credit bureau data. Actually, in that case, the decision logic of *Routing* results in an outcome of *Accept,* so there is no need to evaluate *Routing* at all in this case. We shall reexamine this in Chapter 12.

c. *Decline,* meaning the lending application will be declined without further decisions.

3. A gateway routes the process flow based on the *Strategy* output value. Each gateway output or *gate* is labeled to match one of the decision output values. This is consistent with the BPMN Method and Style rule that a gateway following an activity tests its end state, since *for a decision task the decision output value names the task's end state.*

4. A second decision task *Decide routing* executes the decision *Routing* using the credit bureau data. This decision either accepts or declines the loan application, or possibly refers it to an adjudicator for a human decision. As we saw with *Strategy,* the three output values of *Routing – Accept, Decline,* and *Refer –* match the three gates of the gateway following the Decision task.

5. If *Routing* returns *Refer,* the task *Collect documents* gathers supporting information before the adjudicator makes the *Adjudication,* with output values either *Accept* or *Decline.* We know this is a human decision because it is performed by the BPMN user task *Review application.* A user task signifies it is performed by a person, not a Business Rule Engine. Remember, it is this task, not the gateway that follows, that makes the decision.

Note that there is no single DMN decision node that determines whether the loan application is approved or declined. Instead, the outcome of the business decision as a whole is determined by the BPMN model, Figure 48. As discussed in Chapter 12, this need not be the case.

The *Strategy* Decision

The DRD for the *Decide bureau strategy* decision task is shown in Figure 49. Notice that the service executed by this task actually includes 7 DMN decision nodes: *Strategy, Bureau call type, Eligibility, Pre-Bureau Affordability, Pre-bureau Risk category, Application risk score,* and *Required monthly installment.*

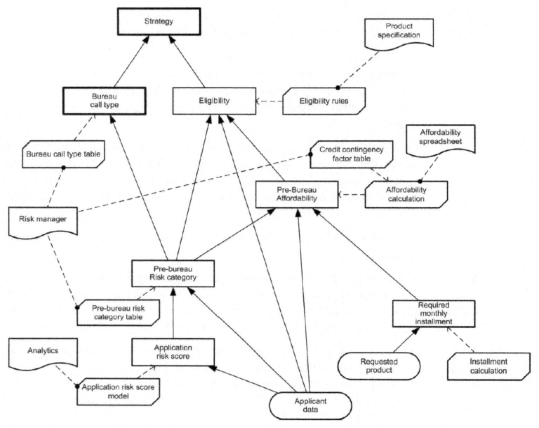

Figure 49. *Strategy* **DRD. Source: OMG**

The *Strategy* decision logic, a decision table with *Unique* hit policy, is shown in Figure 50.

Strategy			
U	Eligibility	Bureau call type	Strategy
1	*INELIGIBLE*	-	*DECLINE*
2	*ELIGIBLE*	*FULL, MINI*	*BUREAU*
3		*NONE*	*THROUGH*

Figure 50. *Strategy* **decision table.**

This is the only decision in the Lending example that does not invoke a BKM. Note the following about this decision:

- In the DRD it has two information requirements, and these correspond to the two decision table inputs, *Bureau call type* and *Eligibility*.

- The tab at the top (*Strategy*) must be the name of the decision, and it should match the output column heading. In DMN, decision outputs are variables used in the value expressions of other decisions, so you need to keep this in mind when naming decisions. Other decision modeling methodologies such as *The Decision Model* use a verb in the decision name, such as "Determine Strategy," but this would not be appropriate in DMN. The DMN spec requires the name of the decision and its output variable to be the same, and a variable name starting with a verb seems awkward.

- The use of italics in the input and output entries signifies a *literal value*. Without the italics (or surrounding quotation marks), this decision table would be incorrect, since there are no *variables* named INELIGIBLE, etc.

- In the *Eligibility* column, the *ELIGIBLE* cells for rules 2 and 3 are merged, meaning both rules 2 and 3 test the condition Eligibility = "ELIGIBLE". This cell merging is a traditional convention in decision tables that simplifies visual scanning of the decision table logic and is considered essential by long-time practitioners of decision modeling. However, many first-generation DMN tools do not yet support it.

- The input entry *hyphen* (-) for *Bureau call type* in rule 1 means that this input is *irrelevant* in the rule. In other words, if Eligibility = "INELIGIBLE", then regardless of the *Bureau call type* value, the decision output is "DECLINE".

- The comma in the *Bureau call type* input entry for rule 2 signifies *OR*. If *Bureau call type* = "FULL" OR *Bureau call type* = "MINI", then the decision output is "BUREAU".

Bureau Call Type

Bureau call type determines whether a Full or Mini credit report is requested from the service bureau, or none at all, based on the *Pre-bureau Risk category,* which in turn is determined from the input data elements *Applicant data* and *Requested product*. Here *Bureau call type* does not directly contain the decision logic. Instead it invokes the BKM called *Bureau call type table.* Note from the DRD Figure 49, there is no information requirement connector drawn from *Pre-bureau Risk category* to the BKM. Instead, *Pre-bureau Risk category* provides its output value to the decision *Bureau call type,* which then maps it to a BKM parameter via invocation. The output of the BKM then becomes the output of the invoking decision.

Bureau call type	
Bureau call type table	
Pre-bureau Risk category	Pre-bureau Risk category

Figure 51. Boxed invocation of *Bureau call type table*

The invocation mapping is defined as a *boxed expression* (Figure 51). The format for a boxed invocation is as follows:

- The tab at the top names the decision, here *Bureau call type.*

- Immediately below that is the name of the BKM, here *Bureau call type table*. Technically, the metamodel says it is an *expression* whose value is the name of a BKM. DMN requires that the names of all DRG elements are unique, so a BKM and a Decision may not share the same name.

- Below that is a list of (parameter, binding expression) pairs displayed as a two-column table. The shaded column on the left lists the BKM *parameters*, which are the variables referenced by the invoked decision logic. The name listed in the invocation must match the parameter name specified in the BKM. The column on the right (unshaded) shows the *binding expression* for each parameter, the mapping of one or more input variables of the invoking decision or BKM to the parameter. As shown in Figure 51, the input variable *Pre-bureau Risk category* of decision *Bureau call type* provides the value assigned to parameter *Pre-bureau Risk category* of BKM *Bureau call type table*. In this case the name of the BKM parameter and the decision input variable are the same, but in general this may not be the case.

Bureau call type table		
U	Pre-bureau Risk category	Bureau call type
1	*HIGH, MEDIUM*	*FULL*
2	*LOW*	*MINI*
3	*VERY LOW, DECLINE*	*NONE*

Figure 52. Decision logic of *Bureau call type table*

Figure 52 shows the decision logic of the BKM *Bureau call type table*, a decision table. Again, the italicized input entries and output entries signify these are literal values, not names of variables.

Pre-bureau Risk category

Pre-bureau Risk category is also a decision table implemented by invoking a BKM, here called *Pre-bureau risk category table*. The boxed invocation (Figure 53) is another trivial mapping. The value of the parameter *Existing Customer* is provided by the input data element *Applicant data.ExistingCustomer*. Here *Applicant data* is a structured variable, and its attribute *Existing Customer* is referenced as a *qualified name*, using the dot notation.

Pre-bureau Risk category	
Pre-bureau risk category table	
Existing Customer	Applicant data.ExistingCustomer
Application Risk Score	Application risk score

Figure 53. Boxed invocation of *Pre-bureau risk category table*

Figure 54 shows the invoked decision table. Input entries for *Application Risk Score* are numeric ranges. The parentheses in the ranges specified in the *Application Risk Score* input entries indicate the endpoint is excluded from the range. So *[100..120)* means greater than or equal to 100 but less than 120.

Pre-bureau risk category table			
U	Existing Customer	Application Risk Score	Pre-bureau Risk category
1		<100	*HIGH*
2		[100..120)	*MEDIUM*
3		[120.130]	*LOW*
4	FALSE	>130	*VERY LOW*
5		<80	*DECLINE*
6		[80..90)	*HIGH*
7		[90..110]	*MEDIUM*
8	TRUE	>110	*LOW*

Figure 54. *Pre-bureau risk category* **decision table**

Eligibility

The *Pre-bureau Risk category* decision is also an input to *Eligibility*. Once again, this is an invocation of a BKM, *Eligibility rules*, a decision table (Figure 55). Here more than one of the rules in the table can match, and they don't all give the same output value. As indicated in the top left cell, this table has a hit policy code *P*, which stands for *Priority*. *Priority* hit policy means that if multiple rules in the table match, producing different output values, the output value to select is the one with the highest priority. The output value priority is determined by the *listed order of the output values*. Listing input and output values in the decision table column headings is optional, but in order to use hit policy *P*, the output values must be specified. In this case, *Ineligible* is listed before *Eligible*, so it has a higher priority. If both values are selected by matching rules, *Ineligible* wins.

Eligibility rules			
P	Pre-bureau Risk category	Pre-Bureau Affordability	Age	Eligibility INELIGIBLE, ELIGIBLE
1	*DECLINE*	-	-	*INELIGIBLE*
2	-	*FALSE*	-	*INELIGIBLE*
3	-	-	<18	*INELIGIBLE*
4	-	-	-	*ELIGIBLE*

Figure 55. *Eligibility* **decision, with** *Priority* **hit policy. Source: OMG**

Notice in Figure 55 that rule 4 has hyphens in all input columns, so this rule *always* will match. When such a rule selects a low-priority output value in a *Priority* Hit Policy table, it effectively acts as an *Else* clause in the decision logic, since its output value is selected only if none of the other three rules is satisfied. The decision logic is

```
if (Pre-bureau Risk category = "Decline" or Pre-Bureau Affordability =
    false or Age < 18) then "Ineligible" else "Eligible"
```

While this style of decision table is favored by Alan Fish, author of the Lending example, DMN Method and Style prefers tables with hit policy of *Unique*. It is possible to translate a table like Figure 55 into a *Unique* table. We discuss this issue further in Chapter 9.

Application Risk Score

The *Application risk score* decision invokes the BKM *Application risk score model* (Figure 56), a multi-hit decision table with a hit policy of *C+, Collect and sum*. In this case, each of the inputs – *Age, Marital Status,* and *Employment Status* – contributes a *Partial score,* and the partial scores are summed to produce the result.

Application risk score model				
C+	**Age**	**Marital Status**	**Employment Status**	**Partial score**
			UNEMPLOYED, EMPLOYED, SELF-EMPLOYED, STUDENT	
	[18..120]	S, M		
1	[18..21]	-	-	32
2	[22..25]	-	-	35
3	[26..35]	-	-	40
4	[36..49]	-	-	43
5	>=50	-	-	48
6	-	S	-	25
7	-	M	-	45
8	-	-	*UNEMPLOYED*	15
9	-	-	*STUDENT*	18
10	-	-	*EMPLOYED*	45
11	-	-	*SELF-EMPLOYED*	36

Figure 56. *Application risk score model* **BKM, a multi-hit decision table. Source: OMG**

Note that here the decision table specifies allowed *input values,* a range of *Age* values and enumerated string values for *Marital Status* and *Employment Status.* When input values are provided, a value that is not included in this list is an error. Although it is possible to define *allowed values* in the variable's *item definition,* best practice is to indicate input and output values for each decision table column as well. Technically, decision table input values refer to allowed values of an *input expression,* while an *item definition's* allowed values refer to a single *input variable,* so you could argue that there is no redundancy here. But remember, in a BKM, the input expression must be an input variable, not an expression.

Because each input in this table contributes a partial score independently of the other inputs, it is possible to convert this table into a set of single-hit decision tables and combine their output values with a simple expression. The Decision Model, for example, recommends such a conversion, but DMN Method and Style does not require it.

Pre-Bureau Affordability

Like the preceding examples, *Pre-Bureau Affordability* invokes a BKM, *Affordability calculation.* The boxed invocation is shown in Figure 57.

Pre-Bureau Affordability	
Affordability calculation	
Monthly Income	Applicant data.Monthly.Income
Monthly Repayments	Applicant data.Monthly.Repayments
Monthly Expenses	Applicant data.Monthly.Expenses
Risk Category	Pre-bureau Risk category
Required Monthly Installment	Required monthly installment

Figure 57. Boxed invocation of *Affordability calculation*

Affordability calculation here is not a decision table. Instead it is modeled as a *context* (Figure 58).

Affordability calculation		
(Monthly Income, Monthly Repayments, Monthly Expenses, Risk Category, Required Monthly Installment)		
Disposable Income	Monthly Income - (Monthly Replayments + Monthly Expenses)	
Credit Contingency Factor	Credit contingency factor table	
	Risk Category	Risk Category
Affordability	If Disposable Income * Credit Contingency Factor > Required Monthly Installment then true else false	
Affordability		

Figure 58. *Affordability calculation* **logic expressed as a boxed function. Source: OMG**

In the boxed expression, the five BKM parameters are enclosed in parentheses in the top row. These names must match those listed in the invocation (Figure 57). But notice that the three variables referenced in the literal expression of *Affordability* are not these parameters. They are instead intermediate variables, local to the context, defined by *context entries*: *Disposable Income, Credit Contingency Factor,* and *Affordability*. The final result just references the variable *Affordability*. This boxed expression could have omitted the context entry *Affordability* and just put the literal expression in the final result box.

Note also that the literal expression in the *Affordability* context entry is an *if..then..else* construct. This is allowed in FEEL but not in S-FEEL.

Now let's look at where these variables referenced by the context entries come from.

- *Monthly Income, Monthly Repayments,* and *Monthly Expenses,* referenced by *Disposable Income,* are passed from *Applicant data,* an input data element.

- *Credit Contingency Factor* invokes another BKM, called *Credit contingency factor table.* Thus its value expression in the context entry is not a simple literal expression but instead an *invocation,* modeled as a nested boxed expression with the name of the BKM (*Credit contingency factor table*) in the top row followed by a list of parameter/binding expression pairs. Here there is only one parameter, *Risk Category,* which is passed to the *Pre-Bureau Affordability* decision by an information requirement, from there mapped to the *Affordability calculation* parameter *Risk Category,* and finally from there to the *Credit contingency factor table* parameter *Risk*

Category. (Hidden underneath those simple *knowledge requirement* connectors in Figure 49 is a lot of parameter mapping!)

- *Required monthly installment* is an information requirement of the *Pre-Bureau Affordability* decision.

Credit contingency factor table is a standard decision tables (Figure 59).

Credit contingency factor table		
U	Risk Category	Credit Contingency Factor
1	*HIGH, DECLINE*	0.6
2	*MEDIUM*	0.7
3	*LOW, VERY LOW*	0.8

Figure 59. *Credit contingency factor table.* **Source: OMG**

Thus the *Affordability calculation* decision logic requires Conformance Level 3. It goes beyond CL2 in several ways:

- It uses a *context* to define intermediate variables.

- It contains a *nested invocation.*

- It contains an *if..then..else* FEEL expression.

Suppose, however, we want to model this decision logic at Conformance Level 2. It is possible, using the following basic strategy:

1. Insert supporting decisions for the intermediate variables and nested invocations.

2. Use a decision table to replace the *if..then..else* literal expression.

The result is shown in Figure 60. In this CL2 version, *Affordability calculation* becomes a one-column decision table with input expression *Disposable income * Credit contingency factor,* input entries *>Required monthly installment* and *<=Required monthly installment,* and corresponding output entries *true* and *false.*

This illustrates the fact that there is often a way to refactor CL3-based decision logic into CL2 by inserting additional supporting decisions in the DRD.

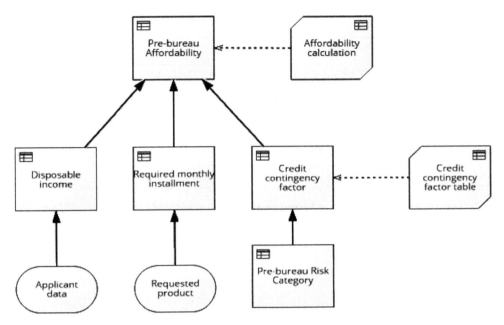

Figure 60. Refactoring allows *Pre-bureau Affordability* and *BKM Affordability calculation* to be CL2-compliant.

Required Monthly Installment

Required monthly installment invokes a BKM *Installment calculation,* which depends only on the input data *Requested product.* Figure 61 illustrates the invocation, and Figure 62 illustrates the decision logic, a boxed context. Context entry *Monthly Fee* is a FEEL literal expression using *if..then..else,* and *Monthly Repayment* here is specified as an *external* function *PMT.* Alternatively, it could have been modeled as a literal expression of *Rate, Term,* and *Amount,* or invocation of an internal function definition.

Required monthly installment	
Installment calculation	
Product Type	Requested product . ProductType
Rate	Requested product . Rate
Term	Requested product . Term
Amount	Requested product . Amount

Figure 61. Invocation of *Installment calculation.* **Source: OMG**

Installment calculation	
(Product Type, Rate, Term, Amount)	
Monthly Fee	if Product Type = "STANDARD LOAN" then 20.00 else if Product Type = "SPECIAL LOAN" then 25.00 else null
Monthly Repayment	PMT(Rate, Term, Amount)
Monthly Repayment + Monthly Fee	

Figure 62. *Installment calculation,* **a boxed context. Source: OMG**

The *Routing* Decision

All of the decision logic discussed so far relates to the *Strategy* decision, which determines what type of credit report to obtain from the external bureau. The *Routing* decision now recalculates *Affordability* and *Risk category* based on the additional credit bureau information. The DRD is shown in Figure 63.

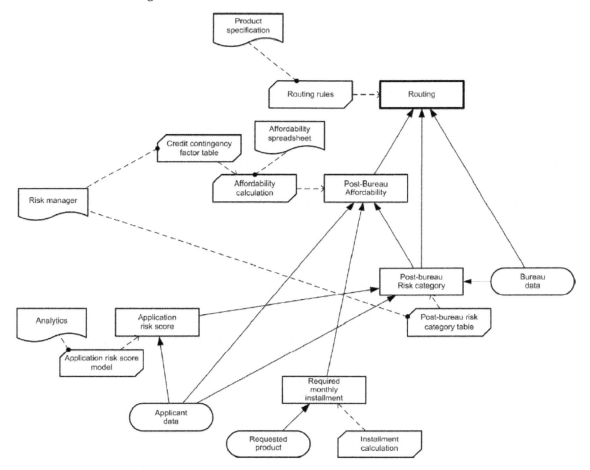

Figure 63. DRD for *Routing* decision. Source: OMG

Routing invokes the BKM *Routing rules*, based on *Bureau data, Post-bureau Risk category,* and *Post-Bureau Affordability* (Figure 64).

Routing	
Routing rules	
Bankrupt	Bureau data.Bankrupt
Credit Score	Bureau data.CreditScore
Post-bureau Risk Category	Post-bureau risk category
Post-Bureau Affordability	Post-Bureau Affordability

Figure 64. Boxed invocation of *Routing rules*

The *Routing rules* decision table is shown in Figure 65. The *Bankrupt* and *Credit score* inputs come from the credit bureau data.

Routing rules					
P	Post-bureau Risk category	Post-Bureau Affordability	Bankrupt true, false, null	Credit Score [0..999], null	Routing DECLINE, REFER, ACCEPT
1	-	*FALSE*	-	-	*DECLINE*
2	-	-	*TRUE*	-	*DECLINE*
3	*HIGH*	-	-	-	*REFER*
4	-	-	-	*<580*	*REFER*
5	-	-	-	-	*ACCEPT*

Figure 65. *Routing* decision table, with *Priority* hit policy

Credit Score is normally a number from 0 to 999, but note that the allowed values include the value *null*, because instances with *Strategy* output of *THROUGH* are passed to *Routing* without a credit score. *Null* here means that the input data *Credit score* for this applicant contains no value. *Null* is supported by FEEL at CL3. See Chapter 5 for more details on use of *null*.

Like the *Eligibility* decision (Figure 55), this is a decision in which multiple rules may match, with different output values. The correct output value is selected by the *Priority* hit policy, code *P* in the top left corner of the table. The *Priority* order is in the order of listed output values: *Decline, Refer, Accept*.

Actually, as mentioned earlier, when the *Strategy* decision outcome is *THROUGH*, *Routing* is evaluated without the *Bureau data*, and in this case not only is the *Credit score* value *null*, but *Bankrupt* is also *null*. While it is not immediately obvious, tracing back through the decision logic reveals this can only occur when *Post-bureau Risk Category* is *Very Low* and *Post-bureau Affordability* is *true*. Again, it is not obvious from the decision table of Figure 65, but this will always result in a *Routing* outcome of *ACCEPT*. Thus, when *Strategy* is *THROUGH*, there is actually no need to evaluate *Routing* at all. While it gives the "right answer," this entanglement of decision factors is not best practice.

Post-Bureau Affordability

The *Post-Bureau Affordability* decision invokes the same *Affordability calculation* BKM as the *Pre-Bureau Affordability*. The only difference is that the *Risk Category* parameter is now populated with the *Post-Bureau* values instead of the *Pre-Bureau* values (Figure 66). This illustrates proper use of BKMs for reusable decision logic.

Post-bureau affordability	
Affordability calculation	
Monthly Income	Applicant data . Monthly . Income
Monthly Repayments	Applicant data . Monthly . Repayments
Monthly Expenses	Applicant data . Monthly . Expenses
Risk Category	Post-bureau risk category
Required Monthly Installment	Required monthly installment

Figure 66. *Post-Bureau Affordability* invocation. **Source: OMG**

Post-Bureau Risk Category

The *Post-bureau Risk category* decision invokes a BKM modeled as a standard decision table (Figure 68), using the *Credit Score* obtained from the credit bureau. The invocation (Figure 67) is the same as the Pre-bureau invocation (Figure 53) except for the addition of the *Credit Score* parameter.

Post-bureau Risk category	
Post-bureau risk category table	
Existing Customer	Applicant data.ExistingCustomer
Credit Score	Bureau data.CreditScore
Application Risk Score	Application risk score

Figure 67. Invocation of *Post-bureau risk category table*

Post-bureau risk category table				
U	Existing Customer	Application Risk Score	Credit Score	Post-Bureau Risk Category
1			< 590	*HIGH*
2			[590..610]	*MEDIUM*
3		< 120	> 610	*LOW*
4			< 600	*HIGH*
5			[600..625]	*MEDIUM*
6		[120..130]	> 625	*LOW*
7	false	> 130	-	*VERY LOW*
8			< 580	*HIGH*
9			[580..600]	*MEDIUM*
10		<= 100	> 600	*LOW*
11			< 590	*HIGH*
12			[590..615]	*MEDIUM*
13	true	> 100	> 615	*LOW*

Figure 68. *Post-bureau risk category table* BKM. **Source: OMG**

The *Adjudication* Decision

The *Routing* decision either approves or declines most applicants, but some fraction will require manual adjudication based on additional supporting documents. The process model (Figure 48) indicates a task to collect those documents and execute the *Adjudication* decision when *Routing* has output value *REFER*. The task that executes the decision, called *Review Application*, is a BPMN user task, indicating a human decision.

In the DRD (Figure 69), we see it has four inputs: *Applicant data, Bureau data, Supporting documents,* and *Routing.* However, *Adjudication* has no decision logic included in the model. As a human decision, its logic is *opaque*, possibly undefined. In that case the information requirements merely represent data that informs the decision-maker. In practice, there is little if any difference between a human decision and input data.

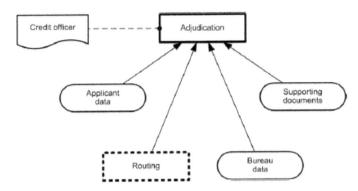

Figure 69. DRD of *Adjudication,* a human decision. **Source: OMG**

In Figure 69, *Routing* is drawn with a dashed border. Such a line style has no defined meaning in DMN, but the spec encourages modelers (and tools) to use line styles and colors to add their own meaning to DRD elements.

CHAPTER 7

Metamodel and Schema

You may have noticed that DMN stands for Decision Model *and* Notation. The "and" means that DMN is more than a diagramming notation. It also provides a *semantic model*: elements with defined names and meanings and relationships to one another described by a formal *metamodel*. The metamodel (in combination with a formal expression language like FEEL) is what allows DMN models to be executed on a decision engine. The XML schema, derived from the metamodel, is what makes DMN models interchangeable between tools. If you are a modeler, the details of the metamodel and schema may be of little interest. But if you are an *implementer* – a developer of modeling tools conforming to the standard – *you need to know this stuff!*

What makes this chapter especially valuable is the fact that, as of this writing, the version of the DMN metamodel and schema available to the general public – DMN 1.0 – is already out of date. The DMN 1.0 schema, in particular, has critical bugs: *it just doesn't work!* While the outward appearance of DMN models – the DRD, decision tables, and boxed expressions – is mostly unchanged, DMN 1.1 has made significant changes to the metamodel and schema. If you are an implementer, forget about the DMN 1.0 metamodel and schema; *you need DMN 1.1.*

The spec defines the metamodel via a set of UML class diagrams relating the semantic elements. The metamodel is serialized in two forms: *xmi*, which is a direct XML representation of the UML; and *xsd*, or XML Schema, used for model interchange and validation. Both are available for download from the OMG website.[48] The spec text discusses the metamodel in terms of the UML class names, which are typically capitalized. The xsd references those same elements in terms of the UML attribute names, which are uncapitalized.

---

[48] The latest publicly released version of DMN can be obtained from http://www.omg.org/spec/DMN/Current. As of this writing, this is DMN 1.0; DMN 1.1 should be released publicly in mid-2016. In the meantime, DMN 1.1 is available to OMG members at http://www.omg.org/cgi-bin/doc?dtc/15-11-10. Implementers are strongly urged to work from the DMN 1.1 specification, not DMN 1.0.

But DMN 1.1 expended considerable effort in aligning the metamodel and xsd, so whichever one you use, the meaning should be the same.

Element References

In the schema, non-containment relationships between elements use pointers as element references. Most elements, in particular those represented in the DRD, are referenced by *id*. Where the referenced element must be in the same decision model as the referencing element, the reference must be IDREF. However, most of the time, the referenced element may be in an imported DMN model. Elements that allow such remote references use the type *tDMNElementReference*.

The syntax of *tDMNElementReference* is unusual:

```
[imported filename]#[local-id]
```

If the referenced element is local (not imported), the imported filename may be omitted, but not the #. It is surprising and a little unfortunate that the DMN task force elected to use a different remote ID pointer format than BPMN uses,[49] but it's not that big a deal.

Item definitions are referenced in the schema by *QName*, with the format:

```
[namespace prefix]:[local-name]
```

The *prefix* is declared in the *definitions* element.

Variables are not referenced directly by schema elements, but may be referenced by expressions. In FEEL, references to variables and BKMs are by *namespace-qualified name*, with the format:

```
[namespace].[local-name]
```

If the variable or BKM is local, the namespace and period are omitted.

DMNElement and NamedElement

In the metamodel, elements that are *subclasses* (i.e., with outgoing open triangle arrow) inherit all the attributes of its *superclass*, and possibly add more. Almost every element in the model belongs to the superclass *DMNElement* (Figure 70), which means it has optional *id* and *label* attributes and optional child elements *description* and *extensionElements*.

- Elements that are referenced by *id* in other elements, such as those in a DRD, should always provide an *id*, which must be unique in the document and is restricted to formats allowed for ID types in XSD.

---

[49] For years, BPMN has successfully used the format [imported namespace-prefix]:[local-id] for remote ID pointers.

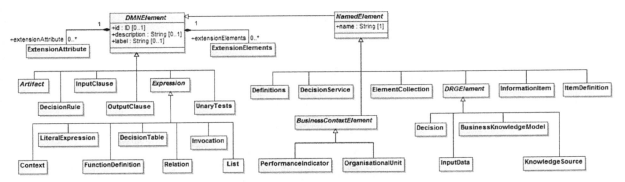

Figure 70. Metamodel, *DMNElement* and *NamedElement*

- *description* is a free text field that can be used in a business glossary or for any other purpose.

- *extensionElements* is a container for additional elements outside of the DMN standard added by the tool vendor or modeler. Each element contained must reference a namespace other than the model namespace.

- *extensionAttribute* similarly means a non-standard (tool-added or modeler-added) attribute, referencing an external namespace, e.g. *@n1:color*, where n1 is the prefix of the external namespace.

The subclass *NamedElement* contains all *DMNElement* members with a *name*. Figure 70 shows which elements have names and which do not. For example, the model (*Definitions*), DRG elements (e.g., *Decision, BKM, InputData*), variables (*InformationItem*), and type definitions (*itemDefinition*) all have a *name*, while *Expressions* (e.g., *LiteralExpression, DecisionTable, FunctionDefinition, Relation*) do not.

definitions

definitions (Figure 71) is the root element of a DMN model. Everything in the model is contained within *definitions*. Its *name* attribute names the decision model. Other attributes of definitions apply to the model as a whole.

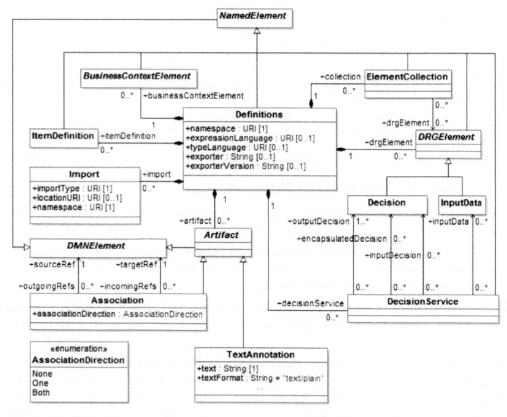

Figure 71. *Definitions* **metamodel**

namespace

definitions/@namespace is a unique identifier of a DMN model. It is important because one DMN model may *import* reusable decision logic or type definitions from another DMN model, and the *namespace* prevents variables in the importing and imported models from having the same *qualified name*.

In XSD, the datatype of *namespace* is *anyURI*, which in most XML serializations would take the form of an absolute URL like *http://methodandstyle/ns/Lending51113*. However, technically, any string without spaces is allowed, and in DMN models using FEEL it is a good idea to make *namespace* a unique string that does not contain spaces, periods, or illegal FEEL name characters like colon. The reason is that when a variable representing an *imported* decision or BKM is referenced in a FEEL expression, it is referenced by a *namespace-qualified name* using a period as the separator between the namespace and the local name.

For example, if a BKM *Payment* is imported from a function library with the namespace *methodandstyleFunctionlib*, FEEL in the importing model references it *as methodandstyleFunctionlib.Payment.*[50]

expressionLanguage and typeLanguage

The optional attributes *definitions/@expressionLanguage* and *definitions/@typeLanguage*, both type *anyURI*, apply to all expressions and type definitions in the model, but may be *overridden* by *expressionLanguage* and *typeLanguage* specifications bound to specific model elements.

Omission of *definitions/@expressionLanguage* and/or *definitions/@typeLanguage* implies the default value, FEEL. For that reason, any DMN tool that does not use FEEL must specify the *expressionLanguage* and type *language* employed.

The following values should be used for common expression and type languages:

- Non-executable: http://www.omg.org/spec/DMN/uninterpreted/20140801

- FEEL/S-FEEL: http://www.omg.org/spec/FEEL/20140401

- XSD (type): http://www.w3.org/2001/XMLSchema

exporter and exporterVersion

Optional attributes *exporter* and *exporterVersion* are string values defined by a DMN tool vendor that uniquely identify the name and version of the tool used to serialize the model. In the case of BPMN, these attributes have proven to facilitate model interchange between tools using minor tool-specific mappings.

import

The complete logic for an end-to-end business decision may be spread across multiple DMN models, and some non-DMN models as well. One DMN model (*definitions*) must define the top level of the end-to-end logic. It can then include the others via one or more *import* elements.

Figure 72 shows the schema for *import*. Each import specifies a *namespace, locationURI,* and *importType.*

- When importing a DMN model, *import/@namespace* references the *definitions/@namespace* of the imported model. When importing an XSD or XML document, *import/@namespace* references the *targetNamespace* of the imported document.

---

[50] Yes this is more than a mouthful. All XML (including DMN) referencing namespaces *must* declare all namespaces used both by *name* and by *prefix,* a short alias for the (usually very long) name.

- *locationURI* is the filespec of the document containing the imported model. Typically it is a filepath relative to the location of the importing DMN document.

- *importType* is a URI identifying the type of model being imported, typically either DMN, XSD, or XML. Normally this is some obscure URL, but it might be nice instead to use a string (without spaces) simply naming the type and version, such as "DMN1.1" or "XSD1.0".

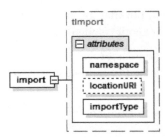

Figure 72. *import* **schema**

definitions/import works at the *document* level. An implementation should be able to access a document named in an *import* element, but *import* does not require actually importing the entire document. Only specific elements defined as *remote references* in the serialization actually need to be fetched into the model.

itemDefinition

Figure 73 shows the schema for *itemDefinition*, specifying the datatype of a DMN *variable* or *expression*. Technically, *base types* in the specified *typeLanguage* do not require an *itemDefinition*, as they are implicitly defined by default. However, any datatypes defined in DMN that specify either a domain of allowed values, a collection, or a data structure require an *itemDefinition*.

- Attribute *name* uniquely names the datatype. The attribute *typeRef* of a *variable* or *expression* points to an *itemDefinition* by *name*, so *itemDefinition/@name* must be unique in the namespace.

- *typeLanguage*, if specified, overrides *definitions/@typeLanguage* for this *itemDefinition*.

- *isCollection* is a Boolean attribute. True signifies a *list* of items of this type.

- Specification of the datatype is a *choice*: either a *typeRef* and *allowedValues* or a list of *itemComponents*.

- The *typeRef* must reference a defined type in the specified *typeLanguage*; *allowedValues* is a list of values or ranges allowed for the *itemDefinition*.

- Each *itemComponent* is itself an *itemDefinition*, i.e. a choice of either a *typeRef* and *allowedValues* or a nested list of *itemComponents*, or a *collection* of these. Using

---

itemComponents, an *itemDefinition* may describe an arbitrarily complex data structure, with each member defined by type and allowed values.

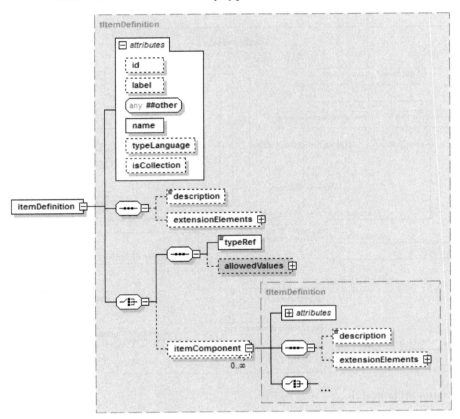

Figure 73. *itemDefinition* **schema**

decision

The metamodel and schema for *decision* are shown in Figure 74 and Figure 75. The two really important parts of *decision* are the *variable* (in metamodel called *InformationItem*) and the *expression*. Based on the *input values* available to the decision, the *expression* determines the *output value* stored in the decision's *variable*. This is the fundamental mechanism at work in DMN.

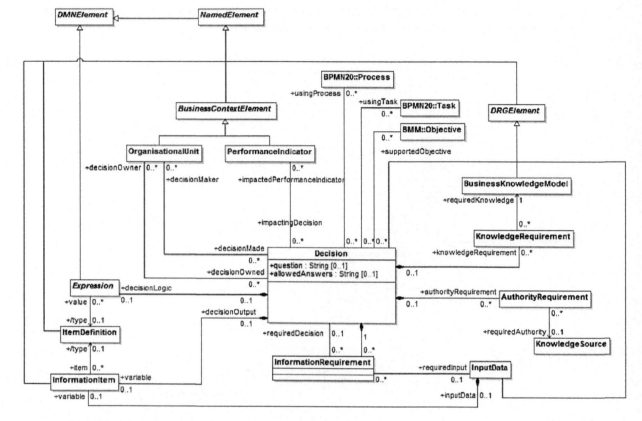

Figure 74. *Decision* **metamodel**

question and allowedAnswers

question and *allowedAnswers* are optional string elements used in modeling methodologies. Best practice is to define every decision as a question (in natural language) with a list of possible answers.

variable and typeRef

In a *decision*, the *variable* must have the same name as the *decision*. In other words, in the serialization,

```
decision/variable/@name = decision/@name
```

This is a requirement of the spec. The *variable* stores the value of the decision's *Expression* and allows it to be referenced by the decision logic of other decisions. DMN expressions reference variables by name. Because the decision *name* must be unique in the model, it follows that the decision variable's *name* must be unique in the model.

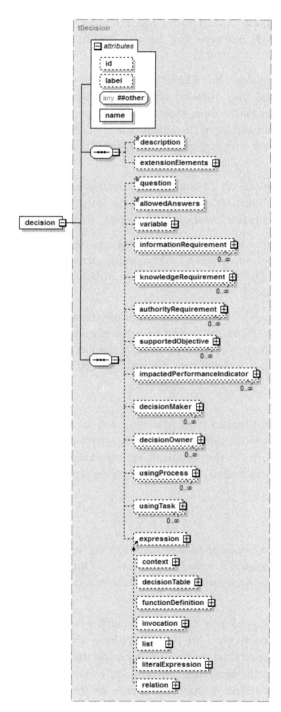

Figure 75. *Decision* **schema**

variable/@typeRef specifies the variable's *datatype* as an XML QName (qualified name, using the [namespace-prefix]:[local-name] syntax). A DMN datatype may be specified in one of four *different* ways:

1. As a *base type* in the specified *typeLanguage*. For FEEL/S-FEEL, the base types are string, number, Boolean, time, date, and two duration types. When specified as a base type, the domain of allowed values is the entire domain of the type. For a base type, *@typeRef* is allowed to omit the namespace of the *typeLanguage*. For example, if *feel* is the declared prefix for http://www.omg.org/spec/FEEL/20140401, either *string* or *feel:string* is valid for *@typeRef*.

2. As a *custom type* defined in the model as an *itemDefinition*. An *itemDefinition* extends a base type either by specifying *allowedValues* or a data structure using *itemComponents*. In this case, *@typeRef* points to *itemDefinition/@name*.

3. As an *itemDefinition* defined in an imported DMN model. In this case, *@typeRef* uses the namespace prefix, e.g., *n1:CreditRiskType*, where *n1* is the prefix corresponding to the namespace of the imported DMN model, and *CreditRiskType* is an *itemDefinition/@name* in the imported model.

4. As a *non-DMN type specification* in an imported document. Typically this would be a datatype specified in an imported XSD. Again, @typeRef uses the namespace prefix, such as *n1:CreditRiskType*, where *n1* is the prefix corresponding to the *targetNamespace* specified by the XSD, and *CreditRiskType* is a global type defined in the XSD.

expression

In the metamodel and schema, *expression* is an abstract class, meaning any of its concrete subclasses may be substituted. DMN defines several different types of *expression*, including *decisionTable, literalExpression, invocation*, and more. In the serialization, one of these concrete elements is used to specify the decision's value expression. We will discuss *expression* in more detail later in this chapter.

informationRequirement

Each *informationRequirement* of a *decision*, corresponding to a solid incoming arrow in the DRD, specifies a *variable in scope* in the decision's value expression. Only variables corresponding to one of the decision's *informationRequirements* may be referenced in its value expression. This is an ironclad rule of DMN.

An *informationRequirement* is either a *requiredDecisionRef* or a *requiredInputRef*, a pointer to the supporting *decision* or *inputData* element, respectively. In the XSD, these are *remote ID pointers*, and the aforementioned variable in scope is the *variable* representing that *decision* or *inputData*. Remote ID pointers allow reference to imported DMN models, so a decision's *informationRequirement* may be a *decision* or *inputData* in another model. In the XSD these remote ID pointers are type *tDMNElementReference*.

knowledgeRequirement

Each *knowledgeRequirement*, corresponding to a dashed arrow connector in DRD, represents an *invocation* of a BKM by the decision. *requiredKnowledgeRef* is a remote ID pointer (*tDMNElementReference*) to the BKM at the tail end of the connector.

authorityRequirement

Each *authorityRequirement*, corresponding to a dashed non-arrow connector in DRD, links the decision to a *knowledgeSource*, such as a policy document or a particular human expert. *requiredAuthorityRef* is a remote ID pointer (*tDMNElementReference*).

Other Info

The other elements of *decision* shown in Figure 75 provide optional ancillary information that help place the decision in a broader business context.

- Each *supportedObjectiveRef* is a remote ID pointer to an *Objective* element in an associated *Business Motivation Model*. BMM is another OMG standard.[51]

- Each *impactedPerformanceIndicatorRef* is a remote ID pointer to a DMN *performanceIndicator* element.

- Each *decisionMakerRef* and *decisionOwnerRef* is a remote ID pointer to a DMN *organizationUnit* element.

- Each *usingProcessRef* and *usingTaskRef* is remote ID pointer to a *process* and *task* in a BPMN process model.

---

[51] http://www.omg.org/spec/BMM/Current/

inputData

Each *inputData* element (Figure 76) defines a *variable* with *name* matching the *name* of the *inputData* element. As with all variables, the *typeRef* attribute specifies the datatype.

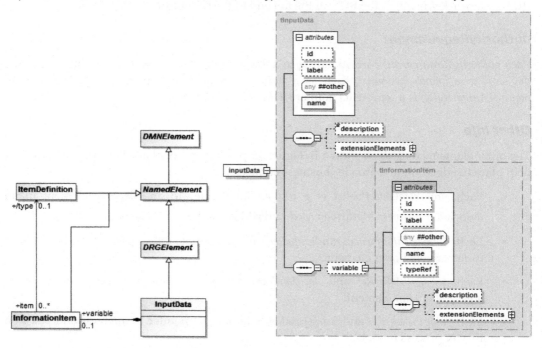

Figure 76. *inputData* **metamodel and schema**

businessKnowledgeModel

The BKM schema is shown in Figure 77. A BKM represents a *function definition*. The BKM's *name* attribute serves as the name of the function. The element *encapsulatedLogic* contains the function specification, comprised of a list of *formalParameter*s and a value *expression* taking any form. Each *formalParameter* is a variable with scope limited to the BKM, so its *name* does not need to be unique in the model, only unique within the BKM. The BKM also defines a *variable* that holds its output value. There is redundancy between *variable/@typeRef* and *encapsulatedLogic/@typeRef*. It is best to omit the latter.

A BKM has no *informationRequirements*. Its input values are passed to it via invocation. It may have one or more *knowledgeRequirements*, signifying other BKMs invoked by this BKM, and possibly one or more *authorityRequirements*.

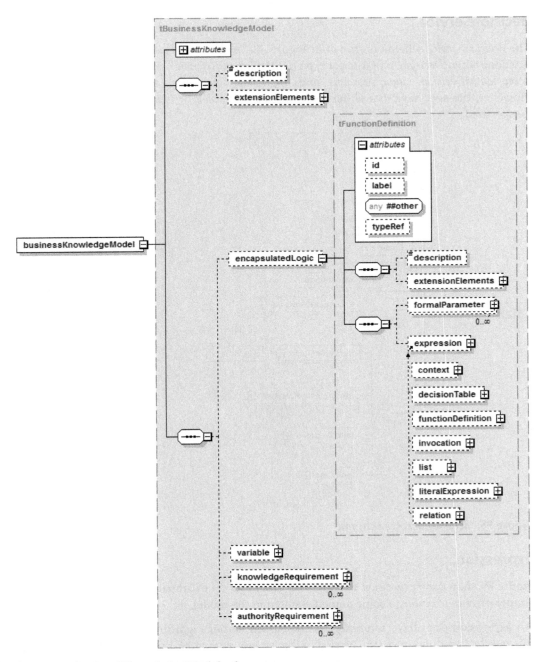

Figure 77. *businessKnowledgeModel* **schema**

decisionService

The *decisionService* schema is shown in Figure 78. A *decisionService* must have a *name* and at least one *outputDecision*, a pointer of type *tDMNElementReference*. It may list also zero or more *encapsulatedDecision*, *inputDecision*, and *inputData* elements, all *tDMNElementReference*. However, the spec says that either the *encapsulatedDecision* or *inputDecision* elements should be specified.

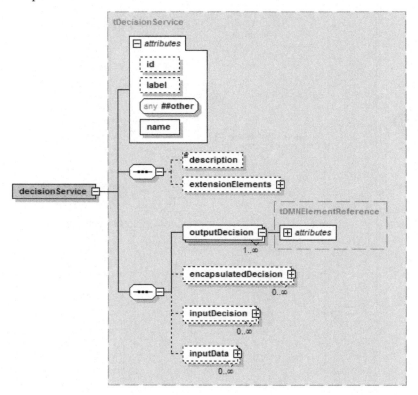

Figure 78. *decisionService* **schema**

expression

Figure 79 shows the *expression* metamodel. Note that an expression does not have a *name;* it simply provides a *value* to some named element in the model.

An expression does have a *typeRef*. As discussed earlier regarding BKMs, most of the time this *typeRef* is redundant to the *typeRef* of the *variable* populated by the expression and should be omitted. There are one or two cases – *inputExpression* in a decision table comes to mind – where the *expression/@typeRef* is useful, but normally it's best to omit *expression/@typeRef*.

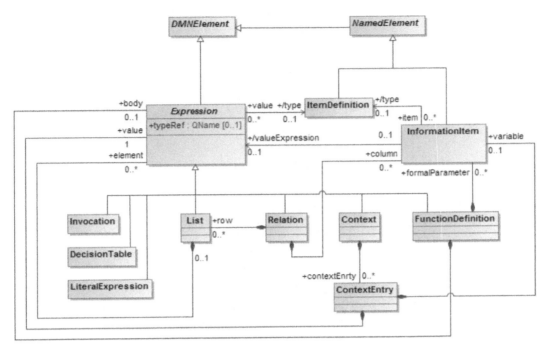

Figure 79. *Expression* **metamodel**

literalExpression

A *literalExpression* is an expression represented as a text string. Figure 80 shows the schema.

- The *expressionLanguage* attribute is omitted unless you need to override the value in *definitions/@expressionLanguage*.

- The expression string is entered in either the *text* element (the normal case) or in *importedValues*.

- *importedValues* allows an expression or value to be imported from an external model. *importedValues/@namespace*, *@locationURI*, and *@importType* should match corresponding values in *definitions/@import*. (Yes there is redundancy, but *definitions/@import* alerts the implementation upfront that access to the imported document is required.

- Whereas *literalExpression/@expressionLanguage* defines the expression language of the expression string, *importedValues/@expressionLanguage* refers to the expression language used to select *importedElement*. For example, if the import is a relation defined in an imported XML document, typically *importedValues/@expressionLanguage* will be XPATH 1.0 or XPATH 2.0.

- *importedValues/importedElement* is an expression string in the above-mentioned expressionLanguage that selects the imported elements.

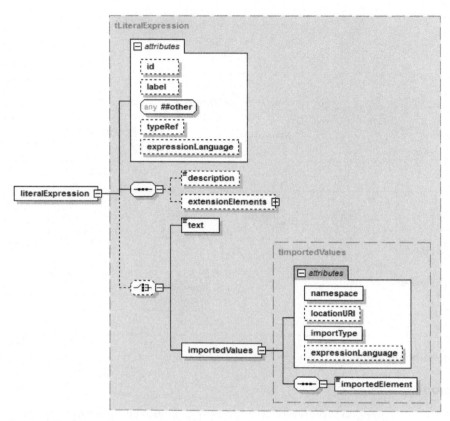

Figure 80. *literalExpression* **schema**

invocation

When a *decision* invokes a BKM, the decision's value expression is *invocation*. The *invocation* schema is shown in Figure 81.

The schema is confusing and may cause some problems. The value of the *expression* element MUST be the *name* of a *functionDefinition*, usually a BKM name (but if nested in a context, possibly another context entry). But instead of making this element *calledFunction,* a string – which it was until the very last minute – it is specified as *any expression*.

The stated intent of this change was to allow the identity of the called function to be determined dynamically at runtime. But this is inconsistent with the rest of the metamodel. For example, the invoking decision's *knowledgeRequirement* points to a specific BKM *id*. Thus the invocation's expression element effectively must be a *literalExpression/text* value matching the *name* of that BKM.

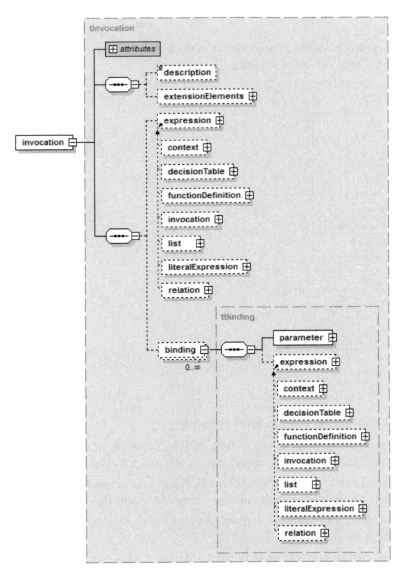

Figure 81. *invocation* **schema**

The rest of the invocation is a list of *bindings*. Each *binding* specifies a *parameter* and an *expression* that maps decision inputs to each *parameter*. Once again the XSD is not ideal. Each *binding/parameter* should be a pointer to a parameter of the called function, but it is not. Instead, *binding/parameter* defines a new *variable*. The problem is that this variable MUST exactly match the definition of a parameter of the invoked BKM. In other words, the following MUST be true for each parameter or the model is invalid:

```
invocation/binding/parameter =
businessKnowledgeModel[@name=invocation/literalExpression/text]/formalParameter
```

decisionTable

The *decisionTable* schema is quite elaborate, so depicting it in the book requires multiple views. Figure 82 shows the attributes and high-level stricture.

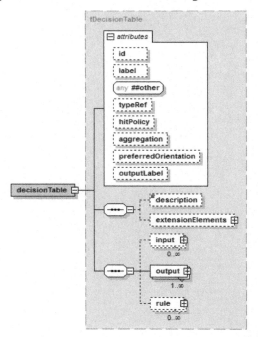

Figure 82. *decisionTable* **attributes and top-level elements**

- *hitPolicy* has enumerated values *UNIQUE, FIRST, PRIORITY, ANY, COLLECT, RULE ORDER, OUTPUT ORDER.* If the attribute is omitted, the default value is *UNIQUE.*

- *Aggregation,* meaningful only with *hitPolicy COLLECT*, has enumerated values *SUM, COUNT, MIN, MAX.* There is no default value, so omission means do not aggregate.

- *preferredOrientation* has enumerated values *Rule-as-Row, Rule-as-Column,* and *CrossTable.* If omitted, the default is *Rule-as-Row.*

- *outputLabel,* a string, can be any text used to label a decision table output. However, expressions must reference the decision table output by its *name,* not the output label.

Figure 83 shows the *decisionTable/input* schema, describing each input column in the table.

- *inputExpression* is a *literalExpression* labeling the input. In CL2 decision tables, it must be a simple expression, either a variable name, arithmetic expression, or comparison. The XSD allows it to be any expression in any expressionLanguage.

- *inputValues* is an optional list of allowed values for the *inputExpression.* If the *inputExpression* is just a variable, its *typeRef* may already list a domain of allowed values. In that case, *input/inputValues* must be a subset of the domain. *inputValues* is type *tUnaryTests*, the same as *inputEntry*.

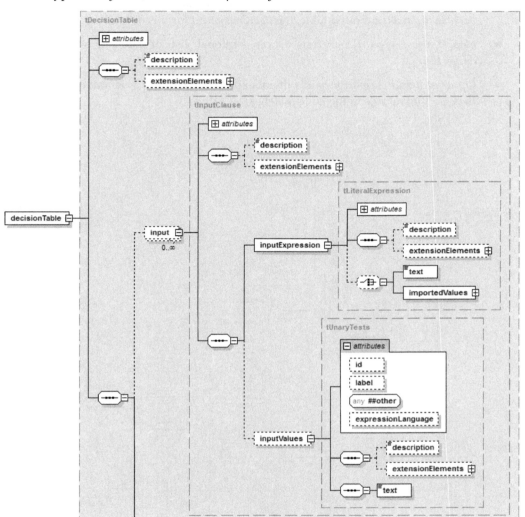

Figure 83. *decisionTable/input* **schema**

Figure 84 shows the *decisionTable/output* schema, describing each output column in the table.

- Attribute *typeRef* is best omitted, as it is redundant to the *typeRef* of the decision *variable* or, in a compound table, the *itemComponent* for this output.

- *outputValues*, type *tUnaryTests*, is an optional list of allowed values for any *outputEntry*.

- Optional *defaultOutputEntry* is a literal expression defining a default output value in the case that no rule in the table matches.

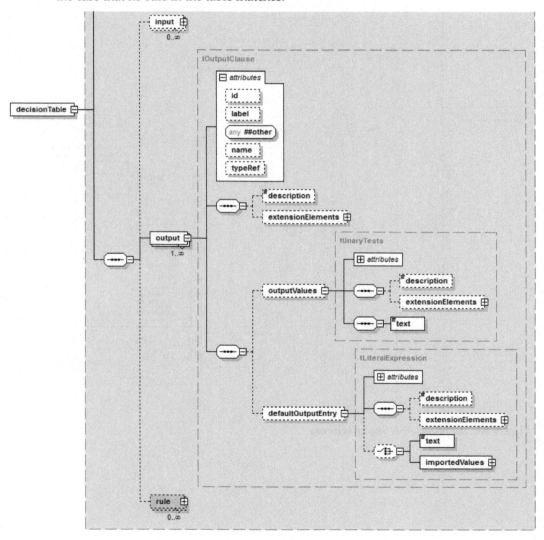

Figure 84. *decisionTable/output* **schema**

Figure 85 shows the *decisionTable/rule* schema. Each *rule* element specifies a list of *inputEntry* and *outputEntry* elements.

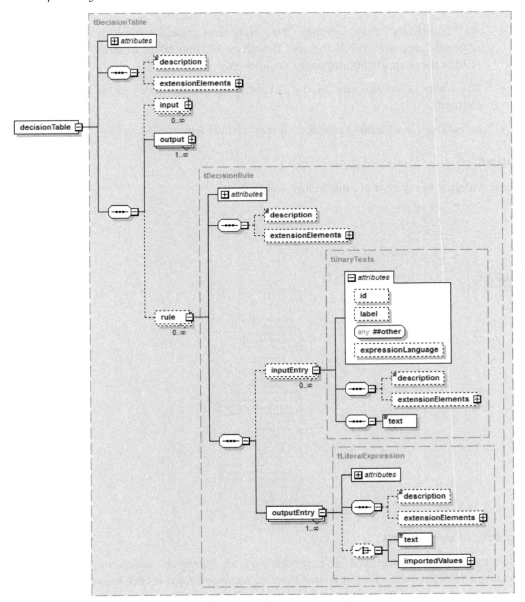

Figure 85. *decisionTable/rule* **schema**

- The order of *inputEntry* elements in the list must match the order of *decisionTable/input* elements. Inputs marked with hyphen (irrelevant) in the decision table must nevertheless be represented by an *inputEntry* in the serialization.

- *inputEntry* is type *tUnaryTests*, a comma-separated list of condition fragments. Concatenation of the *inputExpression* with any item in the list defines a Boolean expression.

- An *inputEntry* may specify an *expressionLanguage* overriding the model *expressionLanguage*. While the spec describes decision tables in terms of FEEL and S-FEEL, other expression languages are allowed.

- The order of *outputEntry* in the list must match the order of *decisionTable/output* elements.

- *outputEntry* is a literal expression. It may include *importedValues*.

context

A *context* (Figure 86) is a list of *contextEntry* elements.

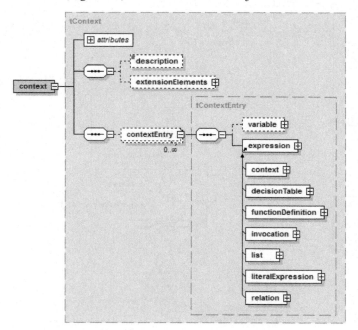

Figure 86. *context* **schema**

Each *contextEntry* is comprised of a *variable* and an *expression*, which may be any type, including another *context*. Through such nesting, a single *context* is able to express arbitrarily complex decision logic. The scope of the *variable* is limited to the *context* that contains it. It is effectively a *local variable*, so its *name* could be the same as some other *variable* outside the *context*.

A *contextEntry* without a variable is typically used to hold the final result of the *context*. In that case, the decision or BKM containing the *context* provides the variable.

list and relation

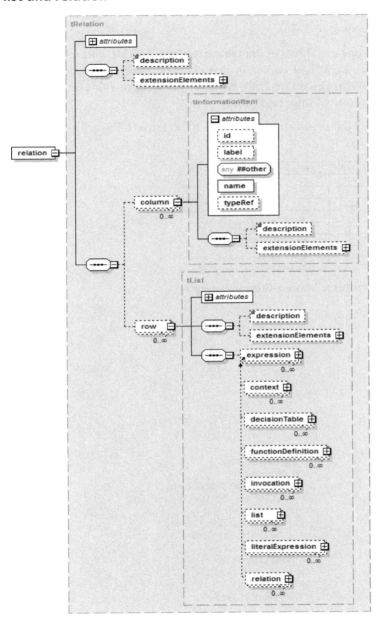

Figure 87. *relation* **schema. Each** *row* **is a** *list*

Figure 87 shows the schema of *relation* and *list*. A *relation* is described in the spec text as a list of similar contexts, but the schema describes it in a more compact way, as a list of *columns* and a list of *rows*. Each column is a *variable*, effectively providing the *name* and *typeRef* of the *contextEntry* in the similar contexts. Each *row* is a *list* (type tList), which is simply a list of *expressions* of any type. Normally a *relation* is a table of literal values, but technically each cell in the table could be an expression.

As an alternative to relation, one could model the table externally in XML and reference it by *literalExpression/importedValues*, described earlier in this chapter. The import automatically maps data from XML types to corresponding FEEL types, so FEEL expressions on the variable are still valid even when expressed as imported XML.

For example, Figure 88 shows the *Ingredients* relation from the Make a Burger example from Chapter 11.

Ingredients	Item	Sodium/mg	Fat/g	Calories	Cost/$
	BeefPatty	50	17	220	0.25
	Bun	330	9	260	0.15
	Cheese	310	6	70	0.1
	Onions	1	2	10	0.09
	Pickles	260	0	5	0.03
	Lettuce	3	0	4	0.04
	Ketchup	160	0	20	0.02
	Tomato	3	0	9	0.04

Figure 88. *Ingredients* **relation from Make a Burger example**

```
<relation typeRef="tns:tIngredients">
  <column name="Item"/>
  <column name="Sodium/mg"/>
  <column name="Fat/g"/>
  <column name="Calories"/>
  <column name="Cost/$"/>
  <row>
    <literalExpression>
      <text>50</text>
    </literalExpression>
    <literalExpression>
      <text>17</text>
    </literalExpression>
    <literalExpression>
      <text>220</text>
    </literalExpression>
    <literalExpression>
      <text>0.25</text>
    </literalExpression>
  </row>
  <row>
    <!-- etc.... -->
  </row>
</relation>
```

```
<ingredientsTable>
  <ingredient>
    <item>BeefPatty</item>
    <Sodium_mg>50</Sodium_mg>
    <Fat_g>17</Fat_g>
    <Calories>220</Calories>
    <Cost>0.25</Cost>
  </ingredient>
  <ingredient>
    <!-- etc. -->
  </ingredient>
</ingredientsTable>
```

Figure 89. Serialization of *Ingredients* **as** *relation* **(left) and XML table (right)**

Figure 89 compares the serialization of *Ingredients* as a *relation* versus an external XML table referenced by *literalExpression/importedValues*. Because a relation is the list of rows, not the table element that encloses the list of rows, the *literalExpression* would be serialized as in (Figure 90).

```
<literalExpression>
  <importedValues namespace="methodandstyleIngredientsTable" locationURI="ingredients.xml" importType="XML1.0">
    <importedElement expressionLanguage="XPath 2.0">//n1:ingredient</importedElement>
  </importedValues>
</literalExpression>
```

Figure 90. Serialization of *literalExpression* of imported XML table

In other words, the *importedElement* is the set of rows named *ingredient*, not the table element *ingredientsTable*. The value of *importedElement* is an XPATH 2.0 expression that selects those rows from the imported document *ingredients.xml*.

PART III:
DMN METHOD AND STYLE

CHAPTER 8

What Makes a Good Decision Table?

Decision tables predate DMN by over three decades, and there is a considerable body of opinion about what makes a *good* decision table. As background to DMN Method and Style, let's take a look at the recommendations of other leading authorities.

Vanthienen

Professor Jan Vanthienen of K.U. Leuven has written extensively about the history, theory, and practice of decision tables. His 1992 paper, "Decision Tables: Refining the Concept and a Proposed Standard,"[52] surveyed the evolution of the technique up to that time and proposed "Ten Commandments" of good decision tables. In 2012, those were updated to Sixteen Commandments.[53] Vanthienen recognized that decision tables are not always the best representation of decision logic; for some logic, a decision tree or nested *If..Then..Else* expressions might be more appropriate. In general, he says, decision tables work best when the conclusion – what he calls the "action" – is selected from an enumerated list. His examples typically are based on "limited action" tables in which each possible output value is displayed as a separate column, with selection of that value indicated by x.

Sixteen Commandments

Here are Vanthienen's Sixteen Commandments, translated into DMN terminology:

1. Decision tables should be *complete* and *consistent*. There should be no combination of inputs not matched by a rule or that results in more than one output value (unless

---

[52]http://www.econ.kuleuven.be/prologa/refsdtpubs/DTDevACM.pdf

[53] J. Vanthienen, "The History of Modeling Decisions using Tables (Part 3), Standardizing Decision Table Modeling," http://www.brcommunity.com/b652.php

filtered by a hit policy).

2. Use *extended-entry* tables, not limited-entry. In the early days, many decision tables were *limited-entry*, meaning their input expressions were limited to Booleans (true or false). But Vanthienen recommends *extended-entry tables*, in which input expressions can have more than two possible values, offering advantages of conciseness, manageability, abstraction power, and overview. Today, we rarely see limited-entry tables.

3. Input entries should be complete and *non-overlapping*. Input entries should test every possible value of each input expression, and any input expression value should satisfy only one input entry value. (Sometimes adjacent rules will have the same input entry value, which is OK, but a single input expression value should not match two different input entry values.)

4. Single-hit tables should have *Unique* hit policy. In DMN terms, only one rule should match for any combination of input values. This eliminates redundancy, conflicts, omissions, and subsumptions automatically.

5. Decision tables may have *compound output*. Some methodologies, like TDM, forbid compound output.

6. Horizontal (rules-as-rows) layout is OK if the number of inputs and outputs is small. If that number is large, *vertical (rules-as-columns) layout* produces more "overview".[54]

7. Rules should be listed in "natural order" to *optimize visual scanning for completeness*.

8. Tables should be optimized via *table contraction*. Contraction refers to combining two or more rules into a single rule, where possible. Often contraction makes use of the input entry *hyphen*, meaning a particular input expression is *irrelevant* in the rule.

9. The order of inputs is irrelevant, but may affect the size of the contracted table.

10. The order of inputs should *minimize the number of rules* in the contracted table.

11. Tables should be *tree-structured*, meaning the input columns should be ordered so that the table can be evaluated "stepwise" from left to right until a specific rule is selected. In the "tree," merging of cells with the same input entry is assumed, allowing the decision table to act as a sort of decision tree. Such a layout also eases visual verification of completeness.

---

[54] Vanthienen notes, "Decision tables often struggle with space. It is important to keep all conditions on one page without having to scroll horizontally. Therefore Rules-as-columns is generally preferred as it easily accommodates 4 or more conditions without scrolling. The major point is that you should never have to scroll conditions because then overview is lost. If the table has few conditions and few rules, the length of input and output names may favour a specific layout with minimal scrolling." Private communication, December 2015.

12. Tables should be *block-oriented*, meaning input entry cells in adjacent rows should be merged as much as possible. DMN supports this cell merging, but many first-generation tools do not yet support it.

13. *Contracted impossibilities.* Some combinations of allowed input values may be in reality impossible to occur. Vanthienen recommends, however, that the decision table be designed as if they could occur, contracted with neighboring conditions to minimize the number of rules. DMN Method and Style makes good use of this commandment, as discussed in Chapter 12.

14. Complex decision logic should be factored into supporting decisions. This is a fundamental assumption of DMN.

15. Avoid "intertabular anomalies." These are not explained.

16. Selection structure. A decision table should simply *select an output value*; it should not include actions within the table definition, such as "restart from top".

Clear and Consistent

Vanthienen emphasizes the basic point that the very structure of a decision table makes decision logic more precise and consistent than it is in text form.

As an example, he quotes from the sports page of his local newspaper from a couple decades back:

> "Clijsters becomes the world's number one if she reaches the final, OR If Davenport doesn't reach the final, OR Mauresmo doesn't win the tournament. Lindsay Davenport stays number one if she wins the tournament AND Clijsters doesn't reach the final, OR she loses the final (against another player than Mauresmo) AND Clijsters loses in the semi-finals. Amélie Mauresmo becomes number one if she wins the tournament and Clijsters loses in the quarter-finals."[55]

By translating this twisted text into a decision table (Figure 91), it's plain to see that certain stated combinations result in two number ones, and other combinations result in zero number ones… both of which are impossible.

---

[55] Jan Vanthienen, "50 Ways to Boost Your Business and Decision Analysis," BBC Conference, 2015. Translated from www.sporza.be.

TennisNumberOne				
U	Clijsters OutEarly, OutSemi, OutFinal, Win	Davenport OutBeforeFinal, Runnerup, Win	Mauresmo Win, NotWin	NumberOne
1	OutEarly	OutBeforeFinal	NotWin	Clijsters
2			Win	Clijsters, Mauresmo
3		Runnerup	NotWin	Clijsters
4			Win	Mauresmo
5		Win	-	Clijsters, Davenport
6	OutSemi	OutBeforeFinal	-	Clijsters
7		Runnerup, Win	-	Clijsters, Davenport
8		Runnerup, Win	Win	-
9	OutFinal, Win	-	-	Clijsters

Figure 91. Decision table exposes inconsistencies in the text-based decision logic

Vanthienen's rules for good decision tables boil down to two simple principles:

1. The decision logic should be clear from visual inspection.

2. The logic should be consistent. A single-hit table should not generate two different outcomes.

Based on these two factors, his conclusion is that decision tables should use *Unique* hit policy.

Consider the decision *SpecialDiscount* decision table of Figure 92. Quick, tell me who gets a 0% discount?

SpecialDiscount				
P	OrderType Web, Phone	Location US, International	CustomerType Wholesale, Retail	SpecialDiscount 10%, 5%, 0%
1	Web	US	Wholesale	10%
2	Phone	-	-	0%
3	-	International	-	0%
4	-	-	Retail	5%

Figure 92. *SpecialDiscount* table makes decision logic hard to see. Source: Adapted from Vanthienen

Did you say, "Phone orders or International"? No, that is incorrect!

Let's make this a *Unique* table. There are 3 inputs, each of which have 2 possible values, making a total of 2x2x2 = 8 combinations:

SpecialDiscount				
	OrderType	Location	CustomerType Wholesale,	SpecialDiscount
U	Web, Phone	US, International	Retail	10%, 5%, 0%
1	Web	US	Wholesale	10%
2	Web	US	Retail	5%
3	Phone	US	Wholesale	0%
4	Phone	US	Retail	5%
5	Web	International	Wholesale	0%
6	Web	International	Retail	5%
7	Phone	International	Wholesale	0%
8	Phone	International	Retail	5%

Figure 93. *Unique*, **non-contracted table**

We can contract this table:

SpecialDiscount				
	OrderType	Location	CustomerType Wholesale,	SpecialDiscount
U	Web, Phone	US, International	Retail	10%, 5%, 0%
1	Web	US	Wholesale	10%
2	-	-	Retail	5%
3	Phone	US	Wholesale	0%
4	-	International	Wholesale	0%

Figure 94. *Unique* **contracted table makes decision logic more easily visible**

Now tell me, who gets a 0% discount? It's a lot easier to see it with *Unique* hit policy.

Ross

Another widely recognized authority is Ron Ross, co-founder and principal of Business Rules Solutions, LLC and executive editor of BRCommunity.com. In "Decision Tables: A Primer – How to Use TableSpeak, v2.0,"[56] he offers his views on what makes a good decision table.

His approach starts from the view that "Many decision tables are too technical. They are aimed at software developers, not business people." TableSpeak is "a set of conventions for business-friendly representation of decision tables and their meaning (semantics) in declarative fashion." Key features of TableSpeak include:

- Optimized choice of table layout based on the number of inputs and possible values for each.

- The principle of *single sourcing*, meaning a single point of change for any decision rule.

---

[56]Ronald Ross, "Decision Tables: A Primer," Business Rule Solutions, http://www.brsolutions.com/b_ipspeakprimers.php, 2013.

- Rules for maintaining integrity of decision table content.

- Naming the decision table as a question.

- Explicitly declared *scope* of the decision.

- Explicit externalization of *exceptions*.

- Precise *business vocabulary*.

A *consideration* in TableSpeak is what DMN calls a decision table *input*. Ross recommends that a single decision table should have no more than 7 considerations, which he calls the *complexity threshold*. Beyond that you need to decompose it into supporting decisions. Enumerated allowed values of a consideration are called *elemental cases*. The set of elemental cases for a consideration should be *exhaustive* (inclusive of all allowed values) and *disjoint*, i.e., non-overlapping. An *intersection case* is the combined values of two or more elemental cases. What DMN calls an output entry is called an *outcome* in TableSpeak.

Layout

Depending on the decision details, Ross might recommend any of the three decision table layouts used in DMN, but for simple decision tables he recommends the *crosstab layout*, for a variety of reasons:

1. No extra cells are required to hold the outcomes.

2. No elemental cases are repeated in the table.

3. Simplifies visual verification of completeness (no empty cells).

4. Single point of change (single-sourcing) for each decision rule.

He considers the alternative rules-as-rows and rules-as-columns layouts to be "less friendly to business people… [and] more prone to certain kinds of anomalies," including incompleteness and single-sourcing violations.

Is it cold?	Is it rainy?	What coat should be worn?
yes	yes	lined raincoat
	no	wool overcoat
	yes	lined raincoat
no	yes	unlined raincoat

Figure 95. Rules-as-rows layout makes it harder to spot completeness and single-sourcing violations. Source: Business Rules Solutions, LLC

For example, Figure 95 illustrates a rules-as-rows table that is both incomplete and has a single-sourcing violation. [57] The intersection case *not cold/not rainy* is not included (incomplete), and the intersection case *cold/rainy* is repeated (single-sourcing violation). This is a trivial example, but Ross maintains that such violations are harder to spot visually using rules-as-rows than with the crosstab layout, and thus decision table validation requires special software.

The recommendation of crosstab layouts is only for simple decision tables. In general, the recommended layout is determined by a complex formula based on the count of *few-case* and *many-case* considerations. A few-case consideration is an input with three or fewer elemental cases (allowed values). A many-case consideration is one with four or more elemental cases.

- *Crosstab* is recommended if there are 4 or fewer few-case considerations and 0 many-case, or 2 or fewer few-case and 2 or fewer many-case.

- *Stacked crosstab* is recommended if there are 5 few-case and 0 many-case considerations, or 3-4 few-case and 1 many-case, or 3 few-case and 2 many-case, or 0-2 few-case and 3 many-case considerations. Stacked crosstab uses a separate table for each elemental case of one of the considerations.

- *Rules-as-rows* (or *rules-as-columns*) is recommended with 4 or more many-case considerations, or if the number of few-case considerations plus the number of many-case considerations is 6-7. Beyond that limit, you need to factor the table into multiple decisions.

Scope, Restrictions, Exceptions, and Defaults

Ross correctly understands the purpose of a decision table is to communicate the *meaning* of the decision logic, clearly and precisely. To that end, his decision table style emphasizes naming, scope, restrictions, defaults and exceptions, and structured business vocabulary.

TableSpeak recommends that the decision table *name* should be the business-relevant *question* that the decision answers. For example, he would name Figure 95, *What coat should be worn?*, not *Coat Table*.

Scope refers to the range of cases considered by the decision. In order to keep tables as simple as possible, TableSpeak recommends that the scope is explicitly stated in the diagram. For example, Figure 95 might be annotated, *gender: female, city: San Francisco*.

Restrictions are rules that govern the integrity of a decision table. *Relevance restrictions* preclude specification of any outcome for certain combinations of inputs (*preemption*) or provide a warning that the specified outcome in those cases may be invalid (*caveat*). In TableSpeak, preempted cells are grayed out and marked *n/a*. *Consideration restrictions* preclude certain combinations of input values. *Outcome restrictions* specify a particular special outcome for certain combinations of input values, or possibly limit the outcomes to a special

---

[57] Ross, "Decision Tables: A Primer," 17.

subset. Like scope, restrictions are intended to simplify decision tables by excluding certain cases. According to Ross, "Defining a restriction not only allows single-sourcing of the related business intent, but also supports its faithful retention and consistent application as the decision table undergoes modifications over time."[58]

Exceptions are cases in scope that use special considerations, not those specified in the decision table. Again, by explicitly indicating exceptions, the decision table for "normal" cases can be kept simple. For example, the normal considerations for issuing and pricing auto insurance are location, driving history, prior insurance, risk score, and credit rating, but the applicant is ineligible if under 18 years of age or has been convicted of a felony involving a motor vehicle. By indicating the age and felony considerations as exceptions, the normal decision table is kept simpler.

Defaults are rules covering combinations of input values that are missing in the decision table. A default is equivalent to a row in the decision table meaning "otherwise". Like restrictions and exceptions, defaults allow more compact decision tables.

Scope, restrictions, exceptions, and defaults all help achieve one of TableSpeak's highest priorities, *single-sourcing*. Based on the premise that decision logic is continually changing, Ross says it is best maintained when a rule is defined in only one place rather than reused in multiple decisions.

Structured Business Vocabulary

In the world of decision modeling, Ron Ross is probably best known for insisting on a precisely defined *business vocabulary* used in decision tables.

> "No form of business rule expression or representation, including decision tables, is viable or complete if not based on a well-defined, well-structured business vocabulary. Knowing the business meaning of the words that appear in expressions or representations is a key element for success."[59]

The vocabulary is defined as a *conceptual data model*, or *concept model* for short. A concept model defines named *entities* representing familiar business-oriented *concepts*, like Customer, Order, and Product, *attributes* of the entities (like name, address, age), and *relationships* between the entities. An entity may have enumerated subtypes that inherit the attributes of the parent and may add their own attributes and subtypes. Concept models are technology-independent and are not required to use any formal notation.

TableSpeak's concept modeling approach, called ConceptSpeak,[60] is based on another OMG standard called *Semantics of Business Vocabulary and Rules*, or SBVR. DMN originally intended

---

[58] Ross, "Decision Tables: A Primer," 36.

[59] Ross, "Decision Tables: A Primer," 50.

[60] http://www.brsolutions.com/b_concepts.php

to leverage SBVR but in the end decided to take a less formal path to formalizing the business vocabulary. In this book, we will discuss data modeling further in Chapter 13.

Procedural Dependencies

A decision table should represent *declarative logic*. Procedural logic should use some other representation:

> "A procedural representation (e.g., a process model, use case, flowchart, etc.) is more natural and effective in capturing and representing logic where:
>
> - The desired determination involves what action to take.
> - The order (sequence) in which the factors are evaluated matters."[61]

One sign of a poorly designed decision table with a procedural dependency, he says, is a blank (in DMN terms, *null*) condition cell. In some cases, a procedural dependency can be converted to a logical dependency. To illustrate, Ross poses the following pricing decision scenario: A company has four classes of product, with associated pricing:

1. Pre-owned, not worked-on (i.e., acquired from supplier and not modified): purchase price plus 12%

2. Pre-owned, worked-on (acquired and modified): hours plus 15%

3. Standard: list price

4. Custom: contract price

What should be charged for a product?	worked-on?	price
pre-owned	no	purchase price + 12%
	yes	hours + 15%
standard		list price
custom		contract price

(left axis label: kind of product)

Figure 96. Poorly designed decision table with blank cells representing procedural dependency. Source: Business Rule Solutions, LLC

Figure 96 illustrates the attempt to model this as a single crosstab decision table, but it has blank cells, since the *worked-on* consideration only applies if the kind of product is *pre-owned*. This implies that the *kind of product* consideration must be evaluated before the *worked-on* consideration. In TableSpeak, a decision table should never have blank cells. (Note: This

---

[61] Ross, "Decision Tables: A Primer," 55.

example could also be handled by a simple *relevance restriction*, graying out the blank cells with the entry *n/a*.)

Ross's recommendation is to break this into two decision tables related by a *logical dependency*, meaning the output of one table provides an input to another. In Figure 97, pre-owned product price is the output of the first table and an input variable (used in output entry) in the second table.

	What should be charged for a pre-owned product?	pre-owned product price
worked-on?	no	purchase price + 12%
	yes	hours + 15%

	What should be charged for a product?	price
kind of product	pre-owned	pre-owned product price
	standard	list price
	custom	contract price

Figure 97. Removing blank cells by creating logically dependent tables. Source: Business Rule Solutions, LLC

This is an example of what Vanthienen calls an *action subtable*. Figure 98 is the DRD of the resulting decision model in DMN. While a single decision table must be declarative in the sense that rules may be evaluated in any order, in a DRD a dependent decision may require prior evaluation of a supporting decision.

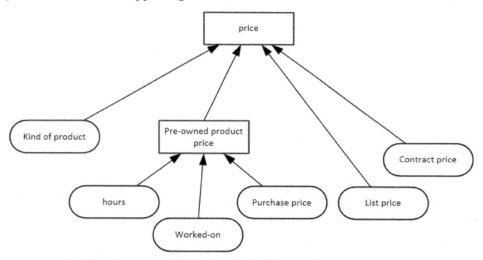

Figure 98. DRD of the factored decision of Figure 97

Anomalies

According to Ross, the following conditions, called *anomalies*, should always be avoided:

- *Redundancy.* Some combination of input values (intersection case) matches multiple rules with the same outcome. This is equivalent to the DMN hit policy *Any*.

- *Multiple outcomes.* Some combination of input values (intersection case) matches multiple rules with different outcomes. This is allowed by the DMN single-hit policies *First* and *Priority*, and by multiple-hit policies.

- *Conflict.* Some combination of input values (intersection case) matches multiple rules with mutually exclusive outcomes.

- *Omission.* Some combination of input values (intersection case) matches no rule and is not covered by an exception, restriction, or default.

- *Subsumable rules.* Two or more rules can be combined in a single rule with no change in outcome. For example, Figure 99 exhibits this anomaly, since the first and fourth rules can be combined, using hyphen in the hazardous materials column.

What is the right delivery method for an order?							
rush order?	any fragile item?	any specialty item?	any high-priced item?	any item involving hazardous materials?	category of customer?	destination of order?	delivery method for order
no	no	no	no	no	silver	—	picked up by customer
yes	yes	no	no	yes	gold	local	shipped by normal service
yes	—	—	—	yes	platinum	remote	shipped by premium service
no	no	no	no	yes	silver	—	picked up by customer

Figure 99. Table with subsumable rules anomaly. Source: Business Rules Solutions, LLC

The Decision Model (von Halle and Goldberg)

The Decision Model (TDM), developed by Barbara von Halle and Larry Goldberg of Knowledge Partners International (acquired in 2014 by Sapiens DECISION[62]), models decision logic – or what they prefer to call *business logic* – based on rigorous principles analogous to the Relational Model for data. It describes notations for both decision tables and the diagram of their dependencies on supporting decision tables, similar to a DRD in DMN. The technique is described in detail in the book *The Decision Model*,[63] published in 2010.

---

[62] http://www.sapiensdecision.com/

[63] von Halle and Goldberg, *The Decision Model*.

Like DMN, TDM seeks to free decision management from the grip of BRE rule language programmers, and empower business users to define and maintain decision models themselves.

> "The Decision Model structure is based on the premise that business logic has its own existence, independent of how it is executed, where in the business it is executed, and whether or not its execution is implemented in automated systems."[64]

TDM Notation

Figure 100 illustrates the TDM notation.

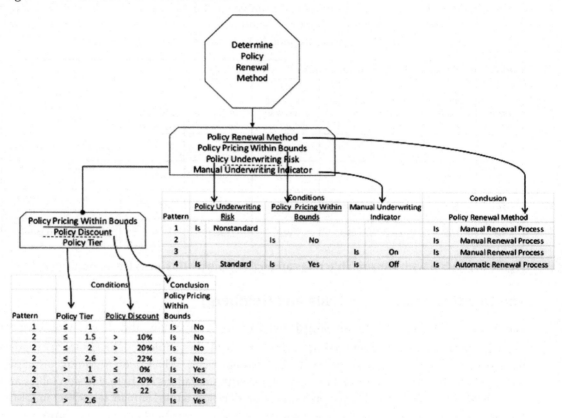

Figure 100. The Decision Model notation. Source: KPI USA[65]

---

[64] von Halle and Goldberg, *The Decision Model*, 8.

[65] Larry Goldberg, Introduction to the Decision Model, 2011, http://www.slideshare.net/IIBA-UK/introduction-to-the-decision-model-larry-goldberg

The octagon at the top is the *decision*, equivalent to a *decision service* in DMN, i.e. a chain of decisions and supporting decisions executed as an atomic stateless action. TDM recommends naming the decision with a verb such as *Determine, Evaluate*, etc. The object of that verb – in Figure 100, *Policy Renewal Method* – names the *decision rule family*, the rectangle with the clipped upper corners that is directly connected to the decision. Connectors with the dot at one end link the decision rule family to other supporting rule families, such as *Policy Pricing Within Bounds*. (Note: The arrows connecting to the decision tables are not TDM, just PowerPoint showing the logic underlying each rule family.) Thus the tree from decision to decision rule family to all the supporting rule families is directly analogous to a DRD in DMN representing the decision's requirements subgraph.

In each rule family, the label above the solid line is the *rule family name*. Listed below it are the *supporting rule families*, what DMN would call *required decisions*. Below the dotted line represent *persistent data*, what DMN calls *required inputs*.

As in DMN, each rule family and persistent data element has a defined data type with specific allowed values, constituting what TDM calls a *fact type*. In TDM, the logic of a rule family is modeled as a decision table, using the rules-as-rows layout, with one or more *conditions* and a single *conclusion*. The head of each condition column names a *fact*, matching either a supporting rule family or persistent data. The conclusion fact name is the name of the rule family.

Unlike DMN, TDM does not define an expression language, but it does require that each condition or conclusion cell in the table is an *atomic logical expression* of the form,

```
[column heading] [operator] [operand],
```

where *operator*, expressed in natural language or symbolic form, is appropriate to the operand and fact type. For example, the operator *Is* compares the fact to a literal value, *Is in* compares the fact to a list of values, *Is greater than* compares the fact to a numeric value, and *Is between* compares the fact to a numeric range. Each TDM-based tool defines its own set of operators. The *operand* may be a literal value, a fact type (i.e., a variable), or a formula, an expression of variables. A *blank* condition cell in TDM corresponds to hyphen in DMN, meaning the fact is irrelevant to the conclusion.

There is one more piece to the TDM notation that plays an important role: *normalization*. The first column of the decision table, called the *rule pattern* number, represents a specific combination of non-blank condition columns. For example, in Figure 100, the rule family *Policy Pricing within Bounds* contains two rule patterns. Rule pattern 1 contains rules involving only the *Policy Tier* fact. Rule pattern 2 contains rules involving both *Policy Tier* and *Policy Discount*. Rule patterns are important in normalizing the decision logic.

TDM Style

TDM prescribes a particular decision table style, which it calls *TDM Principles*. For our purposes, we focus on those that constrain the range and format of decision tables allowed by DMN.

1. **Rules-as-rows.** All rule families in TDM are modeled in this layout. DMN rules-as-columns and crosstab layouts are not allowed.

2. **Condition column headings.** Each condition column heading must be what DMN calls an input variable. Other input expressions are not allowed.

3. **One conclusion fact.** DMN compound outputs are not allowed.

4. **Rule pattern condition key may not be partially empty.** In DMN, this effectively means that rules should be contracted (combined using hyphen) whenever possible.

5. **Inferential relationship between rule families.** In DMN, this effectively means a DRD corresponding to TDM decision must be executable as an atomic stateless action, i.e., a decision service. Thus it may not include human decisions or long-running external decisions.

6. **No inferential dependency between conditions in a rule pattern.** Such a dependency implies redundancy in the decision logic, which can be removed by decomposing into multiple rule patterns. Using DMN notation, here is an example.

U	Age		Past Claims Count		Risk Category ⓘ		Additional Insurance Premium
	Number		Number		{High,Medium,Low}		Percentage
1	>	24	∈	[2..4]	=	Medium	10.00 %
2	>	24	>	4	=	High	20.00 %
3	≤	24	∈	[2..4]	=	Medium	20.00 %

Figure 101. Decision table with possible inferential dependency between inputs

This decision table looks fine at first glance but it suggests a possible inferential dependency between *Past Claims Count* and *Risk Category*, since a count of between 2 and 4 associates with Medium risk and a count of over 4 associates with High risk. One would need to go back to the subject matter experts and ask if one could have, say, a past claims count between 2 and 4 with either High or Low risk, or a count over 4 with a risk other than High. If the answer is no, then these conditions are redundant and one of them should be removed.

7. **Within a rule family, exactly one conclusion value for any combination of input values.** Otherwise the decision table is *inconsistent*. This effectively disallows DMN hit policies *First* and *Priority*.

8. **Within a rule pattern, all input value combinations *in scope* must be covered by a rule.** Thus some incomplete DMN tables may be allowed by TDM if the missing input combinations are declared out of scope.

9. **Within a rule pattern, condition keys should not overlap.** In DMN terms, this means that in a table with hit policy of *Any*, all rules in a rule pattern should together generate no more than one hit.

10. **No transitive dependencies between inferentially related rule families**. This problem is quite common, and is the most difficult to correct. In DMN terms, a *transitive dependency* occurs when the two or more information requirements of a single decision can be traced (via the information requirements of the supporting decision) back to a common decision or input data element. In other words, there are two or more information requirement "paths" leading from a decision or input data to the same decision.

Figure 102, clipped from the Lending example in the DMN spec, illustrates transitive dependency. There are two information requirement connectors out of *Post-bureau Risk category* leading to *Routing*, and two out of *Bureau data* leading to *Routing*. Whenever you can follow two different chains of information requirements from point A to point B in the DRD, you have a transitive dependency.

TDM claims that by careful redesign of the decision model, one can remove transitive dependencies. While that may be true in theory, the effort and skill required to do that will usually be too great, and one should not expect modelers to attempt it. Moreover, according Fish, "it is a matter of opinion whether it is [even] desirable. In [Figure 102], it is natural for business users to frame some routing rules based on risk category and others on affordability, even though affordability is partly derived from risk. In my view this trumps considerations of formal correctness based on database normalization dogma."[66]

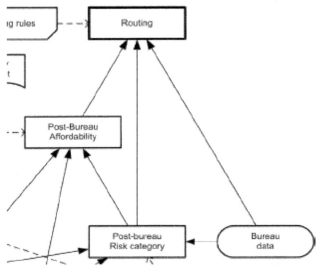

Figure 102. DRD fragment illustrating transitive dependency. Source: OMG

---

[66] Fish, private correspondence, December 2015.

Normalization

Both Vanthienen and TDM have expressed the view that design of good decision tables can benefit from Relational Model principles applied to database design, in particular *normalization*.[67]

> "There is a striking similarity between decision tables and databases. The way in which we model and represent sets of rules can benefit from the insights obtained in database design. Good decision table design and good database design are subject to similar concerns, such as consistency, nonredundancy, normalization, etc."[68]

In a decision table, the combination of condition values constitutes a *key*. For the key to be unique, the decision table must have hit policy *Unique*. Vanthienen concludes,

> "Although there are major differences between decision table knowledge and database dependencies, the analogy is striking, such that the normalization rules of database design provide an excellent guideline to evaluate the design and decomposition of decision tables. Both normalization of relations and of decision tables have as a primary goal to avoid redundancy and to correct anomalies. In addition, the normalization of decision tables simplifies decision tables and increases their readability.... [Normalization] rules can then be used to improve the design and factoring of decision tables."[69]

Normalization provides the theoretical underpinning of TDM as well, which, in analogy with relational data, describes First, Second, and Third Normal Forms for decision tables. The First Normal Form is a requirement in TDM, and each higher Normal Form is considered better.[70]

First Normal Form

In TDM, the *First Normal Form* of a Rule Family (decision table) requires that no row can be decomposed into more than one row reaching the conclusion. Violations of the First Normal Form include tables with compound outputs, i.e., more than one conclusion column or with any rules containing conditions that are OR'ed together.

A decision table with compound output can always be refactored into multiple decision tables with a single output. Worst case, with N outputs one could simply create N tables, duplicating the rules of the original table but each with a single output column. Prohibition of OR'ing condition columns is standard for all decision tables and need not be discussed further here. The way to handle OR'ed conditions is to break the rule into multiple rules.

---

[67] C.J. Date, *An Introduction to Database Systems, 8th ed.*(Pearson/Addison Wesley, 2004).

[68] Jan Vanthienen, "Rules as Data: Decision Tables and Relational Databases," http://www.brcommunity.com/b516.php

[69] Ibid.

[70] von Halle and Goldberg, *The Decision Model.*

Second Normal Form

In TDM, the *Second Normal Form* eliminates conditions that are irrelevant to the conclusion. For example, the table on the top in Figure 103 violates the Second Normal Form because the condition *Age* is actually irrelevant to the conclusion. The conclusion value is determined solely by the condition *Income*. The table on the bottom is equivalent, in the Second Normal Form.

| U | Age | | Income | | Target Market |
	Number		Currency ($)		{A,B}
1	>	18	>	$ 50000	A
2	>	18	≤	$ 50000	B
3	≤	18	>	$ 50000	A
4	≤	18	≤	$ 50000	B

| U | Income | | Target Market |
	Currency ($)		{A,B}
1	>	$ 50000	A
2	≤	$ 50000	B

Figure 103. Second Normal Form violation (top), and corrected version (bottom)

Third Normal Form

The *Third Normal Form* addresses *transitive dependencies* among conditions. The example of Figure 104, discussed earlier in this chapter, suggests a violation of the Third Normal Form, since it is *possible* that *Past Claims Count* and *Risk Category* are not actually independent conditions. If further investigation determines a dependency between them, TDM says that one of those conditions should be removed from the table.

| U | Age | | Past Claims Count | | Risk Category ⓘ | | Additional Insurance Premium |
	Number		Number		{High,Medium,Low}		Percentage
1	>	24	∈	[2..4]	=	Medium	10.00 %
2	>	24	>	4	=	High	20.00 %
3	≤	24	∈	[2..4]	=	Medium	20.00 %

Figure 104. Possible violation of Third Normal Form

Recommendations Compared

We have now seen recommendations for "good" decision tables from three recognized authorities in the field. Naturally, they do not agree! The differences are summarized below.

	DMN	Vanthienen	Ross	TDM
Condition heading	Input expression, possibly involving multiple variables, or comparison test	Variable name or comparison test	Phrased as a question	Variable name
Conclusion heading	Decision name (output variable name)		Phrased as a question	Variable name
Layout	Choice of Rules-as-rows, Rules-as-columns, or Crosstab	Rules-as-columns preferred	Crosstab preferred except for complex tables	Rules-as-rows only
Explicit scope, restrictions, exceptions	No	Not recommended in general; occasionally useful.	Yes	Yes
Incomplete tables	Allowed but not encouraged. Default output optional.	No. Default output sometimes useful but confusing to business users.	OK if default output defined.	No, unless out of scope
Hit policy *Unique*	Default, but not explicitly preferred	Strongly preferred	Preferred	
Hit policy *Any*	Yes	No, "because redundancy is present (not well-normalized)."	No	Yes if hits are in separate rule patterns
Hit policy *First*, *Priority*	*First* allowed, *Priority* is preferred	*First* not allowed; *Priority* discouraged but better.	No	No
Compound output	Yes	Yes	Not recommended	No
Maximize contraction	Not required	Yes, not only for pairs of rules but blocks of rules	Yes	Yes
Optimize cell merging, ordering for visual scanning	Not required	Yes	Not required	No
Variable definitions based on glossary	No	No	Yes	Yes
Unique concern	Executable but business-friendly	Ease of visual scanning for completeness, consistency	Single-sourcing, structured vocabulary	Normalization (remove implicit dependencies)

Figure 105. DMN vs. recommendations/preferences of decision table experts

Condition Heading

Condition heading refers to the label of a decision table input. As we have seen, opinions vary as to whether it should be simply the name of an input variable, a Boolean comparison expression, or a question in natural language. Even though in the DMN spec it is an *input expression*, the examples all use simply an input variable name. But even if an expression is allowed, is it best practice?

There is considerable benefit to restricting the input expression to a (possibly qualified) variable name, since that provides a one-to-one link between the decision table input and an information requirement.

Conclusion Heading

Technically the heading of the decision table output column, called the *output label*, can be anything you like. But best is to label it with the name of the *output variable*, which is the name of the decision or BKM containing the table. In a compound decision table – meaning it has more than one output column – each output column label is the *output component name*, where the output is a sub-element of the output variable. For example, if a decision table *Discount* has output columns *Product Discount* and *Shipping Discount*, the output variable *Discount* contains the components *Discount.Product Discount* and *Discount.Shipping Discount*.

Orientation

There is no agreement among the experts as to which decision table layout is best. There is a definite advantage, however, in standardizing on one layout, and first-generation DMN tool vendors seem to agree, most settling on the rules-as-rows format.

Scope, Restrictions, and Table Completeness

DMN allows a modeler to define a *default output entry* for each output column, to be applied only in the event that no rule matches in the decision. Other than that, DMN provides no way to indicate that the decision table is *intentionally incomplete*. One reason the *isComplete* attribute was eliminated in DMN 1.1 was the difficulty in agreeing on what "completeness" of a decision table entails. In this book I mean by "complete" a decision table that contains a rule matching every possible combination of allowed input values. By that definition, Method and Style recommends that all decision tables should be complete.

Others, however, favor explicitly defining a decision table scope that excludes certain input value combinations. Ross and TDM, for example, are in favor of this, since it is frequently the case that certain combinations simply cannot occur, or must be handled in a special way. Accommodating such cases in a complete decision table makes the table larger and more complex than it would be with explicitly defined scope and possibly restrictions and exceptions, as described by Ross.

Hit Policy

Ross advocates limiting single-hit decision tables to what DMN calls hit policy *Unique*. Vanthienen strongly favors *Unique* as well, although he admits that some tables are more easily defined at first using *Priority*. They can be converted to *Unique* by a simple algorithm. TDM allows *Any* hit policy only if the matching rules are in different Rule Patterns, meaning they test different sets of inputs. On the other hand, Fish's *Knowledge Automation* makes a strong case for *Priority* as being easier to maintain when the underlying rules change.

Even though hit policies like *Any* or *Priority* may simplify the decision table, they are more prone to modeler errors, such as inconsistent logic, and these authors recommend simply conditioning modelers to specifying decision tables using *Unique* hit policy.

Maximum Contraction

Contraction refers to combining specific rules into a single more general rule that leads to the same result. The DMN spec allows it but considers it a matter of methodology and does not either encourage or discourage its use. All three of the decision table experts, however, advocate maximizing contraction. In TDM, it is actually a rule related to normalization.

Table Cells Optimized for Visual Scanning

In a decision table, the order of the rules has no influence on the result. "But," notes Vanthienen, "that does not mean that the presentation order is irrelevant; it is easier for humans if condition entries are presented in a natural order (e.g., from low numbers to high numbers), or if the entries of the lowest conditions vary first. This also allows easy checking for completeness. So indeed, rule order doesn't matter, but gives extra value."[71]

Figure 106 provides an illustration. The top table contains 6 rules; by rearranging the columns, the number of rules reduces to 4. Both tables exhibit the "tree structure" favored by Vanthienen and others. If an input entry is repeated in successive rules, the cells may be merged. In the tree structure, the number of distinct cells in a column increases from left to right.

> "The decision table then corresponds to a tree where the same condition is always evaluated at a certain level of the tree…. Besides the fact that the tree structure principle eliminates "rule ambiguity" (more than 1 column satisfied), it provides an easy way for humans to consult the decision table (top-down) and to guarantee completeness. This principle eliminates the need to examine the rules one by one, from left to right, when making a decision."[72]

---

[71] Vanthienen, "The History of Modeling Decisions Using Tables (Part 3)", http://www.brcommunity.com/b652.php

[72] Ibid.

TypeOfOrder	CustomerLocation	Wholesaler	CustomerClass
Web	US	Y	1
		N	4
	non-US	Y	2
		N	4
Phone	-	Y	3
		N	4

Wholesaler	TypeOfOrder	CustomerLocation	CustomerClass
Y	Web	US	1
		non-US	2
	Phone	-	3
N	-	-	4

Figure 106. Rearranging the order of inputs makes a smaller table that is easier to visually verify. Source: Vanthienen[73]

Standardized Business Vocabulary

One of the most surprising things about DMN is that the specification does not require linking variables to a business glossary. In fact, it makes no reference to another OMG standard called *Structured Business Vocabulary and Rules*, SBVR. SBVR provides a formal way to define the business terms and business rules used in decision models, and when DMN was getting started, SBVR was expected to play an important role.

> "The DMN RFP asks submitters to focus on decision models, and to link to other existing OMG specifications for related concepts such as rules and vocabularies and business processes.... The choice to use the SBVR vocabulary as the basis for the considerations and conclusions of a decision seems obvious. Attractive features of an SBVR vocabulary include its semantic richness (noun concepts, verb concepts, definitions, etc.), support for ordinary business terminology (rather than programming terms), and extensive business documentation features such as notes and examples."[74]

In the end, however, it didn't happen, for several reasons:

1. Rules in DMN are specific to the decision in which they are defined. In SBVR, rules are like policies, applicable to all decisions across the business.

2. Rules in DMN are formulated as *production rules*, suited to invocation from a business process:

---

[73] Ibid.

[74] M. Linehan and C. de Sainte-Marie, "The Relationship of Decision Model and Notation (DMN) to SBVR and BPMN", http://www.brcommunity.com/b597.php.

```
If [condition1] and [condition2] then output = [output entry].
```

SBVR rules, on the other hand, are typically formulated as *constraints*:

```
The age of each registered customer must be greater than 13.
```

3. In DMN, decisions are composed of other decisions. SBVR does not easily allow this.

4. SBVR's method of formalizing the business vocabulary is too complex and "heavyweight" to be readily adopted by business analysts.

DMN does ask modelers to define the datatypes and allowed values of a decision model's input data and decision elements, but otherwise makes no reference to a standard data dictionary or glossary that would help standardize the vocabulary used in decisions across the business. For Ross and TDM, however, such standardization is essential.

In TDM, a *glossary* is basically a two-column table listing fact types (in DMN, variables) and their definitions:

> "A *glossary* of fact types [TDM's term for the variables used in a decision model] is neither a standard nor a specification. It isn't even a model…. It is simply a managed list with an entry for every fact type or literal value in a Decision Model…. The benefit of creating a glossary of fact types is that business people, rather than business analysts or technical people, are at ease with maintaining and consulting a dictionary-like form of the glossary, and it provides rigor…. If a fact type in the glossary becomes complex or there is a need to clarify its context with other fact types, a *fact model* [a diagram showing relationships between business concepts and/or properties] may be useful."[75]

We'll come back to the glossary topic in Chapter 13.

---

[75] von Halle and Goldberg, TDM, 392.

CHAPTER 9

DMN Style

As it does with all of its standards, OMG ultimately will measure the success of DMN by its breadth of adoption by tool vendors and end users. Because of that, OMG standards normally try to avoid anything that smacks of "methodology" or "stylistic recommendations." The thinking is that tool vendors and practitioners in the space simply have too much investment in their own "method and style" to allow OMG to declare elements of that practice invalid unless they violate the metamodel or semantics of the standard.

Maybe so, but some methodology and stylistic guidelines are essential to effective use of DMN. Otherwise, DMN simply provides too many different ways to model the same decision logic. And that works against the larger goal of a single language and notation shared across tools.

DMN Style is my attempt to add constraints on top of those provided by the DMN specification, in order to provide a more uniform look and feel, greater logic transparency and ease of use, and a smaller gap between modeling and implementation. It is "unofficial," not sanctioned by OMG. Ultimately, I would judge its success by adoption of its rules and conventions by modelers.

The principles and rules of DMN Style are mostly applicable to the *decision logic,* such as decision tables. In Chapters 10-16, the *DMN Method* provides additional principles and methodology applicable to modeling *decision requirements*, that is, the DRD.

Naming

There are two DMN Style issues affecting naming, one primarily addressed to implementers, the other to modelers.

Removing the Spaces

I have already discussed the parsing problem incurred by spaces in FEEL variable names. While a decision or input data name containing spaces may indeed be more "business-friendly" in the DRD, including those spaces in the variable name poses difficulties for executable expression languages. Its practical effect may actually be to discourage tool vendors from using FEEL. That would be unfortunate, as executable DMN would no longer be interchangeable between tools.

While it is too late to change DMN 1.1, here are some workarounds that implementers could use to avoid the parsing issue.

1. Use different names for the DRG element (i.e., DRD node) and its associated variable. Because the spec says the names should match, they should be tightly coupled by some formatting rule. In the variable, one might prefix the DRG element name with a special symbol such as $ or # and replace spaces with underscore or camel case. For example, the input data element *Applicant data* would then correspond to a variable named *$Applicant_data*.

2. Keep the variable and DRG element names the same, but in literal expressions use the symbolic prefix and space replacement described above. In S-FEEL decision tables, the spaces are OK. This seems less of a violation of the spec.

3. Use the *label* attribute to name shapes in the DRD, and generate in the tooling an execution-friendly variant to name the DRG element and its associated variable. For example, input data labeled *Applicant data* in the DRD generates variable named *$Applicant_data* used in literal expressions.

Of course, modelers can always elect on their own to use decision and input data names without spaces. One way to avoid spaces is to use camel case, such as *DateOfBirth* instead of *Date of birth*. Another way is to replace them with underscore characters, for example, *Date_of_birth*. This makes it more likely that the variable name used in executable expressions is the same (perhaps except for a leading symbol character) is the same as the label used in the DRD.

Name Should Suggest the Type

Quite aside from the spaces issue, DMN Method and Style recommends a naming convention in which the data type of the variable is suggested by the variable's name. The type is most often indicated by the last fragment of the name, such as *Amount, Percent, Score, Category*, etc., or some abbreviation of those. Organizations should develop their own naming conventions. Examples include:

- *LoanToValuePct* or *LTVPct* for a percent
- *MonthlyFeeAmt* for a numeric amount
- *BorrowerRiskScore* for a numeric score
- *BorrowerRiskCategory* for an enumerated category value
- *isExistingCustomer* for a Boolean

The benefit of this convention is that the end-to-end decision logic is communicated more clearly from the DRD on its own. A decision called *Medical History* is ambiguous. Is this a classification into a category? Is it a list of medical history events? Is it a Boolean meaning, "do we have a record of the medical history"? You cannot tell from the name. Names like *MedicalHistoryCategory, MedicalHistoryEvents,* and *isMedicalHistoryOnFile* more clearly suggest the type of allowed values.

Decision Table Style

Rules-as-Rows

While there are some advantages for the crosstab orientation for very simple decision tables, they are outweighed by the benefit of *standardizing on a single layout* for all decision tables. Users become familiar with a single way to view the decision table logic, independent of the number of inputs and outputs. For that reason, DMN Method and Style recommends the *rules-as-rows* orientation in all cases.

Discount					
			Customer, Delivery		
	Discount	Business	Private		Government
		-	sameday	slow	-
Ordersize	<10	0.05	0	0.05	0.15
	>=10	0.10	0	0.05	0.15

Figure 107. Discount vs Ordersize, crosstab layout. Source: OMG

Discount				
U	Customer	OrderSize	Delivery	Discount
	Business, Private, Government	<10, >=10	sameday, slow	0, 0.05, 0.10, 0.15
1	Business	<10	-	0.05
2		>=10	-	0.10
3	Private	-	sameday	0
4			slow	0.05
5	Government	-	-	0.15

Figure 108. Discount vs OrderSize, preferred rules-as-rows orientation. Source: OMG

Figure 107 and Figure 108 show the same decision table in two orientations, crosstab and rules-as-rows. The crosstab orientation gives a smaller tale and is possibly easier to read, but can only be used in special situations. The rules-as-rows orientation can be used with any decision table and offers a consistent look and feel. While rules-as-rows tables may not fit easily on the page when the number of inputs becomes large, first-generation DMN tools seem to favor rules-as-rows, and it is the layout used by DMN Method and Style.

Input Entry Cell Merging

In an earlier era, when decision tables were created by hand, techniques such as merging input entry cells from adjacent rules having the same cell value greatly eased visual scanning of tables for completeness and consistency. Even though most modern DMN tools are able to verify completeness and consistency automatically, cell merging still simplifies both data entry and reading the decision table. However, few first-generation DMN tools support it so far. Thus, while some decision table experts insist on input entry cell merging, modelers should not necessarily expect their tool to provide it.

Hit Policy

DMN allows a variety of single-hit policies for decision tables: *Unique, Any, Priority,* and *First.* Often a hit policy of *Any, Priority,* or *First* results in a smaller table, one with fewer rules, than a *Unique* table, and one in which the rules are more easily defined. And as Fish has pointed out, *Priority* or *First* tables are more easily modified after the fact. However, DMN Style considers these considerations to be overweighed by *Unique's* advantage, as demonstrated by Vanthienen, in making the decision logic clearly visible and less likely to be incomplete or inconsistent.[76]

Thus, in most cases DMN Style recommends use of *Unique* hit policy for single-hit tables. In such a decision table, only one rule will match for any possible set of input values. (There are exceptions, however, where the complexity of a *Unique* table makes *Priority* a better choice. See, for example, Figure 189.)

In general, a decision table with hit policy of *Any, Priority,* or *First* can be converted to a *Unique* decision table. We'll see examples of how to do this in the discussion of Classification Patterns in Chapter 11.

Compound Output

A decision table with more than one output column is called *compound.* While some methodologies, such as TDM, insist on separating a compound decision table into multiple decisions, each with a single output, DMN Method and Style does not agree. It recommends using compound decision tables whenever the values of multiple outputs are simultaneously

---

[76] Vanthienen comments: "[Modeling all-or-nothing pattern with Priority] is what our tool does automatically. Priority rules are considered intermediate rules (kept for traceability), but are automatically converted into unique tables. So there is a lifecycle of hit policies, rather than a choice. Maintainability is served by a) seeing the final result in the table, and b) being able to trace back each result to its original (priority) rule. So my common advice is: Priority rules do not belong IN the table, but can be used to construct the table." Private communication, December 2015.

determined by a single combination of input values.

Maximum Contraction of Rules

Most of the decision table experts agree that if two or more specific rules in a decision table can be combined in a single, more general rule – called *table contraction* – it should be done. DMN allows it but does not require it. DMN Style, however, requires decision tables to be maximally contracted.

Sometimes contraction involves combining specific rules into a more general rule:

U	Age		Service		VacationAccrual
	Number		Number		Number
1	<	18		-	27
2		[18..45)	<	15	22
3		[18..45)		[15..30)	24
4		[18..45)	≥	30	30
5		[45..60)	<	30	24
6		[45..60)	≥	30	30
7	≥	60		-	30

Figure 109. This decision table is not maximally contracted. Rules 4 and 6 can be combined.

U	Age		Service		VacationAccrual
	Number		Number		Number
1	<	18		-	27
2		[18..45)	<	15	22
3		[18..45)		[15..30)	24
4		[18..60)	≥	30	30
5		[45..60)	<	30	24
6	≥	60		-	30

Figure 110. Contracted representation of *VacationAccrual* table

In other cases, some inputs irrelevant to the decision may be eliminated entirely. This is what TDM calls Second Normal Form.

U	Age		Income		Target Market...
	Number		*Currency (USD)*		*{A,B,C}*
1	>	18	>	$ 50000	A
2	>	18	≤	$ 50000	B
3	≤	18	>	$ 50000	A
4	≤	18	≤	$ 50000	B

U	Income		Target Market...
	Currency (USD)		*{A,B,C}*
1	>	$ 50000	A
2	≤	$ 50000	B

Figure 111. TDM Second Normal Form violation (top), and corrected version (bottom), illustrates another example of maximum contraction.

Input Expressions

DMN Style recommends using a *variable name* for all decision table input expressions, not an expression. There are two reasons for this:

- It creates a more obvious linkage between the decision's information requirement and the decision table input.

- It removes the inconsistency between decision tables in a decision versus decision tables in a BKM. An input expression in a BKM may only be a variable name, not an expression.

In this context, a *qualified name* such as *Customer.MonthlyIncome*, naming an element of a structured variable, is considered a variable name and may be used as a decision table input expression.

For example, the following input expressions are allowed by the DMN spec, but violate DMN Style:

Input Expression, Incorrect in DMN Method and Style	Suggested Alternative
Age>25	isValidAge
Applicant.annual income / 12	monthlyIncomeAmt
Applicant.monthly expenses + Loan.monthly payment	monthlyPaymentAmt
Loan.monthly payment / Applicant.monthly income	paymentToIncomePct

Figure 112. Input expressions incorrect in DMN Method and Style, with suggested alternative

Note the following about the suggested alternatives:

- A single variable name
- No spaces in the name
- Datatype implied by the variable name

In order to use these alternatives as input expressions, they must be variables in scope, defined either by a supporting decision or, in a BKM, an invocation binding.

Input and Output Values

The heading row of a decision table may optionally include lists of input and output values. Like input entries, these lists are type *unaryTests*. They may contain both specific values (literals or names) and ranges like *>0* or *[1..100)*. For numeric, date/time, and enumerated string types, DMN Method and Style generally recommends providing these values, as they permit validating the completeness of the table. For other types, DMN Method and Style recommends specifying the datatype (*typeRef*) of the input expression.

Note that the input and output values for a decision table must be within the domain of values allowed by the associated variable's *typeRef* specification.

In CL3 decision tables, *unaryTests* may include the value *null*, meaning the unavailability of a value for the input expression may be used in the decision logic. According to the spec, if a decision table lists input values and input entries test for *null*, then *null* must be explicitly listed in the decision table input values, something many first-generation tools do not yet allow.

Input Entries

Like input and output values, each input entry is of type *unaryTests*, meaning a list of specific values (literals or names) or ranges like *>0* or *[1..100)*. By itself, an input entry is not a complete *expression*. The *combination* of input expression and input entry defines an expression. Because of that, the *not()* function, if used in an input entry, must apply to the entire list, not just part of it. For example,

```
not(0,1)
```

is a valid input entry, meaning the condition is true if the input expression is not equal to 0 or 1, but

```
not(<0), BalanceAmt
```

meaning the condition is true if the input expression is not less than zero or is equal to the variable *BalanceAmt,* is not allowed.

Input expression	Input entry	Meaning
Customer.name	*John*	Allowed. True if Customer's name is "John"
Customer.name	John	Allowed. True if Customer's name is the same as the variable John. Usually this is not what you mean.
Applicant.age	<18, >=65	Allowed. True if Applicant's age is either under 18 or greater than or equal to 65
Applicant.age	<18 or >=65	**Not allowed.** Conjunctions "and", "or" are not allowed in input entries. Use comma-separated values instead of "or". Use separate input clauses instead of "and".
Applicant.age	[18..65)	Allowed. True if Applicant's age is greater than or equal to 18 or under 65.
Applicant.age	not([18..65])	Allowed. True if Applicant's age is less than 18 or greater than 65. The not() operator, if used, must apply to the whole list, not selected elements.
Borrower.income	>Co-borrower.income	Allowed. True if Borrower's income is greater than Co-borrower's income.
Borrower.income	>3.3*MonthlyPayment	**Not allowed.** Simple expressions are not allowed in an input entry. Value must be a literal or qualified name only.
Borrower.income	>max(Co-borrower[1].income, Co-borrower[2].income)	**Not allowed.** List expressions and FEEL functions like max() are not allowed by DMN spec, even at CL3.

Figure 113. Examples of input entries allowed and not allowed by DMN Method and Style

Not() is the only FEEL function allowed by the spec in input entries, even at Conformance Level 3. The only other difference between input entries at CL3 and CL2 is that CL3 allows the value *null*, meaning the condition is true if no value is provided for the input.

DMN Method and Style adds little to the rules of the DMN spec for input entries (Figure 113).

Output Entries

Output entries at CL2 are limited to simple (arithmetic) expressions, but output entries at CL3 may be any literal expression allowed by FEEL or other specified expression language. DMN Method and Style places no additional constraints on output entries.

Table Completeness and Null

In Chapter 4 we discussed why the Completeness Indicator was eliminated in DMN 1.1. But table completeness remains important. In general, modelers should try to avoid *incomplete* decision tables, those for which some combinations of input values are not matched by any rule. They immediately call into question whether the unmatched conditions were omitted intentionally or by accident.

As described in Chapter 4, DMN allows specification of a *default output entry*, an output value to be used only in the case where no rule matches. But except for error reporting when the lack of rule match is unintentional, DMN Method and Style recommends not using default output entry.

However, there are some occasions where certain combinations of input values do not occur in real scenarios and thus have no meaningful decision outcome. This is the situation described by Ross in Chapter 8 as *decision table scope and restrictions*: If there are certain combinations of inputs that cannot actually occur, then a decision rule specifying an output entry for those combinations makes little sense other than to say, "This rule is only here to fulfill table completeness." One of the techniques Ross recommends is to use a keyword like "n/a" (not applicable) for the output entry of such a rule. His term for "n/a" used in this way is *preemption*, meaning there is no meaningful output for this input combination.

DMN doesn't have such a keyword "n/a", but it does have *null*, meaning the expression has no value. DMN Method and Style recommends using *null* as an output entry for input combinations that would be considered excluded or out of scope. *Null* is part of the full FEEL language but not part of S-FEEL, so decision logic that includes it is beyond CL2. In CL3, a decision table or literal expression can not only use *null* as an output entry but test for the value *null* in the decision logic.

Null in Conditional Decisions

An end-to-end business decision may involve a decision whether to terminate or proceed with further decision logic. The further decision logic thus only occurs if the outcome of the first decision is to proceed. It is *conditional* on the result of the first decision.

Here is a familiar example: The Customer applies for a loan, let's say a home mortgage. If the lender decides to proceed with the transaction, the decision logic then determines the loan rate. If the lender decides not to proceed, there is no loan rate to determine. To keep it simple, we'll say the loan rate is specified as a category, *A, B,* or *C.* The actual interest rate for each category is based on the current 10-year bond rate, outside the scope of this decision model.

As I just described it, you would say these are *two separate decisions*: (1) Accept or reject the loan application; and (2) Define the loan rate category, where the second decision occurs only if the application is accepted. The *LoanRateCategory* decision is *conditional* on the result of *LoanApproval*. The question is how to model this in DMN.

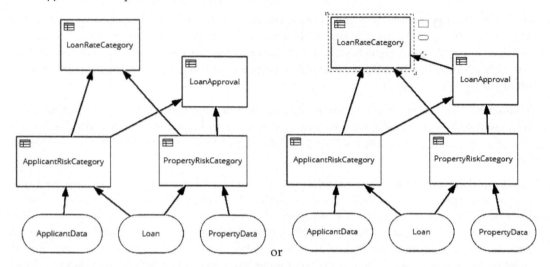

Figure 114. *LoanRateCategory* **is conditional on** *LoanApproval*="**Approved**". **Which DRD is correct?**

Figure 114 shows two different DRDs for this scenario. The one on the left depicts two independent decisions, *LoanRateCategory* and *LoanApproval*. Both depend solely on the input data elements, *ApplicantData, Loan,* and *PropertyData*. The one on the right is exactly the same except that *LoanRateCategory* has a dependency on *LoanApproval*.

Which one is correct?

The Lending decision example in the DMN spec would suggest the one on the left, since the decision *LoanRateCategory* is executed only if *LoanApproval* = "Approved". But Method and Style says the DRD should contain a single top-level decision node that reflects the *business decision as a whole*, the ultimate outcome of the "end-to-end" business decision. In this case, the customer applied for a mortgage. She wants to know, what is the agreed loan rate, or is my application rejected? From the customer's viewpoint, *this is a single business decision by the lender.*

The diagram on the right has one top-level decision node, *LoanRateCategory*. In order to make the decision table complete, we would need to say *LoanApproval* = "Rejected" makes the *LoanRateCategory* output *null* (Figure 115). In this formulation, we would *interpret* a value of *null* for the top-level decision node *LoanRateCategory* as meaning the loan is rejected.

U	ApplicantRiskCategory ⓘ		PropertyRiskCategory ⓘ		LoanApproval ⓘ		LoanRateCate...
	{"High","Medium","Low"}		{"High","Medium","Low"}		{"Approved","Rejected"}		{"A","B","C",null}
1	=	"High"		-	=	"Rejected"	null
2	∈	{"Medium", "Lo...	=	"High"	=	"Rejected"	null
3	=	"Medium"	=	"Medium"	=	"Approved"	"C"
4	=	"Medium"	=	"Low"	=	"Approved"	"B"
5	=	"Low"	=	"Medium"	=	"Approved"	"B"
6	=	"Low"	=	"Low"	=	"Approved"	"A"

Figure 115. Conditional decision table for *LoanRateCategory*, including *null* output entries.

It would actually be better, however, if *LoanApproval* were an explicit *output component* of the top-level decision node, renamed *LoanDecision*. The DRD for that is shown in Figure 116.

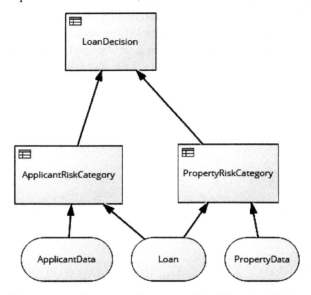

Figure 116. Compound output simplifies the DRD.

The resulting compound decision table (Figure 117) is barely distinguishable from the previous. The only difference is the placement of the double line separating input and output columns of the table.

U	ApplicantRiskCategory		PropertyRiskCategory		LoanApproval	LoanRateCate...
	{"High","Medium","Low"}		{"High","Medium","Low"}		{"Approved","Rejected"}	{"A","B","C",null}
1	=	"High"		-	"Rejected"	null
2	∈	{"Medium", "L...	=	"High"	"Rejected"	null
3	=	"Medium"	=	"Medium"	"Approved"	"C"
4	=	"Medium"	=	"Low"	"Approved"	"B"
5	=	"Low"	=	"Medium"	"Approved"	"B"
6	=	"Low"	=	"Low"	"Approved"	"A"

Figure 117. Improved conditional decision table, *LoanDecision*, with compound output.

Action Subtables

Another way to model conditional decisions is something Vanthienen calls *action subtables*. In an action subtable, an *output entry* for the conditional decision references the name of the supporting decision. That means that if the rule matches, the supporting decision must be evaluated. If that rule does not match, the supporting decision need not be evaluated. It is effectively conditional. Here is an example (Figure 118):

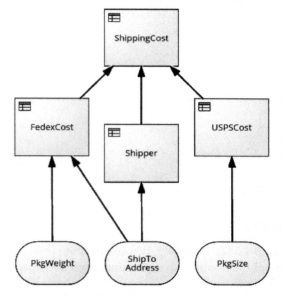

Figure 118. Action subtable example

The decision *ShippingCost* determines the cost to ship an order based on the package size and weight and the ShipTo address. There are two possible shippers, USPS and Fedex, serving different *ShipToAddress* values. The decision *Shipper* selects either USPS or Fedex based on that input data. For Fedex, the shipping cost is based on weight and distance (determined by the *ShipToAddress*). For USPS, the shipping cost is just based on the package size, not weight or distance. So the logic of the *FedexCost* decision is completely different from the logic of *USPSCost*.

Figure 119 shows the decision table. Note that the variables *FedexCost* and *USPSCost* are used not in the input entries but in the *output entries* of this decision. (This is where the term "action subtable" comes from, since the original idea was that the main decision *ShippingCost* would "call" the appropriate supporting decision, *FedexCost* or *USPSCost*, as a "subtable.")

U	Shipper	ShippingCost
	{"Fedex", "USPS"}	Number
1	= "Fedex"	FedexCost
2	= "USPS"	USPSCost

Figure 119. *ShippingCost* **output entries reference variables representing the conditional decisions.**

CHAPTER 10

DMN Method

We're now ready to discuss the DMN Method, a methodology for constructing the end-to-end decision model. As has been mentioned already, OMG is reluctant to include anything that smacks of methodology in its specifications, and DMN is no exception. Modeling methodology is considered part of a service provider's "value add," and the DMN spec tries to avoid suggesting a "right way" to use the standard.

But of course, modelers *need* a methodology to use DMN effectively, and because DMN has features and capabilities missing in other decision modeling approaches, it possibly needs a *new* methodology, different from those applied previously. Moreover, in order to effectively share DMN models with maximum understanding, it is helpful for all stakeholders in the decision model to adhere to the *same* methodology.

Before presenting the DMN Method, let's take a brief look at other decision modeling methodologies described in the literature.

Decision Modeling Methodologies

"Decision Table Methodology"

Many features of DMN Method and Style are part of what Vanthienen calls the *Decision Table Methodology*, outlined in the CODASYL report of 1982 and fleshed out in the 1980s and 1990s. It includes modeling the decision as a whole (without relying on a business process), DRD-like inter-table relationships, and decision table design, including verification, contraction, normalization, and optimization. So these basic ideas go back many years. However, the publications describing this methodology were, in my view, mostly very high level or academic in nature, not practical guidance for business users.

TDM – STEP Methodology

The Decision Model of von Halle and Goldberg (2010) was probably the first detailed publication of a methodology for end-to-end decision modeling. It is the approach that most closely mirrors the objectives of DMN, which is to say detailed decision models that can be created, maintained, and clearly understood by business users. While these authors say that TDM may be used with a variety of methodologies, the one that they have long used in their own practice is called STEP,[77] an acronym for:

- **Separate** the decision logic from the process logic;

- **Trace** the decision logic from business motivation (goals) to code and to processes;

- **Express** the decision logic in a form understandable by all stakeholders, i.e., business users; and

- **Position** the decision logic for change.

In the STEP methodology, decision models are developed iteratively together with BPMN process models and use case models. In the brief summary here, I have attempted to strip out the normal project management activities and focus on activities specific to creating the decision models.

The "top-level entity" in STEP is not an end-to-end business decision, but, more generally, a "project."

1. Step 1 is listing the *decisions* anticipated to be involved in the project and identifying the sources of their information requirements.

2. Step 2 is documenting the *business processes* and use cases, and then "anchoring" decisions at specific points in those activity flows. "Typically," say the authors, "STEP is conducted in parallel with business process modeling efforts, and the decision modeling and process modeling efforts complement each other."[78] (While the process modelers are busy on Step 2, the decision modelers are working on Steps 3 and 4.)

3. Step 3 is building the *business glossary*, possibly linking it to existing data models. The glossary is a business-oriented dictionary of *fact types* used in the decision logic. A fact in TDM is what DMN would call a variable with specified allowed values.

4. Step 4 is building the *decision models*, one for each decision identified in Step 2. Each *decision* in TDM is what DMN would call a *decision service*, a fragment of the end-to-end decision logic that can be executed as a unit in a single stateless action. Each such decision or decision service is then modeled as a DRD-like tree of *rule families*.

5. Step 5 is *analyzing and optimizing* the decision models in accordance with TDM principles, discussed in Chapter 16.

In other words, process modeling (step 2), data modeling (step 3), and decision modeling

---

[77] von Halle and Goldberg, *The Decision Model*, 412ff.

[78] von Halle and Goldberg, *The Decision Model*, 414.

(step 4) are essentially concurrent activities. Beyond that, the TDM book does not elaborate on the modeling methodology.

FICO – Decision Requirements Analysis

Decision Requirements Analysis (DRA) is a methodology developed by Alan Fish of FICO, who is also co-chair of the DMN task force in OMG and contributor of its Decision Requirements Diagram component. DRA, described in Fish's book,[79] is in fact his methodology for constructing the DRD, and as such is highly relevant to the DMN Method. The DRA methodology begins with a *Decision Requirements Analysis Workshop* (DRAW), using top-down decision analysis. As in TDM, the unit of execution is not an individual decision node in the DRD but a *decision service,* a network of decision nodes executed as a single unit.

Fish describes DRAW as "a structured workshop technique for defining the decision-making requirements for a set of decision services and documenting them using DRDs." The primary participants in the workshop, beyond the decision analyst (facilitator) and scribe, are the business domain experts and business analysts. Technical architects may also participate in a part-time supporting role.

The DRAW method encompasses five steps or "stages":

1. Identify the decision points. A "decision point" is a point in the business process that executes the decision service, so Step 1 requires a BPMN model of the end-to-end decision. Each decision point (decision task in BPMN) is specified by a name, the information it requires, and the information it produces as a result.

2. Define the top-level decisions for each decision point. This is a refinement of Step 1, specifying the specific question answered by the decision and its possible values.

3. Decompose the logic for each top-level decision. This in turn refines Step 2 by asking what information is needed to make the decision, and thereby connecting the information requirements of the top-level decision to answers provided by various subdecisions and input data. This is the skeleton DRD structure.

4. Describe all the nodes in detail. For each decision node in the DRD, describe the source of the information, its size and complexity, and how it might be accessed – what DMN calls its authority requirements.

5. Define the rule service boundaries. By this he means "decide which nodes are to be implemented as part of a decision service and which are to remain in external systems." Top-level decisions are assumed to be implemented as decision services, but supporting decisions may be implemented as "external decisions" (i.e., by legacy systems or service providers), or as human decisions.

---

[79] Fish, *Knowledge Automation*

Following definition of the DRDs, DRA goes on to define the decision logic of each decision node. "In our current projects," reports Fish, "BAs are responsible for the process modelling, decision modelling in DRDs, and decision logic definition. Then those are used as specifications by the development / configuration team."[80]

Similarities and Differences

TDM STEP and DRA share several common features:

- The fundamental unit of decision-making is a *decision service,* a network of supporting decisions executed as a single stateless unit.

- The detailed decision logic of a decision service (TDM decision) is defined by *decomposition* into supporting decisions described in a diagram.

- The end-to-end business decision is described as *process model* in BPMN. In both STEP and DRA, the process model is effectively required to describe the logic of the business decision as a whole.

There are a few differences as well:

- DRA describes end-to-end logic extending beyond a single decision service in the form of a DRD; TDM does not have a single decision logic diagram that does that. The DRD may include also external decisions and human decisions. These also are outside the scope of TDM.

- TDM places high importance on standardizing the business vocabulary through a glossary; DRA does not.

- TDM emphasizes optimization of the decision logic according to strict relational principles; DRA does not.

Synthesis and Departure

The DMN Method includes several key elements of TDM and DRA methodology. Like DRA, the decomposition may encompass more than a single decision service. Like TDM, it intends that executable decision logic is *created and maintained by business people.* And like both methodologies, the DMN Method is based on *top-down decomposition,* although it assigns a very different meaning to the "top."

In the DMN Method, the top means the top-level decision node in a DRD representing the *business decision as a whole.* The end-to-end decision logic is fully described by the decomposition of that node into a network of supporting decisions. Although understanding the decision points in the implementation influences the structure of the DRD, the end-to-end decision logic is actually independent of implementation. It is fully described by this DRD

---

[80] Alan Fish, private communication, October 2015.

alone, in combination with the value expressions of its decision nodes. It does not require reference to a companion BPMN model. In this respect it differs significantly from both TDM and DRA.

Historically, process modeling and decision modeling have been done by different teams in the organization. This is probably changing, as the first generation of DMN tool vendors includes a high concentration of BPMN tool vendors expanding into the decision modeling arena. In many cases, they tell me, decision modeling and process modeling are done by the same people.

Even so, my first objection to both TDM and DRA is they depend too heavily on BPMN to describe the end-to-end decision logic. BPMN is not about decision *logic*. In a decision context, BPMN is about decision *implementation*.

> **The DMN Method describes the end-to-end decision logic using DMN alone, without dependence on BPMN.**

This can be done, but it requires a particular Method and Style.

Second, both TDM STEP and DRA place the *project* at the top of their "methodology metamodel." Now this is understandable from the perspective of a consulting service provider, since a project is the typical unit of engagement in that domain. But a project is diffuse in its goals. It may seek to improve a business process *and* improve the decision logic *and* do many other things besides. A project is not decision-specific, and a project may involve more than one business decision.

So a project is not the proper top-level entity for the DMN Method. Nor is a decision service (what TDM would call a decision) in isolation, since it admittedly does not describe the business decision as a whole.

In the DMN Method, the top-level modeling entity is just that: *the business decision as a whole* (subject to the elaborations and exceptions described in Chapter 2). While the phrases "business decision as a whole" and "end-to-end decision logic" appear frequently in this book, they are never mentioned in the DMN specification. The DMN spec, like TDM and DRA before it, instead leans on BPMN to describe the end-to-end decision logic. But that is not necessary, since DMN on its own is fully capable of describing it.

The business decision as a whole means the overall question this decision model is supposed to answer. In all the examples of TDM and DRA, it really is a single question: *Is the loan approved? How much of this claim is payable? What is the next best offer to this customer?* Fundamentally, these are not business processes; they are *business decisions*. For that reason, whether they can be implemented in a single decision service or must be spread over an extended series of decision services, external decisions, and human decisions, the logic of the "business decision as a whole" – this basic question – should be described by a decision model, not a process model.

In the DMN Method, the business decision as a whole should be modeled as one DRD containing a single top-level decision node representing the final outcome.

The lending example in the DMN spec, previously detailed in Chapter 6, does not do it that way. The DMN Method describes an alternative approach.

Top-Down Decomposition

Both TDM STEP and DRA emphasize *top-down decomposition* in the modeling methodology, but in both cases the "top" means the top level of a *decision service* (TDM decision), not the top level of the end-to-end business decision. In contrast, the DMN Method uses top-down decomposition to model *the end-to-end DRD*.

Admittedly, this is *not* the way the decision logic is typically captured in a decision discovery workshop with the stakeholders. On this point, please allow me to relate my experience in the context of process modeling. In BPMN Method and Style, the Method asks the modeler to start by defining the start and end of the end-to-end business process and then decompose the process into ten or fewer *subprocesses* each containing a number of activities. To those who have not done process modeling, that might seem a natural thing to do, but it is in fact *completely alien* to most process modeling practitioners!

The reason is simple: While most business people think *concretely and bottom-up*, the BPMN Method asks the modeler to think *abstractly and top-down*. In the stakeholder workshops that gather the information that goes into the process model, the facilitation is always concrete and bottom-up: *In this process, what happens first? What happens after that?*[81] You need to frame the discussion that way in order to get the stakeholders to contribute. It reflects the way they experience and understand the process. You cannot ask them, in a real-time workshop setting, to decompose the process from the top down.

The top-down decomposition is done later, by a trained business process modeler, who must reorganize the raw material gathered in the workshop. The goal is a process model that can serve as a long-lived digital asset, one that can be shared beyond the immediate project team. In other words, "good BPMN" is not the process model assembled in real time in the stakeholder workshops, but a carefully crafted reorganization of that information.[82]

In the DMN Method, top-down decomposition is similarly performed not in real time at the stakeholder decision discovery workshops, but after the fact by a trained decision modeler.

---

[81] If you are interested in this topic, an excellent resource is Shelley Sweet, *The BPI Blueprint* (Cody-Cassidy Press, 2014), http://www.amazon.com/dp/0982368135

[82] Top-down process model decomposition is described in *BPMN Method and Style*, http://www.amazon.com/dp/0982368119

> In the DMN Method, the top-level decision node in the end-to-end DRD is decomposed into supporting decisions representing distinct aspects of the decision logic. Each of those decisions is likewise decomposed, and this procedure is iterated until the only dependencies are on input data.

This is what the DMN Method means by top-down decomposition.

Decision Logic vs Process Logic

A key reason why BPMN plays a central role in both DRA and TDM is the fact that the business people involved in the decision discovery workshops experience the end-to-end decision as a *process*, that is to say, *procedurally*, not as declarative decision logic. In the workshops, the facilitation is again concrete and bottom-up. *How does the decision work today? What gets decided first? Based on that, what is decided next?* For that reason, the end-to-end decision logic is often described as multiple decisions executed in sequence. While that may be the most practical way to collect this information, we need to keep in mind that it describes a business process not inferential logic!

A decision model is not the same as a process model. Ask yourself, what do those solid arrows in the DRD really mean? In Fish's book, he says that in addition to specifying the information requirements for a decision, they imply an "ordering of tasks: If decision B requires the result of decision A, A must be evaluated before B."[83] *But this is actually not the case.* It is only true with *forward chaining* (see Chapter 2). With *backward chaining*, some instances of B may never require evaluation of A at all, and we will use this fact to convert the example of the DMN spec into "proper DMN" using Method and Style.[84] The solid arrows in a DRD, the information requirements, do not describe a time-ordered relationship, only an inferential relationship.

In fact, the end-to-end decision logic described by a DRD does not prescribe a particular order of execution. That is an aspect of the implementation. The decision modeling world seems to accept without question that whether a decision table is executed with forward chaining, backward chaining, or something in between is a choice made by the execution engine and is not part of the decision logic. The DMN Method applies that same principle to the end-to-end decision logic described by the DRD.

> In the DMN Method, the DRD does not specify or require a particular order of execution.

---

[83] Fish, *Knowledge Automation*, Chapter 4.

[84] To be fair, in private correspondence with me on this point, Fish later walked back this statement from his book, saying: "The precise statement, I suppose, to support both forward and backward chaining, is that if A is required by the logic of B when evaluated for any particular case, the evaluation of A must complete before the evaluation of B can complete. But really I much prefer a declarative interpretation of the arrows, which I generally describe as requirements, rather than sequence flows."

Outline of the DMN Method

With all this as background, we're ready to outline the DMN Method. It consists of the following steps, which will be fleshed out in more detail in subsequent chapters:

1. **Decision discovery.** The first step involves one or more facilitated workshops conducted with subject-matter experts, similar to those used in DRA and TDM. The key decision model elements to be determined in this step are:

   a. The **end-to-end business decision**: its name and possible outcome values. If the outcome specifies multiple output components, the name and possible outcome values of each component should be specified.

   b. The **input data** elements available, again specified by name, datatype, and allowed values. In addition, the source and format of each data element should be specified. If there is reason, such as cost or effort, to defer obtaining certain input data elements until they are required for a particular decision instance, that information should be captured.

   c. The **process logic of the current-state implementation**, a process model depicting activities to collect input data; an activity for each *decision point* involved; and a gateway following any decision point for which the outcome value affects the subsequent decision logic. It is not necessary at this stage that the process model is properly structured BPMN, as long as it indicates the sequence and conditional logic of the decision points.

2. **Top-down decomposition** of the DRD. The DMN Method places a single decision node representing the business decision as a whole at the top of the DRD, and the input data elements at the bottom. Decomposition fills in the nodes in between. If for some reason the end-to-end decision must be implemented in multiple decision points, that will affect the first-order decomposition. Further decomposition is based on principles of the DMN Method in conjunction with common *decision logic patterns*.

3. **Decision logic** for each decision node. Whether modeled as a decision table, literal expression, or boxed context, the logic of almost any decision node in the DRD can be modeled using one of several *decision logic patterns*. The DMN Method describes variety of classification patterns, mathematical computation patterns, table query patterns, iteration patterns, and data validation patterns.

4. **Business glossary and data model.** Beginning at the decision discovery stage and continuing throughout the modeling project, variable names should be collected in a business glossary, along with their datatypes, allowed values, and business meaning. These names and definitions should be used consistently throughout the decision model. Standardization of the business vocabulary used in decision modeling adds valuable discipline to the project. If a glossary and data model for other decision modeling projects exists, reuse of those names and definitions is usually best practice.

5. **Testing and analysis.** Although it is not discussed in the DMN specification, rigorous testing and analysis of the decision model is an essential component of the DMN Method. This includes completeness and consistency checking, test case generation, and simulation.

The next six chapters detail and illustrate the DMN Method.

CHAPTER 11

Decision Logic Patterns

There is no cookbook recipe for decomposing the DRD. Often the same decision logic may be modeled either as a DRD with many decision nodes, each representing some simple logic, or one with few decision nodes, each containing complex logic. Which style you choose is up to you. In the examples in this chapter I probably lean to fewer DRD nodes, but there is nothing wrong with the many-node style.

Whichever decomposition style you adopt, the DMN Method recommends standardizing on a set of common *decision logic patterns* that both modelers and consumers of the decision models will learn to recognize. Once you learn how to model these patterns, breaking down even complicated decision logic becomes far easier.

Several of the patterns can be modeled in a variety of ways, ranging from a *context* in a single decision (CL3) to a DRD composed of multiple simple decisions and BKMs (CL2). The choice may be dictated by your DMN tool, as many first-generation tools do not yet support contexts. Where the pattern requires a context, we will try to suggest a CL2 alternative.

Arithmetic Formula Patterns

One of the most frequently used patterns is *arithmetic computation*. The best way to do it depends on a number of factors: Is the computation conditional or unconditional? Is it for one-time use or reusable? Are elements in the formula literal values, lookups from a table of values, or passed from a decision or input data?

Unconditional Computation

An *unconditional computation* is simply a formula mapping a set of input values to an output value. "Unconditional" means the formula contains no "if-then" logic. When reuse of the formula is not a concern, the decision's value expression should model the formula as a *literal expression*. All of the variables referenced in this formula must be *information requirements* of the decision. S-FEEL expressions are limited to addition, subtraction, multiplication, division, and exponentiation. FEEL allows a much richer assortment of expression types.

For example, in S-FEEL, the amortization formula for the monthly loan payment is

```
MonthlyPmtAmt = (principalAmt *ratePct/12) / (1 - (1 + ratePct/12)**-termMonths)
```

where *principalAmt* is the loan amount, *ratePct* is the interest rate on the loan, and *termMonths* is the number of months in the term of the loan. In Figure 120, the formula is entered as a literal expression defining the decision node *MonthlyPmtAmt*.

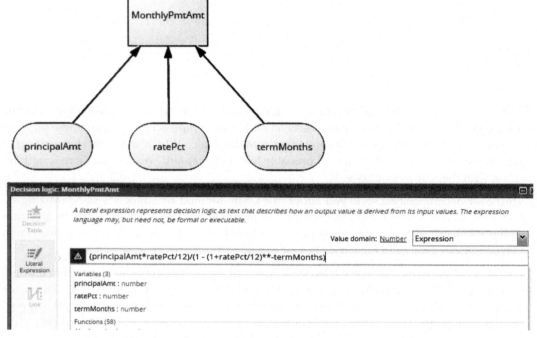

Figure 120. Arithmetic formula as literal expression of input data elements

If the formula is more complicated, instead of a single literal expression referencing the decision inputs, it may be useful to use a *context* that defines intermediate variables. The final result box of the context is then a simpler formula (Figure 121). A CL2 alternative would be to make *LoanPmt*, *TaxPmt*, and *OtherLoans* supporting decisions of *MonthlyPmtAmt* in the DRD.

MonthlyPmtAmt	
LoanPmt	(principalAmt*ratePct/12)/(1-(1+ratePct/12)**-termMonths)
TaxPmt	.0125*Property.value/12
OtherLoans	Borrower.OtherLoansAmt
LoanPmt + TaxPmt + OtherLoans	

Figure 121. Arithmetic formula using a context

Reusable Literal Expression – BKM Invocation

For frequently used formulas, you typically want to allow *reuse* in multiple decision nodes. That means making the formula a *function definition*, in which the variables are *function parameters*. At CL2, a function definition takes the form of a BKM. The name of the BKM becomes the function name.

For example, instead of directly defining the monthly payment formula within the decision node, *MonthlyPmtAmt* could invoke a BKM, *MonthlyPmtCalc* with parameters *p*, *r*, and *n*. There is no need to name the function parameters the same as the variables that supply their values. The value expression of the decision is an *invocation* that *maps* its input variables to the function parameters.

This is illustrated in Figure 122. The decision *MonthlyPmtAmt* invokes the BKM called *MonthlyPmtCalc*, a function of the parameters *p*, *r*, and *n*. The *boxed invocation* (Figure 122, left) maps the decision inputs to the function parameters.

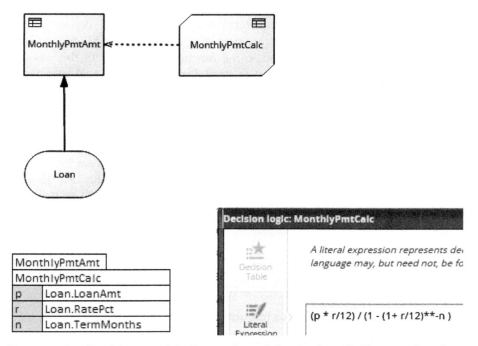

Figure 122. Decision modeled as a boxed invocation (left), mapping inputs to BKM parameters. BKM is a literal expression (right) with parameters *p*, *r*, and *n*.

Literal Function Invocation

A boxed invocation is not the only way to call a reusable formula. A literal expression may invoke a function directly. The *function name* is the name of the BKM or context entry containing the function definition. In the literal expression invoking the function, the syntax is

```
myFunction(param1, param2, param3)
```

The parentheses enclosing a comma-separated list of *parameter values* immediately following *myFunction* identifies it as a *function invocation*. Unlike the boxed invocation, with literal invocation the *values are mapped to parameters in the order they are listed, not by name.*

MonthlyPmtAmt	
Payment	(principalAmt, ratePct, termMonths)
	(principalAmt*ratePct/12)/(1-(1+ratePct/12)**-termMonths)
Payment(Loan.principalAmt, Loan.ratePct, Loan.termMonths)	

Figure 123. Invocation of inline Function Definition from a literal expression

For example, the final result box in Figure 123 illustrates a literal invocation of the function *Payment*. Here the function definition is not a BKM but a *context entry*. That limits the scope of reuse to the containing context, meaning the decision itself. The first parameter value, here *Loan.principalAmt* is passed to the first parameter listed in the function definition, here *principalAmt*, and so on. The order the values are passed in the invocation MUST match the order the corresponding parameters are listed in the function definition. In this case, the function is not reusable outside the decision, but an *iterated invocation*, discussed later, would allow, for example, *Payment* to generate a *list* of monthly payment values for a given list of *Loan* values.

If you want to invoke the *Payment* function outside of this single decision, better to encapsulate the *Payment* function definition in a BKM (Figure 124). Here the boxed expression displays the BKM name in the tab at the top, the function parameter list enclosed in parentheses in the top row, and then the value expression below that. In this case the value expression is a single literal expression, but for more complex formulas could be a context. Now other decisions in the same decision model can invoke *Payment* by name with different parameter values.

Payment	
(principalAmt, ratePct, termMonths)	
(principalAmt*ratePct/12)/(1-(1+ratePct/12)**-termMonths)	

Figure 124. Reusable Function Definition as imported BKM

But reuse should not be limited to decisions in the same decision model. You'd like the *Payment* function to be available to decisions in *any* decision model. To do that, you need to model *Payment* as a BKM and save it in a separate model used as a common *function library*. To use it, the invoking model must first *import* the model containing the function library. Then a literal expression in the invoking decision can simply call the function via its *namespace-qualified name*. For example,

```
methodAndStyleFunctionLib.Payment(Loan.principalAmt, Loan.ratePct,
Loan.termMonths)
```

where *methodAndStyleFunctionLib* is the *namespace* of the function library containing the *Payment* function definition.

Conditional Computation

All of the patterns described above for unconditional computation may be applied to *conditional computation* as well. One way to do it is to use the literal expression or function invocation as a *decision table output entry*. Another way is to use the FEEL *if..then..else* construct. For example, suppose the decision *PaymentAmt* is conditional on the value of the input data *Loan*. Its value may be given by the following literal expression:

```
if Loan.type="Fixed30" then Payment(Loan.principal, Loan.rate30,
360) else if Loan.type="Fixed15" then Payment(Loan.principal,
Loan.rate15, 180) else null
```

Here *Payment* is the function definition described previously.

Classification Patterns

The most basic decision logic pattern concerns *classification* of a fact type into one of its enumerated possible values, such as *Accept, Decline,* or *Refer*. *Decision tables* (Figure 125) are ideally suited to classification, as they make it easy to verify that all possible combinations of input values will generate a classification result, particularly when modeled with a hit policy of *Unique*.

U	Post-BureauAffordabi...		Bankrupt		Post-BureauRiskCate...		CreditScore		Routing
	Boolean		Boolean		Text		Number		Text
1	=	true	=	false	≠	"HIGH"	≥	580	"ACCEPT"
2	=	true	=	false	≠	"HIGH"	<	580	"REFER"
3	=	true	=	false	=	"HIGH"		-	"REFER"
4	=	true	=	true		-		-	"DECLINE"
5	=	false		-		-		-	"DECLINE"

Figure 125. Decision tables are ideally suited to classification

All-or-Nothing Pattern

Vanthienen presents excellent arguments (see Chapter 8) why *Unique* tables are preferred for classification, even when other hit policies enable a table with fewer rules. Not all experts agree. For example, Fish insists that *Priority* hit policy results in tables that are more maintainable.

> "A rule-based categorical decision is, in principle, a very simple thing: the selection of one of a discrete set of alternative categories....You can guarantee the completeness of the rule set by adopting a default decision value and using the rules only to describe exceptions to this decision. Typically the default decision is

"accept" or "continue," and the rules indicate when a case should be referred or declined. This approach seems counterintuitive to some who prefer to think of a default decision of "decline" and a set of conditions for the case being accepted….

Let's say there are 20 conditions for eligibility, starting with: Age >= 18, Residency = local, Not bankrupt. These cannot be framed as separate rules, because it is not true that an applicant over 18 should always be accepted, nor that a local resident should always be accepted. A rule set to accept the case would have to consist of a single rule with 20 conditions:

IF age 18 and residency = local and not bankrupt and [17 more conditions] THEN route = "accept."

This is very unwieldy for maintenance and if the conditions are not met the rule simply fails to fire; you get no information as to the reasons for nonacceptance. The alternative approach, adopting accept as the default decision, gives you:

IF age <18 THEN route = "decline."

IF residency ≠ local THEN route = "decline."

IF bankrupt THEN route = "decline."

and 17 more rules.

This provides 20 independent rules that can be conveniently exposed for editing through a knowledge maintenance interface. Usually, there will be rules for two or more category values in the rule set (for example, refer and decline)…. *There should be a defined set of priorities among these categories*, not among the rules themselves, that should be order-independent. *Each rule can therefore be thought of as proposing a category, and the final result should be the highest priority category proposed by any rule that fires."* [85]

What Fish is describing is a common classification pattern called *all-or-nothing*. In the simplest case, the decision determines a classification value of either *A* or *B*. The value *A* requires that *N* conditions are *all* true; if *any* are false, the value is *B*. The simplest decision table is a *Priority* or *First* table with only *two rules*: one rule with *N* inputs and output value *A*, and an "else" rule – all inputs with hyphen – with output value *B*. But Fish does not recommend that. Instead he recommends an equivalent *any-or-nothing* decision with *N* rules each testing one input independently of the others, all with output *B*, and an else rule with output *A*. This, too, is most simply modeled using *Priority* or *First* hit policy.

But as we saw in the example of Figure 92, *Priority* decision tables can give unintended results that are difficult to detect by quick inspection. For that reason, DMN Method and Style sides with Vanthienen and recommends converting these to *Unique* decision tables. It is always possible to do so, although the algorithm applied by hand can be tedious. (Best is if your DMN tool can do it for you automatically!)

---

[85] Fish, *Knowledge Automation*, Kindle Locations 3168-3203

For example, in Chapter 6, we saw the decision table shown in Figure 126, with *Priority* hit policy. This is modeled as Fish recommends, as an *any-or-nothing* decision.

Eligibility rules

| P | Pre-Bureau Risk Category | Pre-Bureau Affordability | Age | Eligibility |
				INELIGIBLE, ELIGIBLE
1	DECLINE	-	-	INELIGIBLE
2	-	false	-	INELIGIBLE
3	-	-	< 18	INELIGIBLE
4	-	-	-	ELIGIBLE

Figure 126. "Any-or-nothing" decision table using *Priority* hit policy. Source: OMG

This is not the most compact table possible. The *all-or-nothing* formulation of the logic with hit policy *P* or *F* gives a smaller one:

| F | Pre-BureauRiskCateg... | | Pre-BureauAffordabili... | | Age | | Eligibility |
	Text		Boolean		Number		Text
1	≠	"DECLINE"	=	true	≥	18	"ELIGIBLE"
2		-		-		-	"INELIGIBLE"

Figure 127. All-or-nothing formulation gives a more compact table

To convert an *any-or-nothing* table with hit policy *Priority* to a *Unique* table, we start with its equivalent *all-or-nothing* form, changing some of the hyphens to *not()* expressions or equivalent. In other words, starting from an *any-or-nothing* statement of the form,

```
If input1=A OR input2=B OR input3=C then X else Y,
```

change it to its all-or-nothing equivalent:

```
If not(input1=A) AND not(input2=B) AND not(input3=C) then Y else X
```

In other words, if you change all input conditions to their negative (*not()*), change all ORs to ANDs, and swap the output values, you get the same Boolean logic. That means a decision that takes the form

```
If ANY(condition1, condition2, ...) then X else Y
```

is the same as a decision of the form

```
If ALL(not(condition1), not(condition2),...) then Y else X.
```

Thus an any-or-nothing rule always has an all-or-nothing equivalent. A suggested strategy for expressing this pattern in a *Unique* decision table is as follows:

1. Express the logic in the ALL form, i.e., with ANDs not ORs.

```
If input1=A AND input2=B AND input3=C then X else Y
```

2. The first rule in the table is the "all" output entry (*X*).

3. The second rule has *not()* for the first input entry and repeats the entry for the previous rule for all the others, with output entry *Y*.

4. The third rule has hyphen for the first input entry, *not()* for the next input entry, and repeats the entry for the previous rule for all the others, with output entry *Y*.

5. The next rule (if required) has hyphen for the first two input entries, *not()* for the next input entry, and repeats the previous rule for all the others, with output entry *Y*.

6. Add rules in this fashion until all input entries except the last are hyphen, and the last input entry has *not()*.

Figure 128 shows the conversion of Figure 126 to a *Unique* table using this procedure.

U	Age		Pre-BureauAffordability		Pre-BureauRiskCategory		Eligibility
	Number		Boolean		{Decline,High,Medium,Low}		{ELIGIBLE,INELL...}
1	≥	18	=	true	≠	Decline	ELIGIBLE
2	<	18	=	true	≠	Decline	INELIGIBLE
3		-	=	false	≠	Decline	INELIGIBLE
4		-		-	=	Decline	INELIGIBLE

Figure 128. Equivalent decision table with *Unique* hit policy

The *Routing rules* decision table from Chapter 6 (Figure 129) is not all-or-nothing, but converting it to *Unique* (Figure 130) follows the same strategy. While the *Unique* table makes it easier to verify visually the output value for any combination of inputs, it does make modifying the decision logic a little harder. For example, if the *CreditScore* threshold for acceptance should change from 580 to 590, the change must be made to two rules, not one. And if we have made *CreditScore* the first column in the table, we would need to change all 5 rules; this is essentially Fish's argument against *Unique* tables.

Routing rules					
P	Post-bureau Risk category	Post-Bureau Affordability	Bankrupt true, false, null	Credit Score [0..999], null	Routing DECLINE, REFER, ACCEPT
1	-	FALSE	-	-	DECLINE
2	-	-	TRUE	-	DECLINE
3	HIGH	-	-	-	REFER
4	-	-	-	<580	REFER
5	-	-	-	-	ACCEPT

Figure 129. *Routing rules* table with *Priority* hit policy

U	CreditScore	...ost-BureauRiskCategory	Bankrupt	...st-BureauAffordability	Routing
	Number	{HIGH,MEDIUM,LOW,VERY LOW}	Boolean	Boolean	{ACCEPT,DECLINE,REFER}
1	≥ 580	∈ {MEDIUM, LOW, VER...	= false	= true	ACCEPT
2	< 580	∈ {MEDIUM, LOW, VER...	= false	= true	REFER
3	-	= HIGH	= false	= true	REFER
4	-	-	= true	= true	DECLINE
5	-	-	-	= false	DECLINE

Figure 130. Equivalent decision table with *Unique* hit policy

Category-Score Pattern

When many attributes of the input data must be considered in the classification, but not all have equal weight, the *score pattern* is useful. Typically this involves a *multi-hit decision table* with hit policy C+, meaning *collect and sum*. The score decision is typically an input to a classification decision, where various score ranges or "cuts" determine the classification. In the score decision, there is no requirement that all combinations of input values contribute to the score. Just include the ones that affect the subsequent classification.[86]

In the Lending example, various attributes of *Applicant* data – *Age, isMarried,* and *EmploymentStatus* – contribute to the score. The original decision table in the spec (Figure 56) works just fine here.

Although the category-score pattern allows flexible fine tuning of the weight of various factors in the decision logic, it requires careful analysis and testing to be sure that the classification makes sense in all cases.

Category with Reasons Pattern

A classification pattern strongly encouraged in *Knowledge Automation* is called *category with reasons*. The idea is that there may be many different factors that determine whether a loan application, insurance claim, or similar customer request is approved or rejected, and there may be a need to expose in the decision output the specific reason or reasons for the outcome.

This pattern adds a *reason* output to the normal *category* output. Each rule thus not only provides a category value but a reason value as well. For example, referring back to the *Eligibility* decision table (Figure 55), imagine a second output column *Reason* to report the specific cause for disqualification.

---

[86] If your tool reports a completeness violation, you may need to add rules that contribute a score of 0.

Iteration Patterns

The need to apply some bit of decision logic iteratively over items in a list is a very frequent occurrence in decision models. For example, to calculate the price of auto insurance (see Chapter 14), you need to iterate some pricing logic over each car and each driver on the policy. To do this, the iterated logic must first be modeled as a *function definition*. Then it can be invoked iteratively using the FEEL *for..return* construct. This is the basic pattern.

A function definition is modeled either as a BKM or a context entry. Use a BKM if you want the function to be callable from more than one decision. If the iteration is specific to one particular decision, a context entry may be more convenient. The boxed expression of a function definition lists the function *parameters* in a comma-separated list enclosed in parentheses. These parameters are the *only* variables that may be referenced in the function definition's expressions.

For example, consider the loan amortization function

```
payment(principal, rate, numPeriods)
```

When this function is invoked from a literal expression, values are passed to the function in exactly the order listed: *payment, rate, numPeriods*. Even if the meaning is "obvious," you cannot invoke the function with a different order. For example,

```
payment(4%, 360, $300000)
```

does NOT return the correct value!

Normally invocation evaluates the *payment* function for a particular set of *principal, rate,* and *numPeriods* values. But suppose you have a list of loan products that differ in *rate* and possibly *principal* values (since they have different "points" and fees), and you'd like to compare payment for each loan product in the list. (We go through an example such as this in Chapter 15.)

The iteration pattern requires a variable that represents *a list of items*. DMN calls such a variable a *collection*. Often this list is not a list of simple values, but a *relation*, a list of instances of a structured variable, like a list of rows in a relational database table.

The iteration pattern uses the FEEL *for..return* construct in a literal expression to invoke the function once for each item in the list, in this case, for each row in the relation:

```
for item in listVariable return myFunction(item.p1, item.p2,…)
```

Here *item* is a *dummy variable*. It simply means one element in the list *listVariable*, for example, one row of the *Bankrates* table. There is no actual variable named *item*. Nor is there any need for the function definition of *myFunction* to have its parameters reference the name *item*, and normally they will not. The only thing that matters is that the values passed to the parameters enclosed in parentheses in the function invocation reference no names other than *item* (and its child elements).

Here is an example. Suppose we want to create a list of *payment* function values for a loan principal of $300,000 iterated over all the loan products in the relation *Bankrates* (Figure 131).

Bankrates								
LenderName	MortgageType	Conformance Type	MinDown	Term	APR	Rate	Points	FeesAmt
Mount Diablo Lending	ARM 5/1	Conventional	20%	360	2.787%	2.625%	0	$ -
AimLoan	ARM 5/1	Jumbo	20%	360	3.029%	2.750%	0	$ 1,995
Kinecta	ARM 5/1	Jumbo	20%	360	3.127%	2.875%	0.75	$ 1,800
Mount Diablo Lending	ARM 7/1	Conventional	20%	360	3.002%	3.000%	0	$ -
Linear Home Loans	Fixed 10	Conventional	20%	120	2.851%	2.750%	0	$ 795
America One	Fixed 10	Conventional	20%	120	2.937%	2.625%	1	$ 799
America One	Fixed 15	Conventional	20%	180	2.745%	2.375%	0	$ 945
CalFed	Fixed 15	Conventional	20%	180	2.891%	2.750%	0.5	$ 795
Mount Diablo Lending	Fixed 20	Conventional	20%	240	3.502%	3.500%	0	$ -
America One	Fixed 30	Conventional	20%	360	3.577%	3.375%	2	$ 799
Mount Diablo Lending	Fixed 30	Conventional	20%	360	3.629%	3.625%	0	$ -
AimLoan	Fixed 30	Jumbo	20%	360	3.662%	3.625%	0	$ 1,995
America One	Fixed 30	Jumbo	20%	360	3.805%	3.625%	2	$ 799

Figure 131. The relation *Bankrates*

We use the expression

```
for row in Bankrates return payment(300000, row.Rate, row.Term)
```

Let's take a close look at this. First, note the name *row* does not appear either in the relation *Bankrates* or the *payment* function definition! It's just a dummy variable. In the *for..return* expression it means one item in the list, i.e., one row in the *Bankrates* table. *Bankrates* doesn't include a *principal* column, so we use a literal value 300000 for that. The second parameter of payment is the *rate*, so we use the *Rate* column of *Bankrates*, or *row.Rate*. The third parameter is *numPeriods*, which in *Bankrates* is called *Term*, so we write *row.Term*.

Here is an example of the iteration pattern to create a table showing *LenderName*, *MortgageType*, and *Payment* for a $300,000 loan using *Bankrates* data. Following the strategy discussed in the next section on Table Lookup and Query Patterns, we construct the table by using the function definition *tableRow* to define the columns of the table and then a *for..return* expression to populate the rows by iteratively invoking the function. Figure 132 is a little more complicated because the *Payment* column in the *tableRow* function itself invokes a nested function, *payment*.

PaymentsByLender		
payment	(principal, rate, numPeriods)	
	principal * (rate/12) / (1 - (1 + rate/12)**-numPeriods)	
tableRow	(name, mtgeType, r, n)	
	LenderName	name
	MortgageType	mtgeType
	Payment	payment(300000, r, n)
for row in Bankrates return		
tableRow(row.LenderName, row.MortgageType, row.Rate, row.Term)		

Figure 132. *PaymentsByLender* iteratively invokes the *payment* function

The *for..return* construct always returns a list or relation. In this case, *PaymentsByLender* is a relation. We can select from this a column representing list of simple values. For example, *PaymentsByLender.Payment* is a list of monthly payments. We can use FEEL functions such as max(), min(), mean() to extract a single value from that list:

```
min(PaymentsByLender.Payment)
```

Iteration without for..return

The iteration pattern using FEEL *for..return* expressions comes up time and again in decision logic. Unfortunately, there are two problems with it. One is that some business users may find its syntax, including the dummy iterator variable, confusing or "too technical." Another is that many DMN tools do not yet support *for..return*. Let's look at a couple alternatives that could be substituted in those cases.

Multi-Instance Decision Task

One way is to remove iteration from the decision logic and put it in the process logic. You won't be surprised to learn that I am not especially fond of this alternative. In BPMN, a *multi-instance activity* is executed once for each item in a list. Thus, the multi-instance decision task *Determine PaymentsByLender* (Figure 133, left) means execute *PaymentsByLender* (Figure 133, right), equivalent to the *tableRow* function in Figure 132, multiple times, once for each row in *Bankrates*. We can eliminate the context in Figure 132 by making *payment* a separate decision (Figure 134). Now the *PaymentsByLender* elements are just simple expressions (Figure 135).

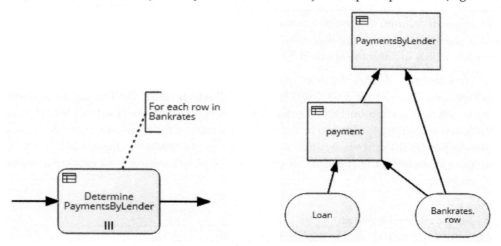

Figure 133. BPMN Multi-instance decision task (left) invokes *PaymentsByLender* decision (right) multiple times, once for each row in *Bankrates*

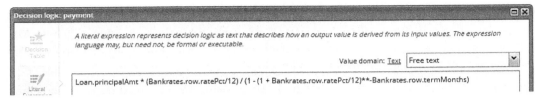

Figure 134. *payment* decision, a literal expression

PaymentsByLender	
LenderName	Bankrates.row.LenderName
MortgageType	Bankrates.row.MortgageType
Payment	payment

Figure 135. *PaymentsByLender* is a single row of a table, executed multiple times

Once again, the problem with this solution is that the meaning of the decision logic is described by BPMN, not DMN.

Multi-Instance Decision

Here is a solution I like much better, a new DRD node type called a *Multi-Instance Decision*, (MID). Unfortunately, it is a proprietary extension in the Signavio tool (Figure 136).

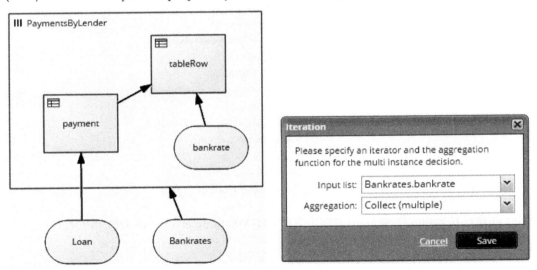

Figure 136. *PaymentsByLender* as Signavio Multi-Instance Decision

Unlike *for..return*, MID iterates over a DRD fragment, not a single decision node, so it works like a *multi-instance decision service*. In the DRD, the MID shape is distinguished by a BPMN-like *multi-instance marker* (three vertical bars) in top left corner. The *iterator* for the MID is a repeating element in one of its information requirements, which must be a *collection*, i.e., a list. The iterator – effectively the dummy variable in *for..return* – is indicated in the DRD by an input data shape inside the MID. For example, in Figure 136 the iterator, called *bankrate*, represents a row in the relation *Bankrates*. Like a multi-hit decision table, Signavio MID allows a variety of *aggregation functions*, including Collect, Sum, Min, Max, and more. We'll see an example of how to use this in Chapter 14.

Even though DMN 1.1 can already handle iteration using *for..return* expressions, something like Signavio MID is a more business-friendly representation, and would be a welcome addition in DMN 1.2.

Sapiens DECISION supports something equivalent in TDM (Figure 137). The circular arrow (like BPMN *loop marker*) in the rule family shape indicates iteration over a *repeating group*, such as *Auto*. OpenRules provides a similar feature.

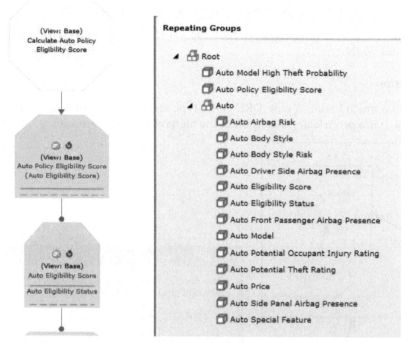

Figure 137. Iteration in Sapiens DECISION (TDM). Source: Sapiens DECISION

Table Lookup and Query Patterns

Quite often decision logic requires looking up a value from a list or table, or possibly selecting multiple items from a list or table, based on some selection criteria. You might say that sounds like it should use SQL, not a decision language like DMN. But just as you should not have to use a completely different language like BPMN to model the end-to-end decision logic, you should also not have to use a completely different language like SQL to model key

---

fragments of the decision logic. Fortunately, FEEL on its own can handle most of the query patterns needed in decisions.

Table Lookup Pattern - Filter Expression

A common pattern in decision models is a *table lookup*. Typically the lookup table is modeled as a relation, such as Figure 138, defined either as an input data element or a *zero-input decision*. As input data, the table must be passed to the decision engine every time it is invoked. As a zero-input decision – a decision node with no information requirements – the table is embedded within the decision model itself.

One way to perform a table query or lookup in FEEL is a *filter expression* on a *list or relation variable*. The syntax is very simple:

```
ListOrRelationVariable [Boolean filter expression]
```

The *predicate*, enclosed in square brackets, is a Boolean expression of elements in the list or relation, perhaps in combination with other variables in scope. For example, if the input data *Order* contains a list of *Items*, the filter expression

```
Order.Item[price < 10]
```

selects all instances of *Order.Item* for which *Order.Item.price* has a value less than 10. What XPATH calls the *context item* – the reference point for named elements in the predicate such as *price* – is the element immediately preceding the predicate (here, *Item*). If we have a list of multiple *Orders*, we could write

```
Order[totalPrice > 100].Item[price < 10],
```

which means from all *Orders* with a *totalPrice* over 100, select all *Items* with a *price* less than 10.

In general, a filter expression returns a list. While the spec does not specify this, we will assume that the order of items returned from the filter is the same as their order in the original list. We can select the first element in any list – filtered or unfiltered – with an integer value in the predicate, indicating the *position* in the list. For example,

```
Order.Item[1]
```

returns the first *Item* in the *Order*. If *Order* contains no *Items*, then *Order.Item*[1] = *null*.

A *relation* is a list of similar *contexts*. By "similar," we mean that all contexts in the relation have the same context entry names and types. The boxed expression for a relation is a table with the context entry names in the top row, with values of the context entry displayed in the corresponding column. A relation in DMN thus acts like a relational table in a database.

Figure 138 depicts a relation defining an input data element *Bankrates*. The variable defined as a relation, here *Bankrates*, is a list of rows in the table. Thus the expression

```
Bankrates[1].LenderName
```

means take the first row in the table and select its *LenderName* value, here *Mount Diablo Lending*.

Bankrates								
LenderName	MortgageType	Conformance Type	MinDown	Term	APR	Rate	Points	FeesAmt
Mount Diablo Lending	ARM 5/1	Conventional	20%	360	2.787%	2.625%	0	$ -
AimLoan	ARM 5/1	Jumbo	20%	360	3.029%	2.750%	0	$ 1,995
Kinecta	ARM 5/1	Jumbo	20%	360	3.127%	2.875%	0.75	$ 1,800
Mount Diablo Lending	ARM 7/1	Conventional	20%	360	3.002%	3.000%	0	$ -
Linear Home Loans	Fixed 10	Conventional	20%	120	2.851%	2.750%	0	$ 795
America One	Fixed 10	Conventional	20%	120	2.937%	2.625%	1	$ 799
America One	Fixed 15	Conventional	20%	180	2.745%	2.375%	0	$ 945
CalFed	Fixed 15	Conventional	20%	180	2.891%	2.750%	0.5	$ 795
Mount Diablo Lending	Fixed 20	Conventional	20%	240	3.502%	3.500%	0	$ -
America One	Fixed 30	Conventional	20%	360	3.577%	3.375%	2	$ 799
Mount Diablo Lending	Fixed 30	Conventional	20%	360	3.629%	3.625%	0	$ -
AimLoan	Fixed 30	Jumbo	20%	360	3.662%	3.625%	0	$ 1,995
America One	Fixed 30	Jumbo	20%	360	3.805%	3.625%	2	$ 799

Figure 138. Input data *Bankrates* defined as a relation

The query

```
Bankrates[Points > 0].LenderName
```

returns the list ["Kinecta", "America One", "CalFed", "America One", "America One"].

To remove the duplicates, you can use the FEEL *distinct values* function:

```
distinct values(Bankrates[Points > 0].LenderName)
```

returns ["Kinecta", "CalFed", "America One"].

To look up in *Bankrates* (Figure 138) the APR for CalFed's Fixed 15-year loan, simply use the expression

```
Bankrates[LenderName="CalFed" and MortgageType="Fixed 15"].APR
```

Table Lookup Pattern – Decision Table

At Conformance Level 2, or if your tool does not support filter expressions, you can still perform table lookups using a decision table. It is slightly less flexible than a filter expression on a relation, for two reasons: First, the lookup table must be embedded within the decision model; it may not be passed as input data. Second, you must explicitly identify table columns as decision table inputs or outputs. But in many cases, these limitations are of no consequence.

Suppose we want to look up the APR for CalFed's Fixed 15-year conventional loan from *Bankrates*, as we did in the previous section. To do this, we turn *Bankrates* into a decision table (Figure 139), with *LenderName, MortgageType,* and *ConformanceType* as input columns and the others as output columns. In this case, the inputs do not constitute a unique key, since a single lender product may be offered with and without points, so the decision table must have hit policy *Collect*. If the inputs constitute a unique key, the table should have a hit policy *Unique.*

To perform the lookup, simply provide values for the inputs, and *Bankrates.APR* provides the desired output value. If CalFed offered this loan with and without points, *Bankrates.APR* would generate a list of APR values.

Bankrates										
C	LenderName	MortgageType	Conformance Type	MinDown	Term	APR	Rate	Points	FeesAmt	
1	Mount Diablo Lending	ARM 5/1	Conventional	20%	360	2.787%	2.625%	0	$	-
2	AimLoan	ARM 5/1	Jumbo	20%	360	3.029%	2.750%	0	$	1,995
3	Kinecta	ARM 5/1	Jumbo	20%	360	3.127%	2.875%	0.75	$	1,800
4	Mount Diablo Lending	ARM 7/1	Conventional	20%	360	3.002%	3.000%	0	$	-
5	Linear Home Loans	Fixed 10	Conventional	20%	120	2.851%	2.750%	0	$	795
6	America One	Fixed 10	Conventional	20%	120	2.937%	2.625%	1	$	799
7	America One	Fixed 15	Conventional	20%	180	2.745%	2.375%	0	$	945
8	CalFed	Fixed 15	Conventional	20%	180	2.891%	2.750%	0.5	$	795
9	Mount Diablo Lending	Fixed 20	Conventional	20%	240	3.502%	3.500%	0	$	-
10	America One	Fixed 30	Conventional	20%	360	3.577%	3.375%	2	$	799
11	Mount Diablo Lending	Fixed 30	Conventional	20%	360	3.629%	3.625%	0	$	-
12	AimLoan	Fixed 30	Jumbo	20%	360	3.662%	3.625%	0	$	1,995
13	America One	Fixed 30	Jumbo	20%	360	3.805%	3.625%	2	$	799

Figure 139. *Bankrates* modeled as a decision table

Table Join Pattern

Many queries require combining information found in multiple related tables linked by a common key field. In SQL this is called a *table join*. Figure 140 illustrates a department table (*dept*) and an employee table (*emp*) linked by the key field *deptno*.

DEPT			EMP		
DEPTNO	DNAME		EMPNO	DEPTNO	ENAME
10	ACCOUNTS		7782	10	CLARK
20	RESEARCH		7934	10	MILLER
30	SALES		7876	20	ADAMS
			7902	20	FORD
			7900	30	JAMES

Figure 140. Simple table join. Source: Oracle[87]

In DMN, *dept* and *emp* would be called relations. *deptno* is an ID field (primary key) in *dept*, and the *emp* table identifies the department of each listed employee by the *deptno*. To get the department name for a particular employee, you need to perform a table join.

To do this in FEEL, you would use a *nested filter expression*. To find the department name of employee *James*, the FEEL expression is

```
dept[deptno = emp[ename = "James"].deptno].dname
```

The inner expression

---

[87] https://docs.oracle.com/cd/B25016_08/doc/dl/bi/B13916_04/joins.htm

```
emp[ename="James"].deptno
```

looks in the *emp* table to find the row corresponding to "James" and selects the *deptno* value for that row. The outer expression looks in the *dept* table to find the department name (*dname*) corresponding to that *deptno* value.

Suppose your decision *EmployeeList* is a relation with columns employee name (*ename*) and department name (*dname*). It should look like this:

Employee List	
dname	ename
Account	Clark
Account	Miller
Research	Adams
Research	Ford
Sales	James

Figure 141. *EmployeeList* **decision result (relation)**

In SQL the query would look like this:

```
select dname, ename
from dept, emp
where
dept.deptno=emp.deptno
```

In DMN with FEEL, it looks like this:

EmployeeList		
empsByDept	(item)	
	dname	dept[deptno=item.deptno].dname
	ename	item.ename
for d in emp return empsByDept(d)		

Figure 142. **DMN equivalent of the table join**

Here is how it works. The context entry *empsByDept* is a *function definition*. Invocation of the function generates a single row in the relation for each instance of its parameter *item*. Note that there is nothing called "item" in either of our source relations, *dept* and *emp*. It is a *dummy variable*; it simply means a row in the table. The function definition says that for any instance of *item* – for any row in the table – put the value of *item*'s attribute *ename* in the *ename* column. For the *dname* column, select the row of the *dept* relation for which the attribute *deptno* matches *item*'s attribute *deptno*, and for that row select the value of *dname*.

To create the list, we need to *iteratively invoke* that function once for each employee in *emp*. For this we use the *for..return* construct, as described previously using the iteration pattern:

```
for d in emp return empsByDept(d)
```

Again *d* here is a dummy variable. We could have called it anything. When you write *"for d in [relation] return [function](d)…"*, that means iterate over each row in [relation] and use that row to supply values of the function parameter *d*. In this case, iterate over each row in *emp* – i.e., once per employee – and call the function *empsByDept* with that employee's values. It doesn't matter that we called the function parameter *d* in the *for..return* expression and *item* in the function definition. They both simply stand for the one parameter of the function.

Here is a variation on this example. Instead of listing all employees, suppose we want to list only those in the Research department. It sounds a little harder, since the employee name is in *emp* and the department name is in *dept*, but it's easy. First we get the *deptno* for Research – it's the key field that links the tables – and then list only the employees for that *deptno* value with a filter in the *for..return* expression (Figure 143).

ResearchEmployeeList		
dnum	dept[dname="Research"].deptno	
researchEmps	(item)	
	dname	item.dname
	ename	item.ename
for d in emp[deptno = dnum] return researchEmps(d)		

Figure 143. Another table join in DMN

Adding ID Field to a Table

It is often important to have one column in a relation that serves to uniquely identify each row in the table. In a database table this is called a *primary key*. Note that the *Bankrates* relation in Figure 138 does not have this. Unfortunately, FEEL does not provide any built-in function to generate a unique ID or even capture the *position* (row number) of an item in the relation (like XPATH *postion()* function). For this reason, when defining a relation in DMN, it is a good idea to create an ID column and provide – manually, if necessary – a unique value for each row.

Sometimes, with input data especially, the decision modeler does not control the data format. As noted, *Bankrates* (Figure 138) does not have an ID field, which would be useful for joining this table with another table, say, one that provides information about the lender. But we can add our own ID field by concatenating some combination of attribute values that uniquely identifies an item in the list.

For example, in *Bankrates*, such a combination would include *LenderName, MortgageType, ConformanceType,* and *Points*. There is at most one row in the table for any combination of those four attributes. It's a bit unwieldy, but we can make it work. In FEEL, the + operator is used to concatenate strings. Since *Points* is a number, we need first to convert it to a string with a constructor function, and we need a separator character not normally part of a field value. Let's use #.

The result is shown in Figure 144. *AddID* is a function definition that constructs an ID field for a row in *Bankrates* and inserts it as the first column. The final result box uses *for..return* to iterate over all the rows.

Bankrates-ID		
AddID	(row)	
	ID	row.LenderName + '#' + row.MortgageType + '#' + row.ConformanceType + '#' + string(row.Points)
	LenderName	row.LenderName
	MortgageType	row.MortgageType
	ConformanceType	row.ConformanceType
	MinDown	row.MinDown
	Term	row.Term
	APR	row.APR
	Rate	row.Rate
	Points	row.Points
	FeesAmt	row.FeesAmt
for row in Bankrates return AddID(row)		

Figure 144. Adding an ID field to a relation

Adding, Removing, Renaming, or Rearranging Table Columns

Figure 144 provides the basic template for adding, removing, renaming, or rearranging *any column* in a table. The decision is a context containing a function definition and a final result box. The function definition has a single parameter, *row*, and defines the structure of a single row in the modified table. Context entries in the function definition specify the columns in the new table and their order. The final result box iterates the function invocation over all rows in the original table, or possibly – using a filter expression – only rows satisfying some condition.

Sorting and Optimization Patterns

From the discussion of iteration and table query patterns, we've seen that DMN is excellent at manipulating lists and tables. For example, given a list of items, DMN can attach a classification or some numeric value to each item in the list. From there it is a short step to determining which item in the list is "best" or "worst," or which items in the list fall above some classification threshold.

Min and Max

If "best" means maximizing or minimizing some numeric field in a relation, you can use the FEEL max() or min() function. The expression

```
min(PaymentsByLender.Payment)
```

finds the minimum value of *Payment* in the relation *PaymentsByLender*.

If you want to output the whole row of *PaymentsByLender* with the minimum value of *Payment*, you could write

```
PaymentsByLender[Payment = min(PaymentsByLender.Payment)]
```

Meets a Threshold

To list instances for which the metric meets some threshold, you can use a filter expression. For example,

```
PaymentsByLender[Payment <= 1500]
```

lists all rows of *PaymentsByLender* for which the *Payment* value is less than or equal to 1500.

Sort Function

The FEEL *sort* function is also useful in optimization. The syntax is

```
sort([list or relation], precedesFunction(x,y)[expression]),
```

where x and y are dummy variables representing items in a list or rows in a relation, and *[expression]* is a comparison indicating their relative ordering in the sorted list. For example, to sort a *simple list* in ascending order, the expression would be $x<y$, meaning if item x in the list is less than item y, it should precede item y in the sorted list. To sort in descending order, the syntax would be

```
sort(myList, precedesFunction(x,y) x>y)
```

To sort rows in a relation, the expression references a particular column in the relation. For example, to sort *Bankrates* (Figure 145) in ascending order of *APR*, write

```
sort(Bankrates, precedesFunction(x,y) x.APR<y.APR)
```

to create the relation *Bankrates-Sorted* (Figure 146).

Bankrates								
LenderName	MortgageType	Conformance Type	MinDown	Term	APR	Rate	Points	FeesAmt
Mount Diablo Lending	ARM 5/1	Conventional	20%	360	2.787%	2.625%	0	$ -
Linear Home Loans	ARM 5/1	no	20%	360	2.870%	2.875%	0	$ 795
AimLoan	ARM 5/1	no	20%	360	3.002%	2.500%	0	$ 1,995
CalFed	ARM 5/1	no	20%	360	3.117%	3.000%	0	$ 795
AimLoan	ARM 5/1	Jumbo	20%	360	3.029%	2.750%	0	$ 1,995
CalFed	ARM 5/1	yes	20%	360	3.080%	3.000%	0	$ 95
Kinecta	ARM 5/1	Jumbo	20%	360	3.127%	2.875%	0.75	$ 1,800
Mount Diablo Lending	ARM 7/1	Conventional	20%	360	3.002%	3.000%	0	$ -
AimLoan	ARM 7/1	Conventional	20%	360	3.103%	2.875%	0	$ 1,995
America One	ARM 7/1	Conventional	20%	360	3.130%	2.875%	1	$ 899
Linear Home Loans	Fixed 10	Conventional	20%	120	2.851%	2.750%	0	$ 795
America One	Fixed 10	Conventional	20%	120	2.937%	2.625%	1	$ 799
America One	Fixed 15	Conventional	20%	180	2.745%	2.375%	0	$ 945
Linear Home Loans	Fixed 15	Conventional	20%	180	2.819%	2.750%	0	$ 795
Mount Diablo Lending	Fixed 15	Conventional	20%	180	2.887%	2.875%	0	$ -
CalFed	Fixed 15	Conventional	20%	180	2.891%	2.750%	0.5	$ 795
AimLoan	Fixed 15	Conventional	20%	180	2.924%	2.750%	0	$ 1,995
IPL Mortgage	Fixed 15	Conventional	20%	180	3.068%	2.990%	0	$ 465
Kinecta	Fixed 15	Conventional	20%	180	3.124%	2.875%	0.625	$ 1,800
Farmers and Merchants	Fixed 15	Conventional	20%	180	3.298%	3.125%	0	$ 1,960
IPL Mortgage	Fixed 15	Conventional	20%	180	3.155%	3.125%	0	$ 895
Farmers and Merchants	Fixed 15	Conventional	20%	180	3.691%	3.625%	0	$ 1,960
Mount Diablo Lending	Fixed 20	Conventional	20%	240	3.502%	3.500%	0	$ -
Linear Home Loans	Fixed 20	Conventional	20%	240	3.555%	3.500%	0	$ 795
AimLoan	Fixed 20	Conventional	20%	240	3.573%	3.500%	0	$ 1,995
America One	Fixed 30	Conventional	20%	360	3.577%	3.375%	2	$ 799
Mount Diablo Lending	Fixed 30	Conventional	20%	360	3.629%	3.625%	0	$ -
AimLoan	Fixed 30	no	20%	360	3.682%	3.625%	0	$ 1,068
America One	Fixed 30	no	20%	360	3.790%	3.750%	0	$ 799
IPL Mortgage	Fixed 30	no	20%	360	3.796%	3.750%	0	$ 895
Kinecta	Fixed 30	no	20%	360	3.808%	3.625%	1.125	$ 1,800
CalFed	Fixed 30	no	20%	360	3.915%	3.875%	0	$ 795
Farmers and Merchants	Fixed 30	no	20%	360	3.974%	3.875%	0	$ 795
AimLoan	Fixed 30	Jumbo	20%	360	3.662%	3.625%	0	$ 1,995
America One	Fixed 30	Jumbo	20%	360	3.805%	3.625%	2	$ 799

Figure 145. Input data *Bankrates* defined as a relation

Bankrates-Sorted								
LenderName	MortgageType	Conformance Type	MinDown	Term	APR	Rate	Points	FeesAmt
America One	Fixed 15	Conventional	20%	180	2.745%	2.375%	0	$ 945
Mount Diablo Lending	ARM 5/1	Conventional	20%	360	2.787%	2.625%	0	$ -
Linear Home Loans	Fixed 15	Conventional	20%	180	2.819%	2.750%	0	$ 795
Linear Home Loans	Fixed 10	Conventional	20%	120	2.851%	2.750%	0	$ 795
Linear Home Loans	ARM 5/1	no	20%	360	2.870%	2.875%	0	$ 795
Mount Diablo Lending	Fixed 15	Conventional	20%	180	2.887%	2.875%	0	$ -
CalFed	Fixed 15	Conventional	20%	180	2.891%	2.750%	0.5	$ 795
AimLoan	Fixed 15	Conventional	20%	180	2.924%	2.750%	0	$ 1,995
America One	Fixed 10	Conventional	20%	120	2.937%	2.625%	1	$ 799
AimLoan	ARM 5/1	no	20%	360	3.002%	2.500%	0	$ 1,995
Mount Diablo Lending	ARM 7/1	Conventional	20%	360	3.002%	3.000%	0	$ -

Figure 146. Truncated view of *Bankrates,* after applying FEEL *sort* function for ascending value of *APR*

Make a Burger Challenge

Even though the FEEL spec had been available since the DMN 1.0 beta in 2014, implementers largely ignored it. So its power in optimization decisions took the decision management world by surprise when Gary Hallmark, chair of the DMN task force and inventor of FEEL, submitted his solution to the *Make a Burger Challenge* on DMCommunity in June 2015.[88] The challenge is reprinted below.

> As the owner of a fast food restaurant with declining sales, you know that your customers are looking for something new and exciting on the menu. Your market research indicates that they want a burger that is loaded with everything as long as it meets certain health requirements. Money is no object to them. The ingredient list in the table below shows what is available to include on the burger:
>
> | Item | Sodium (mg) | Fat (g) | Calories | Item cost ($) |
> |------|------------|---------|----------|---------------|
> | Beef Patty | 50 | 17 | 220 | $0.25 |
> | Bun | 330 | 9 | 260 | $0.15 |
> | Cheese | 310 | 6 | 70 | $0.10 |
> | Onions | 1 | 2 | 10 | $0.09 |
> | Pickles | 260 | 0 | 5 | $0.03 |
> | Lettuce | 3 | 0 | 4 | $0.04 |
> | Ketchup | 160 | 0 | 20 | $0.02 |
> | Tomato | 3 | 0 | 9 | $0.04 |
>
> You must include at least one of each item and no more than five of each item. You must use whole items (for example, no half servings of cheese). The final burger must contain less than 3000 mg of sodium, less than 150 grams of fat, and less than 3000 calories. To maintain certain taste quality standards you'll need to keep the servings of ketchup and lettuce the same. Also, you'll need to keep the servings of pickles and tomatoes the same.
>
> Offer several recipes for a good burger. What is the most and the less expensive burger you can make?

Gary's solution[89] is shown with slight modifications in Figure 147 and Figure 148. Comparison with the others responding to the challenge clearly demonstrates DMN's superior expressive power and elegance!

Ingredients is a relation, either input data or a context entry. *MakeBurger* is a function definition with 6 parameters, the counts of each of the ingredient categories. Each instance of *MakeBurger* creates a row with 10 columns. The first six just report the ingredient counts; the last four are the "optimization" metrics.

To solve the problem, we iteratively invoke the *MakeBurger* function using the *for..return* construct. This list variable here is a list of possible values of the ingredient counts, integers

---

[88] https://dmcommunity.wordpress.com/challenge/make-a-good-burger/, borrowed from http://puzzlor.com/2014-08_GoodBurger.html

[89] https://dmcommunity.files.wordpress.com/2015/06/garyhallmarkburger.pdf

from 1 to 5, called *itemCount,* defined simply as a list of literal values. The context entry *AllBurgers* iterates *MakeBurger* over that list, generating a table with 10 columns and many rows.

Ingredients	Item	Sodium/mg	Fat/g	Calories	Cost/$
	BeefPatty	50	17	220	0.25
	Bun	330	9	260	0.15
	Cheese	310	6	70	0.1
	Onions	1	2	10	0.09
	Pickles	260	0	5	0.03
	Lettuce	3	0	4	0.04
	Ketchup	160	0	20	0.02
	Tomato	3	0	9	0.04

MakeBurger	(nBeef, nBun, nCheese, nOnion, nK-L, nP-T)	
	patties	nBeef
	buns	nBun
	cheese	nCheese
	onions	nOnion
	ketchup-lettuce	nK-L
	pickle-tomatoes	nP-T
	sodium	nBeef*Ingredients[Item="BeefPatty"].Sodium/mg + nBun*Ingredients[Item="Bun"].Sodium/mg + nCheese*Ingredients[Item="Cheese"].Sodium/mg + nOnions*Ingredients[Item="Onions"].Sodium/mg + nK-L*Ingredients[Item="Ketchup"].Sodium/mg + nK-L*Ingredients[Item="Lettuce"].Sodium/mg + nP-T*Ingredients[Item="Pickles"].Sodium/mg + nP-T*Ingredients[Item="Tomato"].Sodium/mg
	fat	nBeef*Ingredients[Item="BeefPatty"].Fat/g + nBun*Ingredients[Item="Bun"].Fat/g + nCheese*Ingredients[Item="Cheese"].Fat/g + nOnions*Ingredients[Item="Onions"].Fat/g + nK-L*Ingredients[Item="Ketchup"].Fat/g + nK-L*Ingredients[Item="Lettuce"].Fat/g + nP-T*Ingredients[Item="Pickles"].Fat/g + nP-T*Ingredients[Item="Tomato"].Fat/g
	calories	nBeef*Ingredients[Item="BeefPatty"].Calories + nBun*Ingredients[Item="Bun"].Calories + nCheese*Ingredients[Item="Cheese"].Calories + nOnions*Ingredients[Item="Onions"].Calories + nK-L*Ingredients[Item="Ketchup"].Calories + nK-L*Ingredients[Item="Lettuce"].Calories + nP-T*Ingredients[Item="Pickles"].Calories + nP-T*Ingredients[Item="Tomato"].Calories
	cost	nBeef*Ingredients[Item="BeefPatty"].Cost/$ + nBun*Ingredients[Item="Bun"].Cost/$ + nCheese*Ingredients[Item="Cheese"].Cost/$ + nOnions*Ingredients[Item="Onions"].Cost/$ + nK-L*Ingredients[Item="Ketchup"].Cost/$ + nK-L*Ingredients[Item="Lettuce"].Cost/$ + nP-T*Ingredients[Item="Pickles"].Cost/$ + nP-T*Ingredients[Item="Tomato"].Cost/$

Figure 147. *Ingredients* **relation and** *MakeBurger* **function definition**

itemCount	[1,2,3,4,5]

AllBurgers	for nBeef in itemCount, nBun in itemCount, nCheese in itemCount, nOnion in itemCount, nK-L in itemCount, nP-T in itemCount return MakeBurger(nBeef, nBun, nCheese, nOnion, nK-L, nP-T)

BurgersByCost	sort(AllBurgers[sodium<3000 and fat<150 and calories<3000], precedesFunction(x,y) x.cost<y.cost)

LeastExpensive	BurgersByCost[1]
MostExpensive	BurgersByCost[-1]

Figure 148. *Make a Burger* **iteration and optimization**

BurgersByCost uses a *sort* function to arrange the rows of *AllBurgers* in ascending order of the *cost* column. The first row in the list is the *LeastExpensive*. The last row, with index -1, is the *MostExpensive*. Of course, if we didn't need a sorted list, we could just use min() and max():

```
LeastExpensive: AllBurgers[cost = min(AllBurgers.Cost)]
```

Action Subtable Patterns

An *action subtable* occurs when you have a decision table in which an output entry references a supporting decision. If the decision rule containing that output entry does not match, there is no need to evaluate the supporting decision. But if it does match, then you must execute the supporting decision – the action subtable – in order to determine the output entry value. The supporting decision is called an action subtable because its execution is effectively triggered by a rule in the parent-level decision in the DRD, a form of backward chaining.

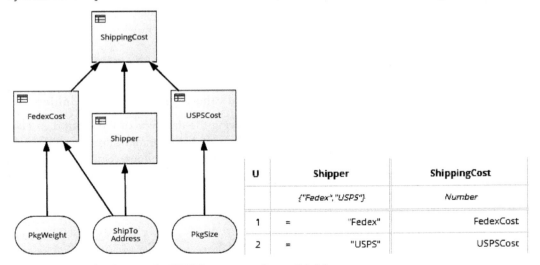

U	Shipper	ShippingCost
	{"Fedex", "USPS"}	Number
1	= "Fedex"	FedexCost
2	= "USPS"	USPSCost

Figure 149. *FedexCost* and *USPSCost* **are action subtables**

Figure 149 shows an example. *FedexCost* and *USPSCost* are action subtables, "called" by the parent decision *ShippingCost*. While some people find them confusing, action subtables provide an elegant way to reduce the size of a decision table.

Validation Patterns

Your decision logic normally assumes that the input data is *valid*, but that is not necessarily the case. Ideally, validation of input data occurs *before* the data is passed to the decision engine, but it is possible to validate it using DMN decision logic. Examples of invalid input data include:

- Value outside of the range or list of allowed values
- Incorrect datatype
- Required element is missing
- Arithmetic error

Invalid Data

If the *item definition* of an input data element specifies a list of *allowed values*, you can validate the input data value using the FEEL *if..in* construct:

LoanValidation	
isTypeValid	if Loan.type in ("Fixed30", "Fixed15", "ARM5/1") then true else false
. . .	

Figure 150. Validation of data element with enumerated allowed values.

This requires explicitly entering the list of allowed values specified by the item definition.

If your tool supports it, the FEEL *instance of* construct makes it easier:

LoanValidation	
isLoanValid	Loan instance of tLoan

Figure 151. Validation of data element structure and values against its item definition.

Here *tLoan* is the name of the item definition specifying the datatype of the input data *Loan*. This simple expression returns true if all components of *Loan* contain allowed values, and false if any component is missing or contains other than allowed values. Unfortunately, item definition does not have a way to say that a component is *optional*, unless you explicitly include *null* as one of the allowed values. Without that, the *instance of* validation expression will return a value of false if one of the component values is blank.

Validation Rules

Even if *null* is an allowed value in the datatype, validation rules may *require* a non-*null* value if some other element has a certain value. For example, suppose a data entry form includes a

---

radio button field (i.e., select one value from a list), the last of which is labeled *Other* and has an associated *text entry field*. And suppose a validation rule says that if the *Other* box is checked, the text entry field may not be blank. Figure 152 illustrates the FEEL literal expression that checks this:

LoanValidation	
isTypeValid	if Loan.type in ("Fixed30", "Fixed15", "Other") then true else false
isOtherValid	if (Loan.type="Other" and not(string length(Loan.otherType)>0)) then false else true

Figure 152. Validation a data element conditional on values of other elements.

To detect blank string fields without enumerated allowed values, the FEEL expression *not(string length()>0)* is more reliable than testing for *null*. To detect blanks in fields of number, date/time, duration, and Boolean types, or strings with enumerated allowed values, you can test for *null*.

Other common validation rules for form data entry implement *arithmetic checks*. For example, a form may have a *Total* field that sums a number of other fields, call them *A*, *B*, and *C*. Depending on the implementation, testing *Total=A+B+C* could possibly report a correct *Total* value as invalid because of rounding. A better way to model *isTotalValid* is to test equality within some acceptable tolerance, such as

```
if Total - sum(A,B,C) in (-0.05..0.05) then true else false;
```

Error List Pattern

The examples above simply generate a value of true or false indicating whether or not the data element is valid. But what we more often want when validating input data is a *list of validation errors*, in which each item in the list provides an error message. It is similar to the *Category with Reasons* pattern described previously.

ErrorList		
ValidationRules	Condition	Message
	not(Loan instance of tLoan)	"Input data Loan has invalid structure or data values."
	not(Loan.type in ("Fixed30", "Fixed15","Other")	"Loan.type is blank or has invalid value."
	Loan.type="Other" and not(string-length(Loan.otherType)>0)	"Loan.otherType is blank."
	. . .	. . .
rawList	for n in ValidationRules return validate(n.Condition, n.Message)	
if count(rawList[Condition != null])>0) then rawList[Condition !=null] else "No errors"		

Figure 153. *ErrorList* pattern iterates over a list of validation rules.

In Figure 153, the relation *ValidationRules* specifies each validation rule as a *Condition* and associated *Message*. *Condition* is a Boolean expression which is true for an error condition. Following the iteration pattern described previously, we use the *for..return* construct to model the *ErrorList* decision. *rawList* iterates the function *validate* over each validation rule. Rules which are not violated generate *null* entries in *rawList*, so these need to be filtered out. The final result box also outputs the message "No errors" if *rawList* contains no non-*null* entries.

The iterated function *validate* is defined by the BKM shown in Figure 154. It is a simple *if..then..else* literal expression that outputs either the *Message* value if the *Condition* is true, or *null* if the *Condition* is false.

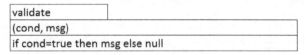

Figure 154. Iterated function *validate* is simple *if..then..else* expression

CHAPTER 12

Top-Down DRD Decomposition

Using the decision logic patterns discussed in the previous chapter, we're ready now to decompose the DRD.

Decomposition Strategy

Decomposition of the end-to-end decision logic is more of an art than a science. There is no fixed template for it, but the Method defines a *top-down strategy*:

1. **Start at the top.** This is the essence of what the Method means by the "business decision as a whole." The "top" just means *the question you are trying to answer*. Whether that is something of interest to the customer, like the monthly premium for an insurance contract (or possibly a decline to offer), or a small internal detail, like the identity of the best tech support rep to handle a particular request, the top should be represented by a *single decision node at the top of the DRD*.

2. **Identify the considerations affecting the top-level decision.** Try to separate these into logically independent categories. For example, in residential mortgage origination, you might list the borrower's creditworthiness, affordability of the loan, condition and location of the property, and market conditions, such as interest rates. *Each of those logically distinct considerations defines a separate branch of the DRD.*

3. **For each high-level consideration, identify detail considerations that affect its outcome.** For example, factors in the borrower's creditworthiness might include the credit score, past bankruptcy or short sale history, quality of income (not all types of income are considered equally by underwriters), steadiness of employment, etc. Some of these detail considerations may be determinative on their own; for example, past bankruptcy may disqualify the borrower all by itself. More often, they simply contribute to some aggregate rating, either positively or negatively. *The classification patterns discussed in the previous chapter provide a number of ways to combine the detail considerations to obtain a useful result.* If it is available, analytics data can provide

excellent guidance on combinations of these detail considerations that lead to successful and/or unsuccessful outcomes.

4. **For each detail consideration, identify the input data required and their source.** These include application forms, data in in-house business systems and databases, service provider data, and human decisions. *These are the input data elements in the DRD.*

5. **For each input data element, determine whether it is needed for all instances of the decision or only some, and whether there is a cost or other disadvantage to obtaining it for all instances in advance.** If not, modeling the end-to-end decision as one that can be executed in a single decision service is preferable to spreading it out over multiple steps separated in time. However, if certain input data is only needed for certain instances, and obtaining that data incurs significant cost, delay, or other disadvantage, it may be better to model the decision logic to allow execution at multiple decision points. *In this case, a process model indicating the decision points and branch points (gateways) is needed to properly structure the DRD.* However, reference to that process model should not be required to understand the resulting DRD. *This step, even though it is last, does impact the first-order decomposition.*

Lending Example Revisited

To illustrate the decomposition, let's take another look at the Lending decision described in Chapter 6 of this book. Figure 155 is the DRD from the spec redrawn without the BKMs and knowledge sources. Note it has two top-level decisions, *Strategy* and *Adjudication*, neither of which represents the business decision as a whole. The business decision as a whole instead is represented by a BPMN model, shown in the Figure 156.

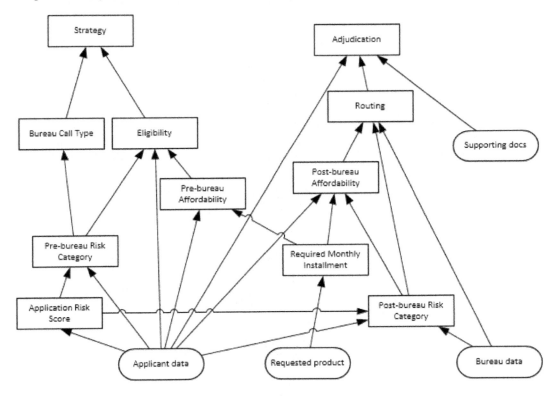

Figure 155. DRD of the original Lending decision example

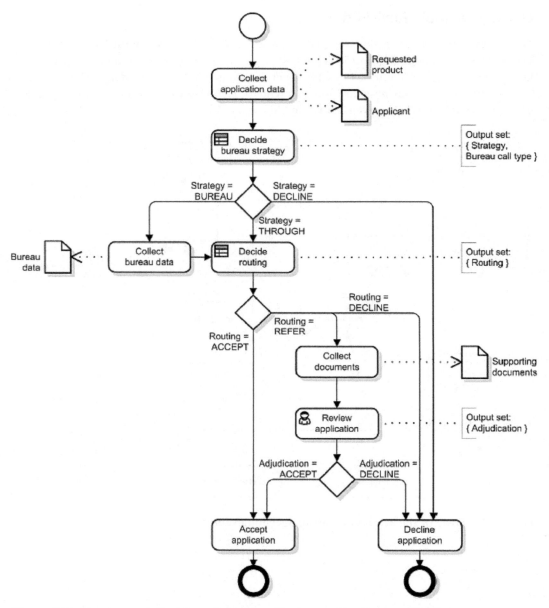

Figure 156. Process model of the original Lending example. Source: OMG

First Order Decomposition

The DMN Method looks at this logic differently. Here the business decision as a whole is to approve or decline a loan application. So the decomposition strategy says the DRD should

---

have a single top-level decision node, *Approval*, with possible outcome values *Approved* and *Declined*.

Next, we need to identify the distinct types of considerations affecting the top-level outcome. In this example, there are two: the borrower's credit risk and the affordability of the loan. In the example, the credit risk decision is a *classification* based on the applicant's age, marital status, employment status, and credit history. The *Category-Score pattern*, described in the previous chapter, is a good way to combine these detail considerations with flexible weighting, ideally aligned with the bank's analytics. That pattern suggests a *RiskCategory* decision supported by a *CreditRiskScore* decision.

Loan affordability is based on a simple *arithmetic computation*, comparing the monthly loan payment to the applicant's monthly income. If that ratio is below some threshold value, the loan is considered affordable, otherwise unaffordable. Thus the affordability decision is a Boolean, *isLoanAffordable*. Our analytics tell us that the threshold value of the ratio is dependent on the applicant's *RiskCategory* value. It is usually best to avoid dependencies between the major considerations, but in this case we cannot avoid it. So we need to make *RiskCategory* a supporting decision of *isLoanAffordable*.

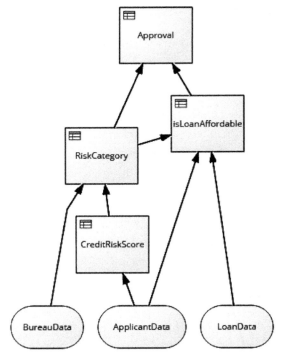

Figure 157. Tentative first-order decomposition of revised Lending example

The input data for the credit risk decision come from the borrower's application and from an external credit bureau. So let's call these elements *ApplicantData* and *BureauData*. The input data for the affordability decision comes from the borrower's application and the details of the loan, i.e., *ApplicantData* and *LoanData*. We now have enough to create a *tentative* first-order decomposition (Figure 157). I say "tentative" because the possibility that we may not want to obtain all of these elements in advance for all instances of the decision will require modifying this DRD.

Now we need to consider whether all of these input data elements are obtained in advance for all instances of the decision. We know from Figure 156 – let's say this represents the current-state decision process described in the decision discovery workshops – that *BureauData* is not obtained in advance.

Why would that be the case? Presumably it is costly to obtain and not needed in every instance of the decision. Thus, we believe it is *more profitable* to obtain and process that input data only for instances that require it. To do it that way requires modifying the DRD. We need to revise the DRD to fit this more profitable implementation, in which the decision logic is possibly executed *twice*, once without the *BureauData* and, for those instances that require it, again with the *BureauData*. Let's call the first pass, without *BureauData*, *Prequalification*, and the second pass, with *BureauData*, *Qualification*.

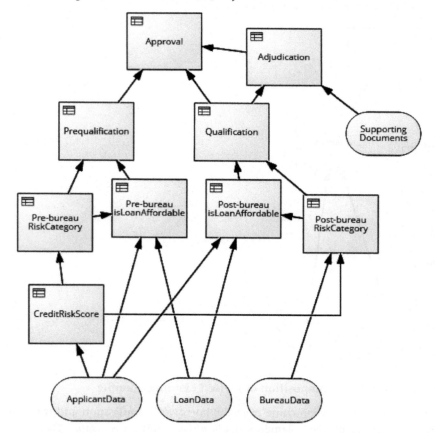

Figure 158. DRD of the Lending example redrawn using DMN Method

From the decision discovery workshop, we also understand that while most loan applications can be approved or declined definitively by the decision logic, some cases are referred to an underwriter for *Adjudication*, a human decision, who reviews the original decisions along with additional *SupportingDocuments*, a new bit of input data. This leads to a revised first-order decomposition (Figure 158).

Here *Post-bureauRiskCategory* requires *BureauData*, while *Pre-bureauRiskCategory* does not. Since the risk category affects the affordability decision, that also must be executed both with and without *BureauData*. The *CreditRiskScore* depends only on *ApplicantData*, so it is executed only once. While it is not obvious from the DRD, *Qualification* and *Adjudication* are *conditional decisions*, executed in only some instances.

	Approval			
U	Prequalification	Qualification	Adjudication	Approval
1	Approve	-	-	Approve
2	Decline	-	-	Decline
3	FullBureauData, MiniBureauData	Approve	-	Approve
4	FullBureauData, MiniBureauData	Decline	-	Decline
5	FullBureauData, MiniBureauData	Refer	Approve	Approve
6	FullBureauData, MiniBureauData	Refer	Decline	Decline

Figure 159. Top-level *Approval* decision

Figure 159 shows the *Approval* decision table. Let's see what it says.

- If *Prequalification* results in either *Approve* or *Decline*, *Qualification* and *Adjudication* are irrelevant to the decision. That's good, because we don't want to execute them in that case.

- If *Prequalification* results in either *FullBureauData* or *MiniBureauData* and *Qualification* results in either *Approve* or *Decline*, *Adjudication* is irrelevant. Again, this is good, because we don't want to perform *Adjudication* unless we absolutely need to do so.

- Only in the case that *Prequalification* results in *FullBureauData* or *MiniBureauData* and *Qualification* results in *Refer* do we need to perform *Adjudication*.

This is exactly the logic described in the BPMN model, Figure 156... except we've done it in DMN on its own. A DMN engine capable of backward chaining would execute this decision table in exactly that way.

Role of BPMN in Decision Modeling

While the DMN Method insists that the end-to-end DRD should fully describe the *decision logic* without reference to a companion BPMN model, *BPMN still plays an important role in decision modeling*, in three ways:

1. In the stakeholder workshops conducted in the "decision discovery" phase, the proven success of both DRAW and STEP methodology demonstrates that eliciting the current-state decision in procedural terms – *What is decided first? Based on that, what happens next?* – still makes sense in the DMN Method. It fits the experience – concrete and bottom-up – of those actually involved in making the decision today. In that sense, a process model is a critical ingredient of the raw material going into the ultimate decision model.

2. A BPMN model aligned with the final DMN model is also important to understanding the actions required to obtain the input data and act on the decision result. For example, even though the decision table of Figure 159 is sufficient to say that *BureauData* and *SupportingDocuments* are irrelevant in some instances of the decision, it does not describe the *action* of obtaining those input data elements when they are needed. Actions – such as obtaining input data, executing external decisions and human decisions, or updating some system with the final decision result – are the province of business process models. Decisions on their own don't take actions. They only select output values.

3. Even though the end-to-end DRD does not *prescribe* a particular order of execution, it must be *consistent with the expected implementation*. This is important when that expected implementation is a sequence of *decision points* separated in time. By "decision point" here we mean simply a single unit of execution, either a decision service, a human decision, or an external decision. In particular, when execution of one decision point is *conditional* on the result of another decision point, that should be reflected in the end-to-end DRD structure. This conditional relationship in the implementation is best described by BPMN. Thus, while reference to BPMN should not be necessary to understand the decision logic, it helps to understand the expected implementation, and it may be necessary to properly design a DRD structure consistent with that implementation.

We can then diagram the *decision process* as in Figure 160. Note that in this diagram there is no decision point corresponding to the top-level decision *Approval*. From an implementation standpoint, it is a *virtual decision*. Its purpose here is merely to aggregate all components of the business decision as a whole into a single variable. If the decision process determined in decision discovery were to require only a single decision point with all input data available from the beginning – and this is best if it incurs no additional cost or effort – then the top-level decision node would represent a *real decision*, not a virtual decision.

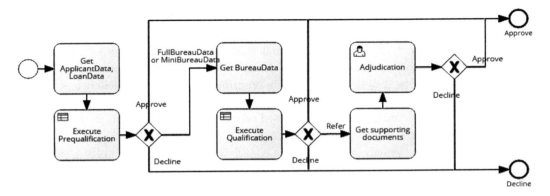

Figure 160. Decision point analysis of the Lending decision process

Priority of Supporting Decisions

Let's take another look at the top-level decision table (Figure 161).

U	Approval Prequalification	Qualification	Adjudication	Approval
1	Approve	-	-	Approve
2	Decline	-	-	Decline
3	FullBureauData, MiniBureauData	Approve	-	Approve
4	FullBureauData, MiniBureauData	Decline	-	Decline
5	FullBureauData, MiniBureauData	Refer	Approve	Approve
6	FullBureauData, MiniBureauData	Refer	Decline	Decline

Figure 161. Top-level *Approval* decision

There is something curious about it. In effect, it says *Prequalification* takes priority over *Qualification*, since if *Prequalification* determines a value of *Approve* or *Decline,* the outcome of *Qualification* is irrelevant. But *Qualification* has more complete and better information than *Prequalification* does; it includes the credit bureau data. It is possible that an applicant deemed *Approve* by *Prequalification* in fact has a low credit score or past bankruptcy, which would cause a *Qualification* outcome of *Decline.* In that case, you could argue that this decision logic gives the "wrong" answer! For the same reason, the human *Adjudication* decision has a lower priority than the automated *Qualification* decision, and a loan application that would be approved by *Qualification* could possibly be declined by *Adjudication* if that decision were allowed to happen.

We justify Figure 161 by saying that *Qualification* is always *null* if *Prequalification* is *Approved* or *Declined,* because that is what the process model of Figure 160 says. But is that process *always* followed? What if the applicant recently was declined for another loan at the bank, and his *Bureau data* is already available? Wouldn't it be better to use it? Or it might be that in the case of a loan over some high threshold, manual *Adjudication* is always required and takes precedence over the automated *Qualification*. Just because Figure 160 describes the normal or typical decision process, it does not necessarily describe correctly the precedence of the three decision nodes *in all cases*. In reality, we would prefer the decisions with more complete information to take precedence over those based on less complete information. But this is not what Figure 161 says.

So instead of Figure 161, we would prefer to create a top-level decision table that reflects the real priority order of the decision nodes… but still works when the normal decision process of Figure 160 is followed. To create that, let's start by expanding the decision table of Figure 161 to separate the "hyphen" (irrelevant) input entries into *null* and non-*null* values. In this decision table (Figure 162), *Qualification*, if not *null*, takes precedence over *Prequalification*, and *Adjudication*, if not *null*, takes precedence over *Qualification*.

Approval				
U	Prequalification (Approve, Decline, FullBureauData, MiniBureauData)	Qualification (Approve, Decline, Refer, null)	Adjudication (Approve, Decline, null)	Approval (Approve, Decline)
1	Approve	null	null	Approve
2	Decline	null	null	Decline
3	FullBureauData, MiniBureauData	Approve	null	Approve
4	FullBureauData, MiniBureauData	Decline	null	Decline
5	FullBureauData, MiniBureauData	Refer	Approve	Approve
6	FullBureauData, MiniBureauData	Refer	Decline	Decline
7	Approve, Decline	Approve	null	Approve
8	Approve, Decline	Decline	null	Decline
9	Approve, Decline	Refer	Approve	Approve
10	Approve, Decline	Refer	Decline	Decline
11	Approve, Decline	null	Approve	Approve
12	Approve, Decline	null	Decline	Decline
13	Approve, Decline	Approve, Decline	Approve	Approve
14	Approve, Decline	Approve, Decline	Decline	Decline
15	FullBureauData, MiniBureauData	Approve, Decline, null	Approve	Approve
16	FullBureauData, MiniBureauData	Approve, Decline, null	Decline	Decline

Figure 162. *Approval* **logic with correct decision precedence if all input data is available**

We can contract this table to the more compact Figure 163.

Approval				
U	Prequalification (Approve, Decline, FullBureauData, MiniBureauData)	Qualification (Approve, Decline, Refer, null)	Adjudication (Approve, Decline, null)	Approval (Approve, Decline)
1	Approve	null	null	Approve
2	Decline	null	null	Decline
3	-	Approve	null	Approve
4	-	Decline	null	Decline
5	-	-	Approve	Approve
6	-	-	Decline	Decline

Figure 163. Contracted representation of the *Approval* decision logic

Note that in all the cases covered by Figure 161, Figure 163 gives the same result. But Figure 163 also includes exception cases ignored by our initial decision process model and thus by Figure 161.

Now we have a top-level decision table that correctly reflects the priority of the supporting decisions, even in the atypical cases. It is best if we update the BPMN model to reflect the possibility of these cases. Let's say we determine that after *Prequalification*, we will execute *Qualification* if (1) *Prequalification* is *Approve* and either we already have *BureauData* or *LoanData.Type* is *SpecialLoan*; or (2) *Prequalification* is *FullBureauData* or *MiniBureauData*, which is the original "normal" reason. And let's say that after *Qualification*, we will execute *Adjudication* if either (1) *LoanData.Type* is *SpecialLoan*; or (2) *Qualification* is *Refer*, which was the original "normal" reason. The corrected BPMN is shown in Figure 164.

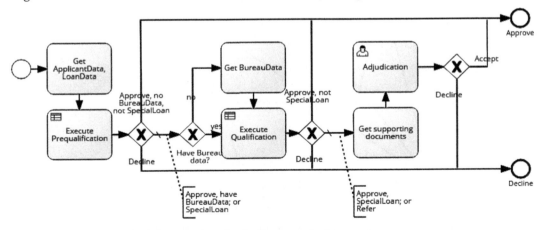

Figure 164. Revised decision process including atypical cases

Full Decomposition

Starting with the first-order decomposition and guided by the decision logic patterns, the Method continues to progressively refine the DRD as it is decomposed. The result should be a network of decision nodes, each defined by easily understood decision logic. What "easily understood" means depends, of course, on the intended audience. Usually some fragment of decision logic may be modeled either as a small number of decisions – often just one – defined as a *context* (Level 3), or as a larger number of decisions, each modeled as a CL2 expression type: a decision table, literal expression, or invocation. So the modeler has a choice in the style of decomposition – a simple DRD containing relatively few nodes, each with more complex decision logic, or a DRD containing many nodes, each with very simple decision logic... or something in between. My own bias is toward simpler DRDs, but the choice is really up to you.

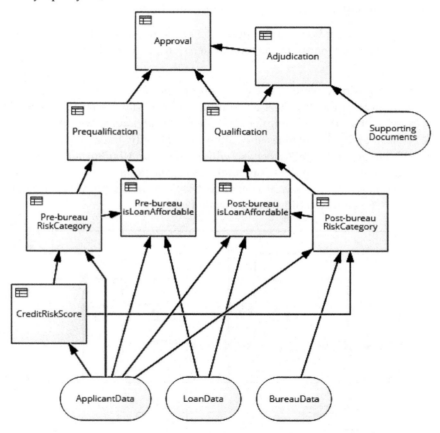

Figure 165. Revised first-order decomposition of Lending decision

To see how this works, let's complete our revision of the Lending decision example, which is largely based on the *classification pattern*. We start with the first-order decomposition. The *category-score pattern* described earlier in this chapter provides flexibility in weighting the various attributes of *ApplicantData* contributing to the *RiskCategory* decisions, so we have interposed *CreditRiskScore* between the two as a supporting decision. However, *Applicant.Age<18* is automatically disqualifying, so *ApplicantData* should also be a direct information requirement to both *RiskCategory* decisions. The resulting modification is shown in Figure 165.

Refining the decomposition requires understanding all the conditions that determine the outcome of the first-order decisions, *Prequalification* and *Qualification*. We cannot simply adopt the decomposition of the current-state implementation, such as might be represented by the original Lending example. In all cases, simplicity, isolation of distinct factors, and ease of understanding should be the overriding concerns. When using the category-score pattern, the "cuts" on the score leading to various classification values should not be arbitrary. Ideally they should be based on analytics data describing past outcomes. But in revising the Lending example, we will not attempt to modify those score cuts.

Prequalification

From decision discovery, we know *Prequalification* has possible output values *Approve, Decline, FullBureauData,* and *MiniBureauData.* The difference between the outcomes *FullBureauData* and *MiniBureauData,* although not explained in the original example, appears to be related to the cost of obtaining the credit report.

Pre-bureauRiskCategory

Working through the original Lending example (Chapter 6), we see the following:

Prequalification is *Decline* if *any* of the following are true:
- *Pre-bureauRiskCategory* = "Decline"
  - *(ApplicantData.isExistingCustomer*=true and *CreditRiskScore<80)* or *ApplicantData.Age <18*
- *isLoanAffordable* = false

Prequalification is *FullBureauData* if *all* of the following are true:
- *Pre-bureauRiskCategory* in ["High", "Medium"]
  - *ApplicantData.Age* >= 18 and
    (ApplicantData.isExistingCustomer = false and *CreditRiskScore<120)* or
    (ApplicantData.isExistingCustomer = true and *CreditRiskScore* in [80..110])
- *isLoanAffordable* = true

Prequalification is *MiniBureauData* if *all* of the following are true:
- *Pre-bureauRiskCategory* = "Low"
  - *ApplicantData.Age* >=18 and
    (ApplicantData.isExistingCustomer = false and *CreditRiskScore* in [120..130])* or
    (ApplicantData.isExistingCustomer = true and *CreditRiskScore* >110)
- *isLoanAffordable* = true

Prequalification is *Approve* if *all* of the following are true:

- *Pre-bureauRiskCategory* = "Very Low"
  - *ApplicantData.Age* >= 18 and
    ApplicantData.isExistingCustomer = false and *CreditRiskScore*>130
- *isLoanAffordable* = true

Figure 166 shows the decision table for *CreditRiskScore*. It is essentially the same as *Application Risk Score* in the original, except that it needs to account for *ApplicantData.Age* values less than 18. Also, even though *ApplicantData.Age* values are integers, FEEL numbers are not restricted to integers, so the Age ranges were specified so that completeness errors are not generated in the tool.

ApplicantData.Age factors into the decision logic in two ways. If less than 18, the outcome is *Decline* automatically, independent of all other inputs. If 18 or more, *ApplicantData.Age* contributes to the *CreditRiskScore*. You could eliminate the *ApplicantData.Age* input in the *Pre-bureauRiskCategory* decision table by assigning a high negative *CreditRiskScore* contribution to *Age* values under 18, but breaking it out as a separate input makes the decision logic clearer. (Technically, the spec says you could define *Age* as a number greater than 0 in its item definition but allow only decision table input values greater than or equal to 18... but my tool does not allow it.)

C+	ApplicantData.Age		...icantData.isMarried		...employmentStatus		...itRiskScore
	Number		Boolean		{Employed,Self-employed,...		**Number**
1	≤	21	-			-	32
2	∈	(21..25]	-			-	35
3	∈	(25..35]	-			-	40
4	∈	(35..50)	-			-	43
5	≥	50	-			-	48
6		-	=	false		-	25
7		-	=	true		-	45
8		-		-	=	Unemployed	15
9		-		-	=	Student	18
10		-		-	=	Employed	45
11		-		-	=	Self-employed	36

Figure 166. *CreditRiskScore* decision table

U	ApplicantData.Age		...sExistingCustomer		CreditRiskScore 🕐		Pre-bureauRiskCategory
	Number		Boolean		Number		{Decline,High,Medium,Low,Very ...}
1	<	18		-		-	Decline
2	≥	18	=	true	<	80	Decline
3	≥	18	=	false	<	100	High
4	≥	18	=	true	∈	[80..90]	High
5	≥	18	=	false	∈	[100..120)	Medium
6	≥	18	=	true	∈	(90..110]	Medium
7	≥	18	=	false	∈	[120..130]	Low
8	≥	18	=	true	>	110	Low
9	≥	18	=	false	>	130	Very low

Figure 167. *Pre-bureauRiskCategory* **decision table**

Figure 167 shows the decision table for *Pre-bureauRiskCategory*. Already the decision logic is clearer than in the original Lending example in Chapter 6. This table does illustrate Fish's point, mentioned earlier, about maintainability of *Unique* decision tables. If the *Age* eligibility threshold should change, say, to 17, all 9 rules would need to be modified. With *Priority*, only one rule would need changing.

Figure 168 shows the decision table for *Prequalification*.

U	Prelim isLoanAffordable 🕐		Prelim CreditRiskCategory 🕐		Prequalification
	Boolean		{Decline,High,Medium,Low,Very Low}		{Approve,Decline,FullBurea...
1	=	false		-	Decline
2	=	true	=	Decline	Decline
3	=	true	∈	{High, Medium}	FullBureauData
4	=	true	=	Low	MiniBureauData
5	=	true	=	Very Low	Approve

Figure 168. *Prequalification* **decision table**

Pre-bureauIsLoanAffordable

Now let's look at the *Pre-bureauIsLoanAffordable* decision, which compares the monthly loan payment to the applicant's income to determine the outcome. We'd like to have this decision support the *Qualification* decision as well, but a minor component of the calculation, the *CreditContingencyFactor*, depends on the credit bureau data. We could put the reusable decision logic in a BKM *isAffordable*, called both Pre-bureau and Post-bureau. Here the simplest thing is to define supporting decisions *PaymentAmt*, *FeeAmt*, and *LoanToIncome*, independent of the credit bureau data, and isolate the *BureauData* dependencies in the two *isLoanAffordable* decisions.   Figure 169 shows the revised DRD decomposition for *Prequalification*.

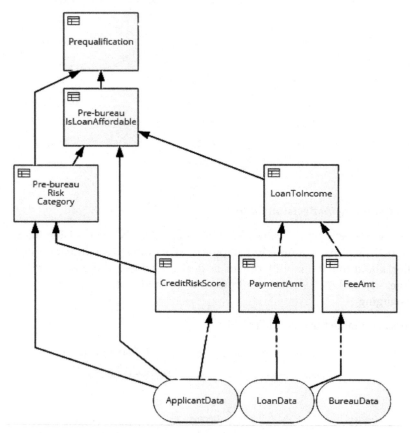

Figure 169. DRD decomposition, *Prequalification*

PaymentAmt is the familiar amortization formula:

```
LoanData.LoanAmt * (LoanData.RatePct/12) / (1 - (1 +
LoanData.RatePct/12)**-LoanData.TermMonths)
```

FeeAmt is a simple conditional expression:

```
If LoanData.Type = "Standard loan" then 20 else if LoanData.Type =
"Special loan" then 25 else null
```

LoanToIncome is an unconditional arithmetic computation:

```
PaymentAmt / (ApplicantData.MonthlyIncome -
ApplicantData.MonthlyExpenses - ApplicantData.MonthlyRepayments)
```

Pre-bureauIsLoanAffordable is most simply modeled as a decision table (Figure 170). You might ask what happened to the function call *CreditContingencyFactor*? The value of adding something like that is to isolate the factor values for various risk categories in a single decision

– what Ross calls "single sourcing" – instead of hard-coding factor values in both *Pre-bureauIsLoanAffordable* and *Post-bureauIsLoanAffordable* (and being sure you do it consistently). Strictly speaking, that is probably better, but here we chose simplicity over single-sourcing.

U	...au Risk Category		LoanToIncome	Pre-bureauIsLoanAffordable
	{Decline,High,Medium,Lo...		Number	*Boolean*
1	∈	{Decline, High}	< 0.6	true
2	∈	{Decline, High}	≥ 0.6	false
3	∈	Medium	< 0.7	true
4	=	Medium	≥ 0.7	false
5	∈	{Low, Very low}	< 0.8	true
6	∈	{Low, Very low}	≥ 0.8	false

Figure 170. *Pre-bureauIsLoanAffordable* **decision table**

This completes the decomposition of *Prequalification*.

Qualification

The *Qualification* decision is similar to the *Routing* decision in the original. Now *BureauData.CreditScore* and *BureauData.hasBankruptcy* are included in the risk score and category determination.

Once again, we have the same two independent factors, *Post-bureauRiskCategory*, which now includes *CreditScore* and *hasBankruptcy*, and *Post-bureauIsLoanAffordable*, a slightly different calculation of *isLoanAffordable* based on the possibility that the revised risk category changes the *LoanToIncome* threshold for affordability. The DRD is shown in Figure 171.

Again, referring to the original Lending example, we see that:

Qualification is "Decline" if *any* of the following are true:
- *Post-bureauIsLoanAffordable* = false
- *BureauData.hasBankruptcy* = true
    - We can include this as *Post-bureauRiskCategory*="Decline"
- *ApplicantData.Age* <18
    - We can include this as *Post-bureauRiskCategory*="Decline"

Qualification is "Refer" if *all* of the following are true:
- *Qualification* is not "Decline"
- *Post-bureauRiskCategory* = "High" OR *BureauData.CreditScore*<580
    - We can combine these as *Post-bureauRiskCategory*="High"

Qualification is "Approve" if all of the following are true:
- *Qualification* is not "Decline"
- *Qualification* is not "Refer"

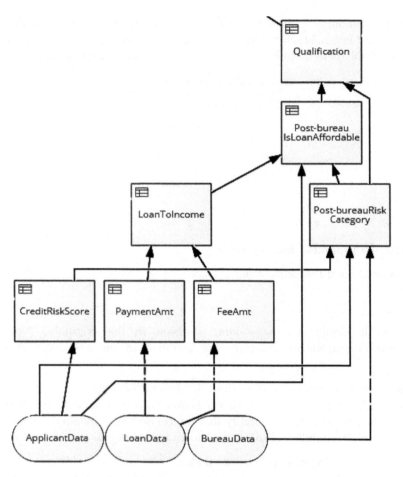

Figure 171. DRD decomposition, *Qualification*

The decision table for *Qualification* is shown in Figure 172. The decision table for *Post-bureauRiskCategory* is shown in Figure 173.

U	Post-bureauIsLoanAffordable ⓘ		Post-bureauRiskCategory ⓘ		Qualification
	Boolean		*{Decline,High,Medium,Low,Very Low}*		*{Approve, Decline, Refer}*
1	=	false		-	Decline
2	=	true	=	Decline	Decline
3	=	true	=	High	Refer
4	=	true	∈	{Medium, Low, Very Low}	Approve

Figure 172. *Qualification* decision table

U	ApplicantData.Age	...ata.hasBankruptcy	...sExistingCustomer	CreditRiskScore ⓘ	...uData.CreditScore	Post-bureauRiskCategory
	Number	Boolean	Boolean	Number	Number	(Decline, High, Medium, Low, Ver...
1	< 18	-	-	-	-	Decline
2	≥ 18	= true	-	-	-	Decline
3	≥ 18	= false	-	-	< 580	High
4	≥ 18	= false	= false	< 120	∈ [580..590)	High
5	≥ 18	= false	= false	< 120	∈ [590..610]	Medium
6	≥ 18	= false	= false	< 120	> 610	Low
7	≥ 18	= false	= false	∈ [120..130]	∈ [580..600)	High
8	≥ 18	= false	= false	∈ [120..130]	∈ [600..625]	Medium
9	≥ 18	= false	= false	∈ [120..130]	> 625	Low
10	≥ 18	= false	= false	> 130	≥ 580	Very Low
11	≥ 18	= false	= true	≤ 100	∈ [580..600]	Medium
12	≥ 18	= false	= true	≤ 100	> 600	Low
13	≥ 18	= false	= true	> 100	∈ [580..590)	High
14	≥ 18	= false	= true	> 100	∈ [590..615]	Medium
15	≥ 18	= false	= true	> 100	> 615	Low

Figure 173. *Post-bureauRiskCategory* decision table

This completes the decomposition of *Qualification*.

Summary of the Decomposition

The complete DRD decomposition for our revised Lending decision is shown in Figure 174.

- It has a single top-level decision node representing the business decision as a whole, with outcomes *Approved* and *Declined*.

- There are two major considerations, representing risk category and loan affordability. If all the input data required to determine the outcomes of these considerations, the first order decomposition would have those two branches.

- In this case, we prefer instead to approve or decline certain applicants without obtaining credit bureau data, requiring decision logic for some applicants to be executed twice. This changes the first-order decomposition, which now contains a *Prequalification* decision, which does not require *BureauData*; a *Qualification* decision, which does incorporate *BureauData*; and a third branch, *Adjudication*, representing a human decision using additional *SupportingDocuments*.

- The three-step execution of *Approval* is reflected in the DRD by overlaying rounded rectangles indicating decision services, one for *Prequalification* and another for *Qualification*. The decisions *LoanToIncome*, *CreditRiskScore*, *PaymentAmt*, and *FeeAmt* are common to both services.

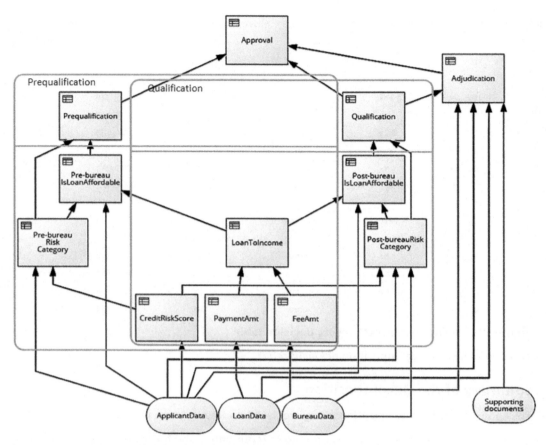

Figure 174. Fully decomposed DRD, showing decision services

- Even though under normal circumstances, *Qualification* and *Adjudication* are not executed (i.e., their outcome is *null*) if *Prequalification* either approves or declines the applicant, our top-level decision logic includes the possibility that they are executed, and gives them the proper relative priority.

- Decomposition of *Prequalification* and *Qualification* uses the original two major considerations, risk category and loan affordability. In *Prequalification*, the decisions are *Pre-bureauRiskCategory* and *Pre-bureauIsLoanAffordable*, and in *Qualification*, they are *Post-bureauRiskCategory* and *Post-bureauIsLoanAffordable*.

- Ideally, risk category and loan affordability are completely independent. However, in this example, the risk category affects the loan-to-income threshold for affordability, so we need to make the risk category decision a supporting decision of affordability.

- In order to flexibly weight the factors determining the risk category, we adopt the *category-score pattern*. In our decomposition, *CreditRiskScore* depends only on

ApplicantData, so we only execute it once, and use the result in both *Prequalification* and *Qualification*.

- In order to simplify the DRD while remaining faithful to the decision logic of the original, we needed to understand all the detailed conditions determining the outcomes of *Prequalification* and *Qualification*. Based on this, our intermediate risk category decisions are modeled slightly differently from the original.

- The affordability decisions compare an *arithmetic computation* to a threshold value determined by the risk category. The simplest way to model this would be a context, but in the interest of creating a CL2 solution, we broke out the computation into the decisions *LoanToIncome*, *PaymentAmt*, and *FeeAmt*.

- The *LoanToIncome* affordability threshold for various risk category values was hard-coded into the affordability decisions. In order to make those values more easily changed using "single-sourcing," we could have supplied them as additional input data or as a zero-input decision, e.g., *LTIThreshold.High*, *LTIThreshold.Medium*, etc.

CHAPTER 13

Data Modeling and Business Glossary

Decisions deal with information, that is to say, data. A rigorous program of decision management requires some form of standardization of the *business vocabulary*, the data element names, datatypes, domain of possible values, and relationship to other information elements. Experience with decision modeling methodologies such as TDM and DRA suggests this standardization should be focused on *business concepts* and not tied to details of physical databases and systems. Because DMN's default expression language FEEL is strongly typed, modelers executable of decision logic must pay attention to the datatype and allowed values of all variables referenced in DMN expressions.

Data Modeling for DMN

Logical Data Model

Data modeling is often associated with database design, and takes a variety of forms. So-called *conceptual data models* describe basic entities like *Customer, Order,* or *Claim* in business terms. These entities contain few attributes, but the models do indicate relationships between the entities. *Logical data models* specify the entities more completely, including their datatypes, attributes, optionality (required or not), and cardinality (more than one allowed), but independent of database design, storage location, or other technical characteristics captured in *physical data models*.

By this definition, the data modeling required for DMN would be classified as a *logical data model*.

A popular form of logical data model is the *Entity-Relationship (E-R) Diagram*, for which there are many different notations. The *Crow's Foot Notation* illustrated in Figure 175 reveals the cardinality of the relationships between entities (via the various tickmarks and "crow's feet"), but does not elaborate on the datatype or allowed values of the attributes, which are important in DMN.

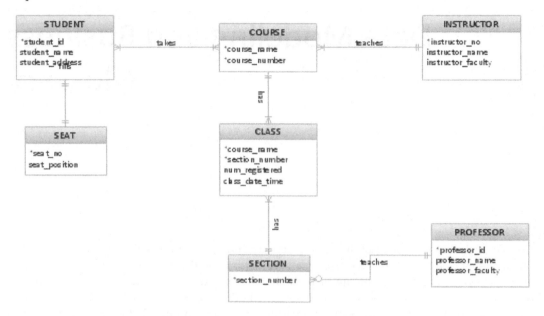

Figure 175. E-R Diagram with Crow's Foot Notation. Source: ConceptDraw[90]

For use in executable DMN models (CL2 or CL3), E-R models such as Figure 175 must first be translated either into FEEL or a DMN-importable data model format such as XSD.

DMN Data Models

Every *variable* referenced in a DMN expression must specify a *typeRef* defining its datatype, which may be one of the following:

- A *base type* of the specified *type language*. For FEEL (the default), the base types are string, number, Boolean, date, time, and two types of duration. For base types, allowed values include the full domain of the type.

- A *custom type*, called an *item definition*. An item definition is either a *simple type* (base type, imported type, or another item definition) restricted to a set of *allowed values*, or a list of *item components* specifying a *complex type*, i.e., a data structure. An item definition may also indicate that it represents a *collection*, i.e., a list. Each item component is a named component of the item definition. The component's datatype is another *typeRef*, either a simple type (possibly with specified allowed values), or a nested list of item components. This nesting allows a DMN variable to be an

---

[90] http://www.conceptdraw.com/How-To-Guide/picture/Entity-relationship-diagram-crows-foot-notation.png

arbitrarily complex data structure. Because item definitions are referenced by name in the DMN schema, their names must be valid XML names containing no spaces, unique in their namespace.

- An item definition defined in an *imported DMN* model. There is no need to declare the item definition in the importing DMN model. A *typeRef* simply references it by namespace-qualified name (QName).

- A datatype defined in an *imported XML Schema Document* (XSD). Again, there is no need to declare the item definition in the importing DMN model. A *typeRef* simply references it by QName. XSD types are automatically mapped to the FEEL domain for use in FEEL expressions.

	Group	Make	Model
cars	"G1"	"Ford"	"Pickup"
	"G1"	"Ford"	"T"
	"G1"	"Ford"	"Taurus"
	"G1"	"Austin"	"Mini"
	"G1"	"Hyundai"	"Santa Fe"
	"G2"	"Ford"	"Pickup"
	"G2"	"Ford"	"T"
	"G2"	"Ford"	"Taurus"
	"G2"	"Hyundai"	"Tucson"
	"G2"	"Hyundai"	"Santa Fe"

Figure 176. Boxed expression representation of a relation in a DMN context element. Source: Gary Hallmark, via DMCommunity[91]

A boxed expression format for item definitions was suggested in DMN 1.1 but did not make it into the final specification. Each tool, therefore, must provide its own user interface for defining and visualizing structured data. The spec does, however, define a boxed expression representation of *instance data*, such as a data table (*relation*) referenced in decision logic (Figure 176), or an *instance of input data* used for logic testing (Figure 177).

---

[91] https://dmcommunity.files.wordpress.com/2015/09/garyhallmarkcars.pdf

applicant	age		51
	maritalStatus		"M"
	existingCustomer		false
	monthly	income	10000
		repayments	2500
		expenses	3000
requested product	product type		"STANDARD LOAN"
	rate		0.25
	term		36
	amount		100000.00

Figure 177. Boxed expression representation of input data. Source: OMG

XSD Data Models

XML Schema (XSD) provides a convenient alternative to FEEL for modeling datatypes, data tables, and instances of input data. While XSD is a tagged text format with no standard graphical representation, XML tools typically provide such graphical representations, which are more user-friendly.

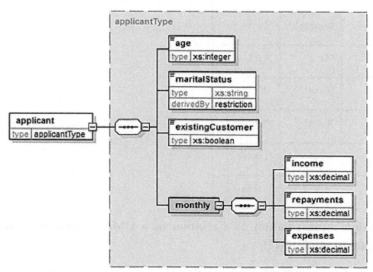

Figure 178. As an alternative to an item definition with item components, *applicantType* could be defined in XSD and imported into DMN.

For example, Figure 178 is a graphical representation of the XSD complex type *applicantType* in Altova XMLSpy. Note that *maritalStatus* is a string with a *restriction*, in this case the enumerated values "M" and "S". XSD provides a richer and more varied array of possible restrictions, including *regular expression patterns*, than does DMN's enumeration of item definition allowed values. While DMN specifies how XSD basic types are mapped to FEEL types, modelers should not assume that restrictions on those types are mapped to FEEL. If *maritalStatus*, for example, is used in a decision table, it might be best to enumerate the allowed input values explicitly in the decision table, even though they are already specified in the imported schema.

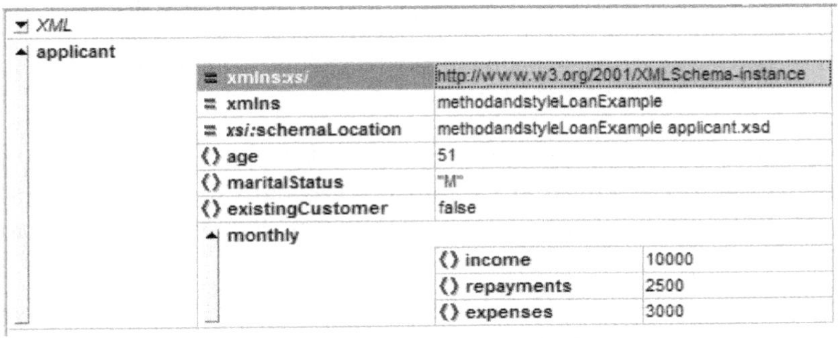

Figure 179. Instance of input data *applicant* specified in imported XML document, as displayed in XMLSpy Grid view

As an alternative to the FEEL definition shown in Figure 177, Figure 179 shows an instance of the input data *applicant* as defined in an imported XML document and displayed in XMLSpy Grid view. Note the namespace *methodandstyleLoanExample*. In the importing DMN model, any expression referencing applicant would need to prefix it with the namespace, for example:

```
methodandstyleLoanExample.applicantData.maritalStatus.
```

Business Glossary

I don't think anything has stirred up as much angst in the BDM community as the news that DMN 1.1 would not be providing a specification for a *business glossary*.[92] The RTF's position, which I agree with, is that the DMN metamodel and schema already contain all the elements needed to construct a business glossary, and that any further specification of the glossary's metadata, user interface, or access methods would likely be ignored by tool vendors.

While most modeling tool vendors and consultants seem to believe that some sort of decision-oriented business glossary is a good thing, there is no common agreement as to what it should include.

Take TDM, for example. In the book, a sample *Fact Type Glossary* is simply a list of *Fact Types*, specifying just the name and descriptive text. According to the book,

> "The benefit of creating a glossary of fact types is that businesspeople, rather
> than business analysts or technical people, are at ease with maintaining and

---

[92] https://www.linkedin.com/groups/4225568/4225568-6021429200609701890

consulting a dictionary-like form of the glossary, and it provides rigor to a corresponding Decision Model." [93]

In DMN terms, a Fact Type is a variable or a sub-element of a variable (qualified name). For example, the Fact Type *Insured Board Change* (in DMN Method and Style, *Insured.BoardChangeInd*) is defined in the glossary as:

> "**Insured Board Change**: An indicator for a named insured to denote a change in the board of directors of the named insured that may contribute to determining risk. Such changes may include the resignation or addition of one or more board members."[94]

The book distinguishes such a Fact Type Glossary from a *Fact Model*, which is effectively a logical data model of Fact Types, as described in the previous section: a diagram specifying the datatype and allowed values. But it then goes on to say that the Fact Model may *replace* the Fact Type Glossary, particularly when the decisions will be automated.

Name	Data Type
Auto Additional Coverage Annual Premium	AMOUNT
Auto Age Annual Premium	AMOUNT
Auto Age in Years	QUANTITY
Auto Airbag Risk	CODE
Auto Annual Premium	AMOUNT
Auto Base Annual Premium	AMOUNT
Auto Body Style	INDICATOR
Auto Body Style Risk	INDICATOR
Auto Classification	CODE

Figure 180. Sapiens DECISION glossary example. Source: Sapiens DECISION[95]

So should a business glossary include datatype specifications or not? Even within TDM, it's not always clear. The company that developed TDM was acquired by Sapiens DECISION in 2014, and in response to the UServ Product Derby Challenge posted on DMCommunity in December 2014,[96] the Sapiens solution included the "business glossary" shown in Figure 180, a table of datatypes.

---

[93] von Halle and Goldberg, *TDM*, 392.

[94] von Halle and Goldberg, *TDM*, Table 7.7, 160.

[95] https://dmcommunity.files.wordpress.com/2015/05/sapiens-decision-document-userv-product-derby-case-study.pdf

[96] https://dmcommunity.wordpress.com/challenge/challenge-dec-2014/

All of this is merely to establish the point that a business glossary can take many forms, appropriate for different user populations, and that it was sensible for DMN not to try to standardize its content or format. Figure 181 below summarizes the DMN metamodel elements that can be used to populate a glossary. The user interface for such a glossary and data model will depend on the DMN tool.

DMN Elements Supporting a Glossary and Data Model

Element	Description
variable / itemComponent name	The *name* of the *variable* representing the value of a *DRG element* such as a *decision, business knowledge model,* or *input data* must be the same as the name of the DRG element. The name of a business knowledge model also serves as the name of the reusable function definition it represents. Elements of structured variables, called *item components*, are referenced by *qualified name*, for example, *ApplicantData.monthlyIncome*. In a *context*, each *context entry* also defines a local variable with the scope of the context. Each *parameter* of a BKM also represents a local variable with the scope of the BKM.
[parent]	The parent element of a variable determines its scope. Parent elements containing variables include decision, input data element, business knowledge model, and context.
namespace	The names of imported variables and types must be namespace-qualified. In FEEL, qualification uses a dot notation, for example, *methodandstyleLibrary.ApplicantData.monthlyIncome*.
description	DMN includes a *description* element for each Information Item.
datatype, with optional type language	The variable's *typeRef* attribute is a pointer to its datatype. Base types in the specified *type language* are identified by name. Custom types, either with specified *allowed values* or *item components*, are specified by the name of an *item definition* containing the type specification. Imported XSD types are specified by qualified name.
allowed values	Variables and item components represented by simple types may specify a list of *allowed values*. These may be enumerated literal values, or, for number, date, time, and duration types, ranges.

Figure 181. DMN metamodel elements supporting a glossary and data model

CHAPTER 14

Example: Auto Insurance Premium

UServ Product Derby

At the Business Rules Forum conference over a decade ago, Business Rule Engine vendors were challenged to demonstrate their capabilities by modeling a decision scenario called the *UServ Product Derby*. In November 2014, the DMCommunity website reprised that challenge[97] online and published 7 submitted solutions.[98] We'll model the scenario here using DMN Method and Style, and you can compare it to the other solutions posted on DMCommunity.

The scenario determines eligibility and annual premium for automobile insurance. The decision scenario is specified as a list of business rules. Our solution features a single DRD for the end-to-end decision logic, and uses the FEEL *iteration pattern* to aggregate the contributions of multiple automobiles and drivers on the policy.

UServ is a fictional provider of insurance and banking products. According to the scenario,

> "UServ plays a balancing act between rewarding their best clients and managing the risk inherent in providing on-going service to clients whose portfolios are profitable, but violate the eligibility rules of individual products.... The business rules address eligibility, pricing and cancellation policies at both the individual product and portfolio level. This case study focuses on UServ's vehicle insurance products, but differentiates the basic business rules from those that apply to preferred and elite clients." [99]

---

[97] https://dmcommunity.wordpress.com/2014/11/25/userv-product-derby-is-getting-second-life-as-a-dm-challenge/

[98] https://dmcommunity.wordpress.com/challenge/challenge-dec-2014/

[99] http://ai.ia.agh.edu.pl/wiki/_media/hekate:2005_product_derby.pdf

The main portion of the scenario deals with eligibility and base pricing for an automobile insurance policy covering multiple automobiles and multiple drivers. Our DMN solution deals only with that.

Rules

The decision requirements were specified as sets of business rules determining eligibility and pricing based on the type of vehicle being insured and the characteristics of the drivers. The rules are summarized below.

Automobile – Potential Theft Category

- If the car is a convertible, then the car's potential theft rating is high.

- If the car's price is greater than $45,000, then the car's potential theft rating is high.

- If the car model is on the list of "High Theft Probability Auto", then the car's potential theft rating is high.

- If all of the following are true, then the car's potential theft rating is moderate.
    - car's price is between $20,000 and $45,000,
    - car model is not on the list of "High Theft Probability Auto"

- If all of the following are true, then the car's potential theft rating is low:
    - car's price is less than $20,000
    - car model is not on the list of "High Theft Probability Auto"

Automobile – Potential Occupant Injury Category

- If the car has no airbags, then the car's potential occupant injury rating is extremely high.

- If the car only has driver's air bag, then the car's potential occupant injury rating is high.

- If the car has driver's and front passenger air bags, then the car's potential occupant injury rating is moderate.

- If the car has driver's front passenger and side panel air bags, then the car's potential occupant injury is low.

- If the car is a convertible and has no roll bar, then the potential occupant injury is extremely high.

Automobile Eligibility

- If the Potential Occupant Injury Rating is extremely high, then the auto eligibility is "not eligible".

- If the Potential Occupant Injury Rating is high, then the auto eligibility is "provisional".

- If the Potential Theft Rating is high, then the auto eligibility is "provisional".

- If none of the following is true, then the auto eligibility is "eligible"
  - Auto eligibility is "not eligible"
  - Auto eligibility is "provisional"

Driver – Age Category

- If the driver is male and is under the age of 25, then young driver.

- If the driver is female and is under the age of 20, then young driver.

- If young driver and driver has training certification, then eligible driver.

- If the driver is over the age of 70, then senior driver.

- If senior driver and driver has training certification, then eligible driver.

- If the following are not true, then eligible driver
  - Young driver
  - Senior driver

- If driver has taken driver's training from school then driver has training certification.

- If driver has taken driver's training from a licensed driver training company, then driver has training certification.

- If driver had taken a senior citizen driver's refresher course, then driver has training certification.

Driver – Driving Record Category

- If the driver has been convicted of a DUI, then the driver qualifies as a High Risk Driver

- If the number of accidents the applicant has been involved in is greater than 2, then the driver qualifies as a High Risk Driver.

- If the driver has had more than 3 moving violations in the last two years, then the driver qualifies as a High Risk Driver.

Eligibility Scoring

Eligibility for insurance is determined by scoring the various categories (Figure 182). The lower the score, the better the eligibility rating.

	Rating	Eligibility Score
For each Auto:	Not eligible	+100
	Provisional	+50
	Eligible	+0
For each Driver	Young, not Eligible	+30
	Senior, not Eligible	+20
	Eligible	+0
	High Risk	+100

Figure 182. UServ Product Derby Eligibility Scoring

- If eligibility score is less than 100, then client is eligible for insurance

- If eligibility score is between 100 and 250 inclusive, then the client's application/policy renewal must be reviewed by underwriting manager who will determine whether the client is eligible for auto insurance.

- If eligibility score is greater than 250, the client is not eligible for auto insurance.

- If a long term client, the client is always eligible for auto insurance, as is every person and car directly covered by a long term client's auto policy. A long term client has maintained a UServ portfolio for 15 years.

Premium – For Each Automobile

- If compact car, then base premium is $250.

- If sedan, then base premium is $400.

- If luxury car, then base premium is $500.

- If car is new, then increase premium by $400.

- If the model year is the same as the current year, then new car.

- If the model year is the same as next year, then the car is new.

- If car is less than 5 years old, then increase premium by $300.

- If car is between 5 and 10 years old, then increase premium by $250.

- If uninsured motorist coverage is included, then increase premium by $300.

- If medical coverage is included, then increase premium by $600.

- If Potential Occupant Injury is Extremely High, then increase premium by $1,000.

- If Potential Occupant Injury is High, then increase premium by $500.

- If Potential Theft is High, then increase premium by $500.

Premium – Automobile Discounts

- If the car only has Driver airbags then lower the premium by 12 %.

- If the car has Driver and Passenger airbags then lower the premium by 15 %.

- If the car has Driver, Passenger and Side airbags then lower the premium by 18 %.

- If the car's potential theft rating is high and the car is equipped with an alarm system, then lower the premium by 10%.

Accumulate all applicable discount percentages before applying to the automobile premium.

Premium – For Each Driver

- If young driver and married and located in CA, NY, or VA, then increase premium by $700.

- If young driver and single and located in CA, NY, or VA, then increase premium by $720.

- If young driver and married and not located in CA, NY, or VA, then increase premium by $300.

- If young driver and single and not located in CA, NY, or VA, then increase premium by $300.

- If senior driver and located in CA, NY, or VA, then increase premium by $500.

- If senior driver and not located in CA, NY, or VA, then increase premium by $200.

- Driver is a Typical Driver is all of the following are true:
  o Not a Young Driver
  o Not a Senior Driver

- If a Typical Driver, then increase premium by $0.

- If a High Risk Driver, then increase premium by $1,000.

- Raise the premium by $ 150 per accident

Fact Model

The scenario conveniently also provides a Fact Model (Figure 183). The triangle arrowheads denote subtypes of the entity. The V arrowheads denote attributes.

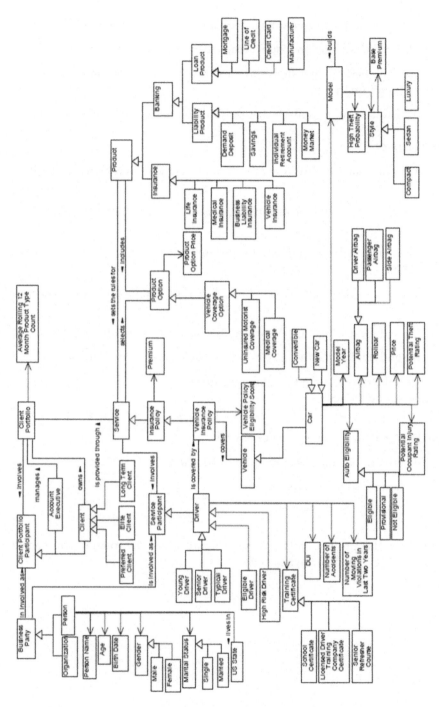

Figure 183. UServ Product Derby Fact Model. Source: BusinessRules Forum

Decision Process

The decision process, redrawn in proper BPMN Method and Style, is shown in Figure 184.

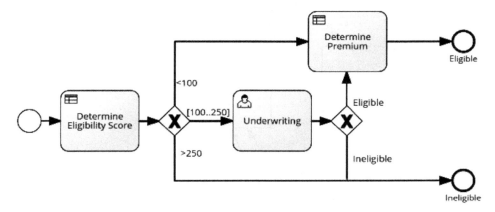

Figure 184. UServ Product Derby decision process

First-Order Decomposition

We will use the scenario to construct our decision model using DMN Method and Style.

The business decision as a whole, let's call it *AutoPolicy*, contains two components: *isEligible*, a Boolean; and *Premium*, a number. If *isEligible* is false, *Premium* is *null*. In this case, *isEligible* and *Premium* are separate and reasonably complex decisions, so they should be separated in the first-order decomposition. Here *isEligible* is based on *EligibilityScore, Underwriting,* and an input data element *isLongTermClient*.

The first-order decomposition of the decision model is shown in Figure 185, and the decision tables for *AutoPolicy* and *isEligible* are shown in Figure 186. Even though the process determined in decision discovery indicates *Underwriting* only occurs for *EligibilityScore* values between 100 and 250, the decision logic gives it precedence over the *EligibilityScore* in all cases.

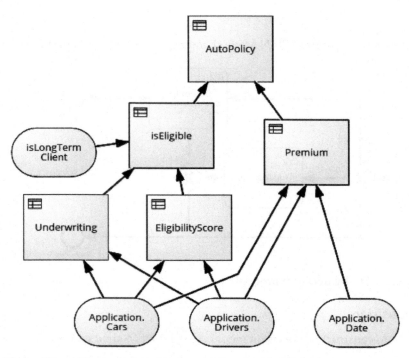

Figure 185. UServ *AutoPolicy* DRD, first-order decomposition

AutoPolicy			
U	isEligible	AutoPolicy	
		isEligible	Premium
1	TRUE	TRUE	Premium
2	FALSE	FALSE	null

isEligible				
U	isLongTermClient	Underwriting	EligibilityScore	isEligible
1	TRUE	-	-	TRUE
2	FALSE	"Eligible"	-	TRUE
3	FALSE	"Ineligible"	-	FALSE
4	FALSE	null	<100	TRUE
5	FALSE	null	>250	FALSE

Figure 186. UServ *AutoPolicy* and *isEligible*, top-level decision logic

Fact Model

The Fact Model supplied by the scenario (Figure 183) helps us create our own FEEL fact model applicable for this decision. It is best practice to separate the input data fact types from the outputs and parameters of decisions and BKMs. In this case, we have an application for insurance containing a list of drivers and cars, and a submission date. The *Application* fact model then looks something like this:

Application
- *Date* [date]
- *Cars* [isCollection]
  - Make-Model [string]
  - ModelYear [number]
  - Style [string, allowed values "compact", "sedan", "luxury"]
  - Price [number]
  - isConvertible [Boolean]
  - hasDriverAirbags [Boolean]
  - hasPassengerAirbags [Boolean]
  - hasSideAirbags [Boolean]
  - hasRollbar [Boolean]
  - has Alarm [Boolean]
  - PolicyOptions.UninsuredMotorist [Boolean]
  - PolicyOptions.Medical [Boolean]
- *Drivers* [isCollection]
  - Name [string]
  - Age [number]
  - Gender [string, allowed values "M", "F"]
  - isMarried [Boolean]
  - StateCode [string]
  - TrainingCertificateType [string, allowed values "School", "Certified training co", "Senior refresher", "None or other"]
  - hasDUI [Boolean]
  - ViolationCount [number]
  - AccidentCount [number]

In addition, we have two more input data elements:
isLongTermClient [Boolean]
HighTheftList [isCollection, string naming Make-Model]

The decision logic defines a number of additional fact types, including:

For each driver:
AgeCategory [string, allowed values "Young", "Senior", "Typical"]
hasTrainingCertification [Boolean]
isHighRiskDriver [Boolean]
isEligibleDriver [Boolean]

For each car:
onHighTheftList [Boolean]
PotentialTheftCategory [string, allowed values "High", "Moderate", "Low"]

PotentialOccupantInjuryCategory [string, allowed values "Extremely high", "High", "Moderate", "Low"]

AutoEligibilityRating [string, allowed values "Eligible", "Provisional", "Not eligible"]

EligibilityScore without Iteration

From the scenario, the *EligibilityScore* depends on the *AutoEligibilityRating* of each car on the policy, combined with various derived attributes of each driver. What makes this complicated is that the decision logic must be *iterated* over each car and driver. If the application involves a single automobile and a single driver, the logic is straightforward. We'll start there, and then add the iteration afterward.

Assuming one automobile and one driver, the business rules suggest the following decomposition of *EligibilityScore*:

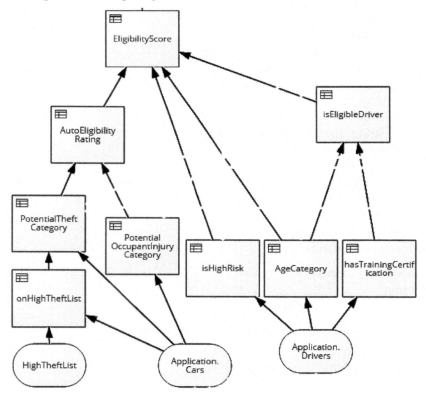

Figure 187. DRD decomposition of *EligibilityScore* (assuming one car, one driver)

Automobile Component

Figure 188 and Figure 189 show the decision tables for the two categories supporting the *AutoEligibilityRating* decision. The Boolean decision *onHighTheftList* is a table lookup, as described in Chapter 11. The input data *HighTheftList* is simply a list of high-theft automobiles, specified by make-model. So *onHighTheftList* is simply the literal expression,

```
if Application.Cars.Make-model in HighTheftList then true else false
```

U	onHighTheftList ⓘ		Application.Cars.Price		Application.Cars.IsConvertible		PotentialTheftCategory
	Boolean		*Currency ($)*		*Boolean*		*{High,Moderate,Low}*
1	=	true		-		-	High
2	=	false	>	$ 45000		-	High
3	=	false	≤	$ 45000	=	true	High
4	=	false	∈	$ [20000..45000]	=	false	Moderate
5	=	false	<	$ 20000	=	false	Low

Figure 188. Decision table, *PotentialTheftCategory*

The logic of Figure 188 has a hit policy of *Unique*, but for Figure 189, the added complexity of a *Unique* table may not be worth it, so in this case we've broken the usual style rule and used a hit policy of *Priority*. While the rules in the scenario don't explicitly cover all combinations of automobile attributes, the clear implication is that combinations resulting in a higher risk category take precedence over those resulting in a lower risk category, and the *Priority* hit policy does this.

P	...s.hasDriverAirbags		...sPassengerAirbags		...ars.hasSideAirbags		...on.Cars.hasRollbar		....Cars.isConvertible		...OccupantInjuryCategory
	Boolean		*Boolean*		*Boolean*		*Boolean*		*Boolean*		*{ExtremelyHigh,High,Moderat...*
1	=	false	=	false	=	false		-		-	ExtremelyHigh
2		-		-		-	=	false	=	true	ExtremelyHigh
3	=	true	=	false	=	false		-		-	High
4	=	true	=	true	=	false		-		-	Moderate
5	=	true	=	true	=	true		-		-	Low

Figure 189. Decision table, *PotentialOccupantInjuryCategory*

Figure 190 shows the decision table for *AutoEligibilityRating*, once again organized to allow a *Unique* hit policy.

U	Potential OccupantInjury Categ...		PotentialTheft Category ⓘ		AutoEligibilityRating
	{ExtremelyHigh,High,Moderate,Low}		*{High,Moderate,Low}*		*{Not eligible,Provisional,Eligible}*
1	=	ExtremelyHigh		-	Not eligible
2	=	High		-	Provisional
3	∈	{Moderate, Low}	=	High	Provisional
4	∈	{Moderate, Low}	∈	{Moderate, Low}	Eligible

Figure 190. Decision table, *AutoEligibilityRating*

Driver Component

Figure 191 through Figure 193 show decision tables for the Boolean decisions supporting eligibility for each driver, *isHighRisk, hasTrainingCertification,* and *DriverAgeCategory.*

U	Application.Drivers.hasDUI		Application.Drivers.Ac...		Application.Drivers.Viol...		IsHighRisk
	Boolean		Number		Number		Boolean
1	=	true	-		-		true
2	=	false	>	2	-		true
3	=	false	≤	2	>	3	true
4	=	false	≤	2	≤	3	false

Figure 191. Decision table, *isHighRisk*

U	Application.Drivers.TrainingCertificateType		hasTrainingCertification
	{"School","Certified trainer","Senior refresher","None or other"}		Boolean
1	∈	{"School", "Certified trainer", "Senior refresher"}	true
2	=	"None or other"	false

Figure 192. Decision table, *hasTrainingCertification*

U	Application.Drivers.G...		Application.Drivers.Age		AgeCategory
	{"M","F"}		Number		{"Young","Senior","Typical"}
1	=	"M"	<	25	"Young"
2	=	"M"	∈	[25..70]	"Typical"
3	=	"F"	<	20	"Young"
4	=	"F"	∈	[20..70]	"Typical"
5		-	>	70	"Senior"

Figure 193. Decision table, *AgeCategory*

U	AgeCategory	hasTrainingCertificat...	IsEligibleDriver
	{"Young","Senior","Typical"}	Boolean	Boolean
1	= "Young"	= true	true
2	= "Senior"	= true	true
3	= "Typical"	-	true
4	= "Senior"	= false	false
5	= "Young"	= false	false

Figure 194. Decision table, *isEligibleDriver*

Based on these decisions, the *EligibilityScore* decision table for an application with one driver and one car is shown in Figure 195. The hit policy indicates multi-hit, collect and sum.

C+	AutoEligibility Rating	IsHighRisk	IsEligibleDriver	AgeCategory	EligibilityScore
	{Not eligible,Provisional,El...}	Boolean	Boolean	{"Young","Senior","Typical"}	[0..1000]
1	= Not eligible	-	-	-	100
2	= Provisional	-	-	-	50
3	= Eligible	-	-	-	0
4	-	= true	-	-	100
5	-	-	= false	= "Young"	30
6	-	-	= false	= "Senior"	20
7	-	-	= true	-	0

Figure 195. Decision table, *EligibilityScore* (assuming one car, one driver)

Premium without Iteration

In similar fashion, we can compute the *Premium* assuming one car and one driver. The DRD is shown in Figure 196. Several of the supporting decisions of *EligibilityScore* are also supporting decisions of *Premium*. This will add a bit more complexity when it comes time to iterate over cars and drivers on the application.

Car Component

The car component of the premium depends on both input data and attributes determined by intermediate decisions. The intermediate decisions shown below illustrate the fact that conditional decision logic does not always require a decision table; it may also be modeled as literal expression:

Base:

```
if car.Style="compact" then $250 else if car.Style="sedan" then $400
    else if car.Style="luxury" then $500
```

CarAgeCategory:

```
if Application.Date.Year - car.ModelYear in [-1..0] then "New" else
    if Application.Date.Year - car.ModelYear in (0..5] then "Recent"
    else if Application.Date.Year - car.ModelYear in (5..10] then
    "Older" else "Really old"
```

CarAgePremium:

```
if CarAgeCategory = "New" then $400 else if CarAgeCategory = "Recent"
    then $300 else if CarAgeCategory = "Older" then $250 else 0
```

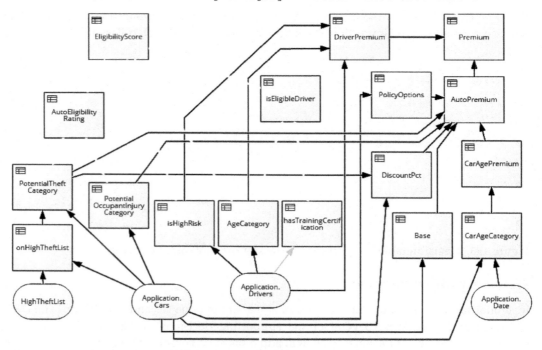

Figure 196. DRD, *Premium* decision, assuming one car, one driver

We can also use a *context* to model the decision logic as a literal expression of intermediate variables (Figure 197):

PolicyOptionsPremium	
UninsuredPremium	if PolicyOptions.UninsuredMotorist=true then $300 else 0
MedicalPremium	if PolicyOptions.Medical=true then $600 else 0
UninsuredPremium + MedicalPremium	

DiscountPct	
AirbagDiscountPct	if hasDriverAirbags=true and hasPassengerAirbags=false and hasSideAirbags=false then .12 else if hasDriverAirbags=true and hasPassengerAirbags=true and hasSideAirbags=false then .15 else if hasDriverAirbags=true and hasPassengerAirbags=true and hasSideAirbags=true then .18 else 0
AlarmDiscountPct	if PotentialTheftCategory="High" and hasAlarm=true then .10 else 0
AirbagDiscountPct + AlarmDiscountPct	

Figure 197. Boxed expressions for *PolicyOptions* and *DiscountPct*, assuming one car

The *AutoPremium* decision logic (Figure 198) pulls in the supporting decisions *PotentialOccupantInjuryCategory* and *PotentialTheftCategory* and sums all the components.

AutoPremium	
Injury	if PotentialOccupantInjuryCategory="ExtremelyHigh" then $1000 else if PotentialOccupantInjuryCategory="High" then $500 else 0
Theft	if PotentialTheftCategory="High" then $500 else 0
(Base + CarAgePremium + PolicyOptions + Injury + Theft) * (1 - DiscountPct)	

Figure 198. Boxed expression for *AutoPremium*, one car

Driver Component

The driver component of *Premium* is given by the decision table of Figure 199, with hit policy *Collect and sum*.

DriverPremium						
C+	AgeCategory	StateCode	isMarried	isHighRisk	AccidentCount	
1	"Young"	CA, NY, VA	TRUE	-	-	$700
2	"Young"	CA, NY, VA	FALSE	-	-	$720
3	"Young"	not(CA, NY, VA)	-	-	-	$300
4	"Senior"	CA, NY, VA	-	-	-	$500
5	"Senior"	not(CA, NY, VA)	-	-	-	$200
6	"Typical"	-	-	-	-	0
7	-	-	-	TRUE	-	$1,000
8	-	-	-	-	-	AccidentCount * $150

Figure 199. Boxed expression for *DriverPremium*, one driver

Adding Iteration

We first looked at the DRD decomposition without iteration in order to better understand the dependencies among the decision logic elements. Now we need to add the iteration. DMN can handle iteration over multiple cars and drivers in a single DRD, but it requires significant restructuring of the diagram. We need to iteratively call the *AutoPremium* logic in a BKM, once for each car, and we need to iteratively call the *DriverPremium* logic in a second BKM, once for each driver. Certain intermediate decisions in Figure 196 are used in both BKMs, adding further complexity.

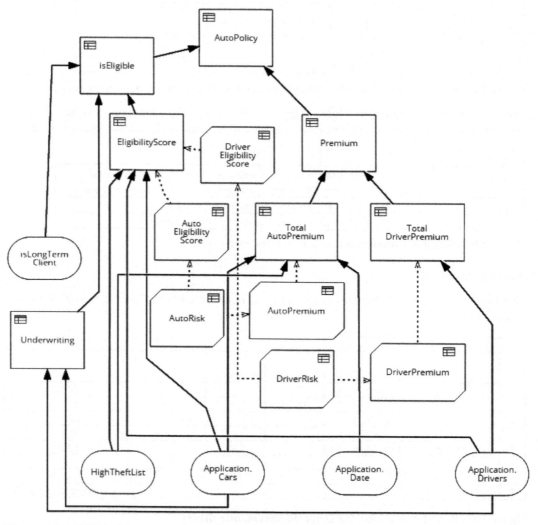

Figure 200. DRD of *AutoPolicy* decision, including iteration

In FEEL, iteration can be accomplished using the *for..return* construct as described in Chapter 11, for example:

```
for car in Application.Cars return AutoPremium(car)
```

Referring back to the input data structure, we see that *Application.Cars* is a list. Here *car* is a dummy index into that list, meaning just a single car in that list. The *for..return* expression means execute the BKM *AutoPremium* for each *car* in that list, and return a *list* of *AutoPremiums*, one per car. The *TotalAutoPremium* decision sums that list.

The structure of the end-to-end DRD now looks like Figure 200. Most of the decision logic is inside the BKMs *AutoEligibilityScore, DriverEligibilityScore, AutoPremium,* and *DriverPremium,* each of which computes an eligibility score or premium amount for a single car or driver. The decision *isEligible* iteratively invokes the eligibility BKMs, and the decision *TotalAutoPremium* and *TotalDriverPremium* iteratively invoke the premium BKMs. Certain supporting decisions in Figure 187 and Figure 196 are used in both the eligibility BKMs and the premium BKMs. These are consolidated into the BKMs *AutoRisk* and *DriverRisk* in Figure 200, which are invoked by the parent BKMs.

Unfortunately, in DMN 1.1, a BKM must be a single value expression, not a DRD.[100] Its details, which can be complex, must be described instead as a boxed context. Non-standard DMN extensions, such as Signavio's MID described previously, allow a more CL2-like alternative.

AutoRisk						
(car)						
onHighTheftList	if car.Make-model in HighTheftList then true else false;					

PotentialTheftCategory	U	onHighTheftList	car.Price	car.isConvertible	
	1	TRUE	-	-	High
	2	FALSE	>$45000	-	High
	3	FALSE	<=$45000	TRUE	High
	4	FALSE	$[20000..45000]	FALSE	Moderate
	5	FALSE	<$20000	FALSE	Low

PotentialOccupant InjuryCategory	P	car.hasDriverAirbags	car.hasPassengerAirbags	car.hasSideAirbags	car.hasRollbar	car.isConvertible	
	1	FALSE	FALSE	FALSE	-	-	ExtremelyHigh
	2	-	-	-	FALSE	TRUE	ExtremelyHigh
	3	TRUE	FALSE	FALSE	-	-	High
	4	TRUE	TRUE	FALSE	-	-	Moderate
	5	TRUE	TRUE	TRUE	-	-	Low

AutoEligibility	U	PotentialOccupant InjuryCategory	PotentialTheft Category	
	1	ExtremelyHigh	-	Not eligible
	2	High	-	Provisional
	3	Moderate, Low	High	Provisional
	4	Moderate, Low	Moderate, Low	Eligible

Figure 201. BKM *AutoRisk*

---

[100] A proposal to allow this was deferred to DMN 1.2.

The BKM *AutoRisk* (Figure 201) is modeled as a context containing the decision logic for *onHighTheftList*, a table lookup, and *PotentialTheftCategory*, *PotentialOccupantInjuryCategory*, and *AutoEligibility*, all decision tables.

DriverRisk	
(driver)	
AgeCategory	if ((driver.Gender="M" and driver.Age<25) or (driver.Gender="F" and driver.Age<20)) then "Young" else if driver.Age>70 then "Senior" else "Typical"
hasTrainingCertificate	if driver.TrainingCertificateType in {"School", "Certified trainer", "Senior refresher"} then true else false
isHighRisk	if (driver.hasDUI = true and driver.AccidentCount>2 and driver.ViolationCount>3) then true else false
isEligibleDriver	if ((driver.AgeCategory="Young" and driver.hasTrainingCertificate=true) or (driver.AgeCategory="Senior" and driver.hasTrainingCertificate=true) or (driver.AgeCategory="Typical")) then true else false

Figure 202. BKM *DriverRisk*

The BKM *DriverRisk* (Figure 202) is also a context. It defines *AgeCategory*, *hasTrainingCertificate*, *isHighRisk*, and *isEligibleDriver* using literal expressions.

AutoEligibilityScore		
(car)		
Risk	AutoRisk	
	thisCar	car
if Risk.AutoEligibility="Not eligible" then 100 else if Risk.AutoEligibility="Provisional" then 50 else 0		

Figure 203. BKM *AutoEligibilityScore*, which invokes *AutoRisk*

In the *AutoEligibilityScore* BKM (Figure 203), the context entry *Risk* invokes the *AutoRisk* BKM. The child element *AutoEligibility* determines a numeric score. Similarly, in *DriverEligibilityScore* (Figure 204), the context entry *DriverInfo* invokes the *DriverRisk* BKM, and the child elements are used to determine a numeric score.

DriverEligibilityScore		
(driver)		
DriverInfo	DriverRisk	
	thisDriver	driver
HighRisk	if DriverInfo.isHighRisk=true then 100 else 0	
AgeScore	if DriverInfo.isEligibleDriver=false and DriverInfo.AgeCategory="Young" then 30 else if DriverInfo.isEligibleDriver=false and DriverInfo.AgeCategory="Senior" then 20 else 0	
HighRisk + AgeScore		

Figure 204. BKM *DriverEligibilityScore*, which invokes *DriverRisk*

The *AutoPremium* BKM (Figure 205) determines the premium for a single car, including discounts. Context entries determine the various premium components. Once again, the context entry *Risk* invokes the BKM *AutoRisk*, and child elements are used to compute premium components. The final result box sums the premium components.

AutoPremium	
(car)	
BasePrem	if car.Style="compact" then $250 else if car.Style="sedan" then $400 else if car.Style="luxury" then $500 else $0
CarAgeCategory	if Application.Date.Year - car.ModelYear in [-1..0] then "New" else if Application.Date.Year - car.ModelYear in (0..5] then "Recent" else if Application.Date.Year - car.ModelYear in (5..10] then "Older" else if Application.Date.Year - car.ModelYear >10 then "Really old"
AgePrem	if CarAgeCategory="New" then $400 else if CarAgeCategory="Recent" then $300 else if CarAgeCategory="Older" then $250 else 0
UninsuredPrem	if car.PolicyOptions.UninsuredMotorist=true then $300 else 0
MedicalPrem	if car.PolicyOptions.Medical=true then $600 else 0

Risk	AutoRisk	
	thisCar	car

InjuryPrem	if Risk.PotentialOccupantInjuryCategory="ExtremelyHigh" then $1000 else if Risk.PotentialOccupantInjuryCategory="High" then $500 else 0
TheftPrem	if Risk.PotentialTheftCategory="High" then $500 else 0
AirbagDiscountPct	if car.hasDriverAirbags=true and car.hasPassengerAirbags=false and car.hasSideAirbags=false then .12 else if car.hasDriverAirbags=true and car.hasPassengerAirbags=true and car.hasSideAirbags=false then .15 else if car.hasDriverAirbags=true and car.hasPassengerAirbags=true and car.hasSideAirbags=true then .18 else 0
AlarmDiscountPct	if Risk.PotentialTheftCategory="High" and car.hasAlarm=true then .10 else 0
TotalDiscountPct	AirbagDiscountPct + AlarmDiscountPct
(BasePrem + AgePrem + UninsuredPrem + MedicalPrem + InjuryPrem + TheftPrem) * (1 - TotalDiscountPct)	

Figure 205. BKM *AutoPremium*, **which invokes** *AutoRisk*

The BKM *DriverPremium* (Figure 206) calculates the premium for a single driver, based on a decision table. The context entry *DriverInfo* invokes the BKM *DriverRisk* to supply some of the decision table inputs.

The decision *EligibilityScore* (Figure 207) performs iteration over cars and drivers to compute a total score. Iteration requires two steps: First, a *for..return* expression creates a *list* of scores. Then a *sum* expression totals the scores on the list. This is done first for cars, then for drivers, and the final result box computes the total score.

DriverPremium (driver)						
DriverInfo		DriverRisk				
1	"Young"	CA, NY, VA	TRUE	-	-	$700
2	"Young"	CA, NY, VA	FALSE	-	-	$720
3	"Young"	not(CA, NY, VA)	-	-	-	$300
4	"Senior"	CA, NY, VA	-	-	-	$500
5	"Senior"	not(CA, NY, VA)	-	-	-	$200
6	"Typical"	-	-	-	-	0
7	-	-	-	TRUE	-	$1,000
8	-	-	-	-	-	AccidentCount * $150

Figure 206. BKM *DriverPremium*, which invokes *DriverRisk*

EligibilityScore	
AutoScoreList	for car in Application.Cars return AutoEligibilityScore(car)
TotalAutoScore	sum(AutoScoreList)
DriverScoreList	for driver in Application.Drivers return DriverEligibilityScore(driver)
TotalDriverScore	sum(DriverScoreList)
TotalAutoScore + TotalDriverScore	

Figure 207. Decision *EligibilityScore*

The decision *isEligible* (Figure 208) is the same as we determined in our first-order decomposition, discussed earlier in this chapter.

isEligible				
U	isLongTermClient	Underwriting	EligibilityScore	isEligible
1	TRUE	-	-	TRUE
2	FALSE	*Eligible*	-	TRUE
3	FALSE	*Ineligible*	-	FALSE
4	FALSE	null	<100	TRUE
5	FALSE	null	>250	FALSE

Figure 208. Decision *isEligible*

The decision logic for *TotalAutoPremium* and *TotalDriverPremium* (Figure 209) iterates the premiums over cars and drivers, using the two-step formula discussed above. *Premium* merely sums those results.

TotalAutoPremium	
AutoPremiumList	for car in Application.Cars return AutoPremium(car)
sum(AutoPremiumList)	

TotalDriverPremium	
DriverPremiumList	for driver in Application.Drivers return DriverPremium(driver)
sum(DriverPremiumList)	

Premium
TotalAutoPremium + TotalDriverPremium

Figure 209. *Premium* **decision**

The top-level *AutoPolicy* decision (Figure 210) is the same as we determined in the first-order decomposition, discussed earlier in this chapter.

AutoPolicy			
U	isEligible	AutoPolicy	
		isEligible	Premium
1	TRUE	TRUE	Premium
2	FALSE	FALSE	null

Figure 210. Top-level decision

Level 2 Solution

While it involves a lot of details, the UServ Product Derby decision model is complicated only in its requirement for iteration using the FEEL *for..return* construct. With the help of extensions like Signavio's Multi-Instance Decision, described in Chapter 11, we can create a quasi-CL2 solution that does not use contexts, BKMs, or *for..return* expressions. The DRD, shown in Figure 211, is only moderately more complex than our CL3 solution, Figure 200. The advantage is I can now use Simulation in the tool to obtain output for any list of drivers and cars (Figure 212).

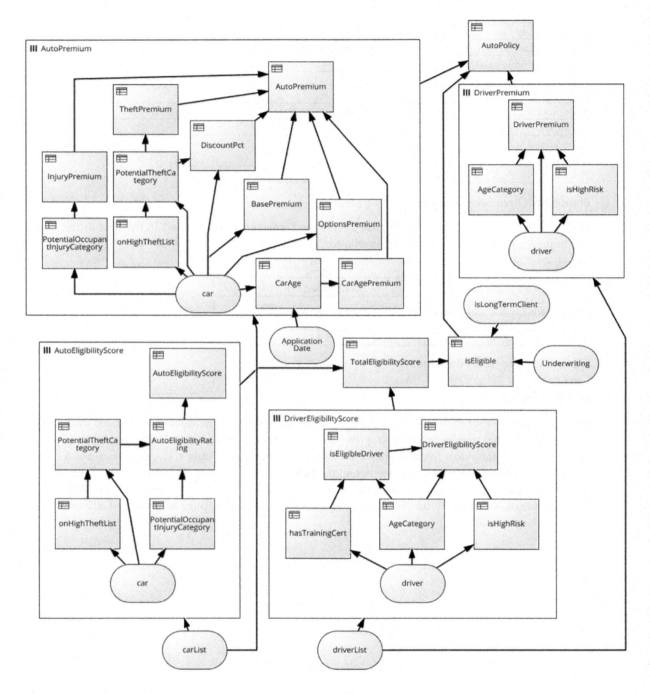

Figure 211. Quasi-CL2 solution using Signavio MID

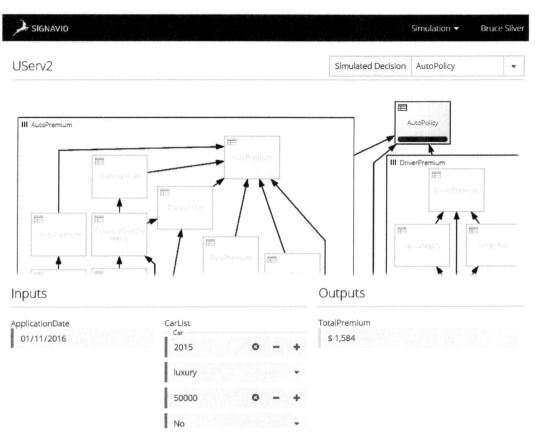

UServ2

Simulated Decision   AutoPolicy   ▼

Inputs

Outputs

ApplicationDate

01/11/2016

CarList
Car

2015   ✕ — ✚

luxury   ▼

50000   ✕ — ✚

No   ▼

TotalPremium

$ 1,584

Figure 212. UServ *TotalPremium* value for test case list of driver and auto data using Signavio Simulation feature

Example: Mortgage Recommender

In 2014, Gil Ronen, now of Sapiens DECISION, published an early case study of DMN used to automate the recommendation of home mortgage products. The decision logic ranked available lender products based on the customer's stated objectives, such as lowest monthly payment, lowest rate, or fastest increase in equity.[101] That scenario is reworked here using FEEL and DMN Method and Style, and adding important features of real mortgage products such as "points" and other fees.

Decision Process

The decision process works as follows: The form submitted by the customer includes the requested loan amount, down payment percentage, type of mortgage (e.g., *Fixed 30-year* or *ARM 7/1*), and the customer's objective, a particular metric used to rank available lender products. The decision logic suggests additional alternative mortgage types oriented to the customer's objective, creating additional loan products to consider. Alternatives include mortgage types with a different term, fixed vs adjustable rate, and rate vs points and fees.

The decision logic then matches the mortgage types in that list with a table of available lender products. Finally, the decision logic calculates the financial metrics for each matching lender product, and ranks them according to the customer's stated objective. The decision output is an ordered list of lender products and their associated financial metrics for the customer's submitted parameters. All of the input data needed for this decision – the customer form and the daily table of lender products and pricing – are available at the start, so this can be executed as a single decision service.

---

[101] https://dmcommunity.files.wordpress.com/2014/06/case-study-mortgage-recommender-final2.pdf

DRD Decomposition

The DRD for the end-to-end decision is shown in Figure 213.

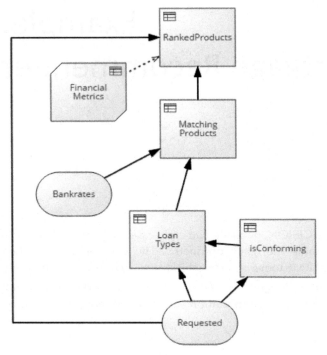

Figure 213. DRD for Mortgage Recommender

- *Requested* includes the customer's loan amount, down payment percentage, type of loan, and product selection objective.

- *isConforming* determines whether a Jumbo loan is required, based on the requested loan amount and property location.

- *LoanTypes* creates a list of possible loan types fitting the customer's stated objective and loan parameters.

- *Bankrates* is a published table of available lender products for each loan type.

- *MatchingProducts* iteratively queries *Bankrates* to select lender products for each item in the *LoanTypes* list.

- *RankedProducts* iteratively invokes the BKM *FinancialMetrics* for each item in *MatchingProducts* to create a list of lender products with associated metrics, and then sorts the list to rank it according to the customer's stated objective.

Fact Model

The fact types below correspond to the input data and decision/BKM variables in Figure 213:

Requested
- MortgageType [*tProductType* (string, allowed values "Fixed 40", "Fixed 30", "Fixed 20", "Fixed 15", "Fixed 10", "ARM 7/1", "ARM 5/1", "ARM 3/1", "ARM 1/1")]
- Objective [string, allowed values "Payment", "Equity", "Rate", "Down"]
- DownPct [number]
- LoanAmt [number]
- PropertyZIP [string]

Bankrates (isCollection) [*tBankrates*]
- LenderName [string]
- MortgageType [*tProductType*]
- ConformanceType [item definition *tConformanceType,* allowed values "Conventional", "Jumbo"]
- MinDown [number]
- Term [number] (specified in months)
- APR [number] (specified in percent)
- Rate [number] (specified in percent)
- Points [number] (specified in percent)
- FeesAmt [number]

LoanTypes (isCollection) [*tLoanTypes*]
- MortgageType [*tProductType*]
- ConformanceType [*tConformanceType*]
- DownPct [number]

MatchLoanType [*tBankrates*]

MatchingProducts (isCollection) [*tBankrates*]

FinancialMetrics [itemDefinition *tFinancialMetrics*]
- LoanAmt
- DownAmt
- Rate
- Points
- FeesAmt
- PaymentAmt
- EquityPct

ProductMetrics, RankedProducts (isCollection) [*tRankedProducts*]
- LenderName
- MortgageType [tProductType]
- ConformanceType [string, allowed values "Conventional", "Jumbo"]
- FinancialMetrics [tFinancialMetrics]

C	...quested.Objective	...ted.MortgageType	isConforming	...equested.DownPct	...rtgageType	...manceType	DownPct
	{Rate,Payment,Down,Equi...	{Fixed 40,Fixed 30,Fixed 2...	Boolean	Percentage	{Fixed 40,Fixed 3...	{Conventional,Ju...	Percentage
1	= Payment	∈ {Fixed 30, Fixe...	-	< 20.00 %	ARM 3/1	Conventional	20.00 %
2	= Payment	∈ {Fixed 30, Fixe...	= false	≥ 20.00 %	ARM 3/1	Jumbo	#Requested.D...
3	= Payment	∈ {Fixed 30, Fixe...	= true	≥ 20.00 %	ARM 3/1	Conventional	#Requested.D...
4	= Payment	= Fixed 15	-	< 20.00 %	Fixed 20	Conventional	20.00 %
5	= Payment	= Fixed 15	= false	≥ 20.00 %	Fixed 20	Jumbo	#Requested.D...
6	= Payment	= Fixed 15	= true	≥ 20.00 %	Fixed 20	Conventional	#Requested.D...
7	= Payment	= Fixed 20	-	< 20.00 %	Fixed 30	Conventional	20.00 %
8	= Payment	= Fixed 20	= false	≥ 20.00 %	Fixed 30	Jumbo	#Requested.D...
9	= Payment	= Fixed 20	= true	≥ 20.00 %	Fixed 30	Conventional	#Requested.D...
10	= Payment	= Fixed 30	-	< 20.00 %	Fixed 40	Conventional	20.00 %
11	= Payment	= Fixed 30	= false	≥ 20.00 %	Fixed 40	Jumbo	#Requested.D...
12	= Payment	= Fixed 30	= true	≥ 20.00 %	Fixed 40	Conventional	#Requested.D...
13	= Payment	∈ {ARM 7/1, AR...	-	< 20.00 %	ARM 3/1	Conventional	20.00 %
14	= Payment	∈ {ARM 7/1, AR...	= false	≥ 20.00 %	ARM 3/1	Jumbo	#Requested.D...
15	= Payment	∈ {ARM 7/1, AR...	= true	≥ 20.00 %	ARM 3/1	Conventional	#Requested.D...
16	= Payment	= ARM 3/1	-	< 20.00 %	ARM 1/1	Conventional	20.00 %
17	= Payment	= ARM 3/1	= false	≥ 20.00 %	ARM 1/1	Jumbo	#Requested.D...
18	= Payment	= ARM 3/1	= true	≥ 20.00 %	ARM 1/1	Conventional	#Requested.D...
19	∈ {Rate, Equity}	= Fixed 30	-	< 20.00 %	Fixed 20	Conventional	20.00 %
20	∈ {Rate, Equity}	= Fixed 30	= false	≥ 20.00 %	Fixed 20	Jumbo	#Requested....
21	∈ {Rate, Equity}	= Fixed 30	= true	≥ 20.00 %	Fixed 20	Conventional	#Requested....
22	∈ {Rate, Equity}	= Fixed 20	-	< 20.00 %	Fixed 15	Conventional	20.00 %
23	∈ {Rate, Equity}	= Fixed 20	= false	≥ 20.00 %	Fixed 15	Jumbo	#Requested....
24	∈ {Rate, Equity}	= Fixed 20	= true	≥ 20.00 %	Fixed 15	Conventional	#Requested....
25	= Equity	= Fixed 15	-	< 20.00 %	Fixed 10	Conventional	20.00 %
26	= Equity	= Fixed 15	= false	≥ 20.00 %	Fixed 10	Jumbo	#Requested....
27	= Equity	= Fixed 15	= true	≥ 20.00 %	Fixed 10	Conventional	#Requested....
28	= Equity	∈ {ARM 7/1, AR...	-	< 20.00 %	Fixed 20	Conventional	20.00 %
29	= Equity	∈ {ARM 7/1, AR...	= false	≥ 20.00 %	Fixed 20	Jumbo	#Requested....
30	= Equity	∈ {ARM 7/1, AR...	= true	≥ 20.00 %	Fixed 20	Conventional	#Requested....
31	= Rate	∈ {Fixed 30, Fixe...	-	< 20.00 %	ARM 5/1	Conventional	20.00 %
32	= Rate	∈ {Fixed 30, Fixe...	= false	≥ 20.00 %	ARM 5/1	Jumbo	#Requested....
33	= Rate	∈ {Fixed 30, Fixe...	= true	≥ 20.00 %	ARM 5/1	Conventional	#Requested....
34	= Rate	∈ {ARM 7/1, AR...	-	< 20.00 %	ARM 1/1	Conventional	20.00 %
35	= Rate	∈ {ARM 7/1, AR...	= false	≥ 20.00 %	ARM 1/1	Jumbo	#Requested....
36	= Rate	∈ {ARM 7/1, AR...	= true	≥ 20.00 %	ARM 1/1	Conventional	#Requested....
37	-	-	= true	-	#Requested....	Conventional	#Requested....
38	-	-	= false	-	#Requested....	Jumbo	#Requested....

Figure 214. *LoanTypes* decision table

LoanTypes

Figure 214 shows the decision logic for *LoanTypes*, which adds alternative mortgage types for consideration, in addition to the requested type, based on the stated objective. For *Requested.DownPct* values below 20%, an alternative configuration with 20% down is also added. The decision table hit policy is *Collect*, generating a list.

The decision *isConforming* is a table lookup that determines whether the requested loan amount conforms to limits set by the secondary market. The limit, either $417,000 or $625,500, depends on the *PropertyZIP* value. Loan amounts above that limit require a *ConformanceType* of "Jumbo." Jumbo loans have a minimum 20% down payment and more stringent credit requirements.

Now we have a list of possible loan types specified by *MortgageType, ConformanceType,* and *DownPct.*

Bankrates

Bankrates (Figure 215) is a published list of lender products for various loan types, along with their current prices. The published APR in *Bankrates* uses a fixed loan amount for conventional and jumbo loans in each product category, so in general the customer's actual APR will be different. Figure 215 displays actual Bankrate.com data published in the newspaper. Note there are no listings for down payments below 20%. Mortgage products for those do exist and can be obtained from the bankrate.com website. In this decision model, *Bankrates* is input data.

Bankrates								
LenderName	MortgageType	Conformance Type	MinDown	Term	APR	Rate	Points	FeesAmt
Mount Diablo Lending	ARM 5/1	Conventional	20%	360	2.787%	2.625%	0	$ -
Linear Home Loans	ARM 5/1	Conventional	20%	360	2.870%	2.875%	0	$ 795
AimLoan	ARM 5/1	Conventional	20%	360	3.002%	2.500%	0	$ 1,995
CalFed	ARM 5/1	Conventional	20%	360	3.117%	3.000%	0	$ 795
AimLoan	ARM 5/1	Jumbo	20%	360	3.029%	2.750%	0	$ 1,995
CalFed	ARM 5/1	Jumbo	20%	360	3.080%	3.000%	0	$ 95
Kinecta	ARM 5/1	Jumbo	20%	360	3.127%	2.875%	0.75	$ 1,800
Mount Diablo Lending	ARM 7/1	Conventional	20%	360	3.002%	3.000%	0	$ -
AimLoan	ARM 7/1	Conventional	20%	360	3.103%	2.875%	0	$ 1,995
America One	ARM 7/1	Conventional	20%	360	3.130%	2.875%	1	$ 899
Linear Home Loans	Fixed 10	Conventional	20%	120	2.851%	2.750%	0	$ 795
America One	Fixed 10	Conventional	20%	120	2.937%	2.625%	1	$ 799
America One	Fixed 15	Conventional	20%	180	2.745%	2.375%	0	$ 945
Linear Home Loans	Fixed 15	Conventional	20%	180	2.819%	2.750%	0	$ 795
Mount Diablo Lending	Fixed 15	Conventional	20%	180	2.887%	2.875%	0	$ -
CalFed	Fixed 15	Conventional	20%	180	2.891%	2.750%	0.5	$ 795
AimLoan	Fixed 15	Conventional	20%	180	2.924%	2.750%	0	$ 1,995
IPL Mortgage	Fixed 15	Conventional	20%	180	3.068%	2.990%	0	$ 465
Kinecta	Fixed 15	Conventional	20%	180	3.124%	2.875%	0.625	$ 1,800
Farmers and Merchants	Fixed 15	Conventional	20%	180	3.298%	3.125%	0	$ 1,960
IPL Mortgage	Fixed 15	Conventional	20%	180	3.155%	3.125%	0	$ 895
Farmers and Merchants	Fixed 15	Conventional	20%	180	3.691%	3.625%	0	$ 1,960
Mount Diablo Lending	Fixed 20	Conventional	20%	240	3.502%	3.500%	0	$ -
Linear Home Loans	Fixed 20	Conventional	20%	240	3.555%	3.500%	0	$ 795
AimLoan	Fixed 20	Conventional	20%	240	3.573%	3.500%	0	$ 1,995
America One	Fixed 30	Conventional	20%	360	3.577%	3.375%	2	$ 799
Mount Diablo Lending	Fixed 30	Conventional	20%	360	3.629%	3.625%	0	$ -
AimLoan	Fixed 30	Conventional	20%	360	3.682%	3.625%	0	$ 1,068
America One	Fixed 30	Conventional	20%	360	3.790%	3.750%	0	$ 799
IPL Mortgage	Fixed 30	Conventional	20%	360	3.796%	3.750%	0	$ 895
Kinecta	Fixed 30	Conventional	20%	360	3.808%	3.625%	1.125	$ 1,800
CalFed	Fixed 30	Conventional	20%	360	3.915%	3.875%	0	$ 795
Farmers and Merchants	Fixed 30	Conventional	20%	360	3.974%	3.875%	0	$ 795
AimLoan	Fixed 30	Jumbo	20%	360	3.662%	3.625%	0	$ 1,995
America One	Fixed 30	Jumbo	20%	360	3.805%	3.625%	2	$ 799

Figure 215. Input data *Bankrates*, showing lender product in each mortgage category with lowest published APR. Source: "Bankrate.com Mortgage Guide," *LA Times*, November 8, 2015

MatchingProducts

MatchingProducts queries the relation *Bankrates* to find lender products matching the *MortgageType, ConformanceType,* and *DownPct* values of each item in the *LoanTypes* list. The function definition *MatchLoanType* follows the *table query* pattern:

```
Bankrates[MortgageType=t.MortgageType and
ConformanceType=t.ConformanceType and MinDown<=t.DownPct]
```

where *t* is a single item in the *LoanTypes* relation. Invoking *MatchLoanType* generates a relation, a list of lender products matching a particular row in *loanTypes*. Now we need to iterate this function over all rows in the *LoanTypes* list.

MatchingProducts	
MatchLoanType	(t)
	Bankrates[MortgageType=t.MortgageType and ConformanceType=t.ConformanceType and MinDown<=t.DownPct]
for t in LoanTypes return MatchLoanType(t)	

Figure 216. *MatchingProducts* **combines table query and iteration**

FinancialMetrics

From the list of *MatchingProducts*, we have the current pricing information for each lender product. We'll use this to compute the BKM *FinancialMetrics*, which lets us rank the lender products according to the customer's stated objective.

To compute the monthly payment, we use the amortization formula

```
Payment = LoanAmt * r / (1 - (1 + r)⁻ⁿ)
```
$$\text{Payment} = \text{LoanAmt} * r / (1 - (1 + r)^{-n})$$

```
LoanAmt = P0 * (1 + PointsPct) + FeesAmt
```

where *LoanAmt* is the loan principal, adjusted to include points and fees, *r* is the loan rate per month, *n* is the term in months, and *P0* is the portion of *LoanAmt* excluding points and fees.

For the equity metric, we use the borrower's equity (original value minus loan balance) at the end of three years. We start by calculating P36, the loan balance remaining after 36 months. This is given by the amortization formula[102]

$$P36 = \text{LoanAmt} * (1+r)^{36} - \text{Payment} * ((1+r)^{36}-1) / r$$

Assuming no price inflation, the property value V is given by the formula,

```
V = P0 / (1 - DownPct)
```

We could assume an annual price inflation rate, but for purposes of ranking the loan products this makes no difference, so we will assume 0% price inflation. Thus,

```
EquityPct = 1 - P36/V
```

---

[102] https://en.wikipedia.org/wiki/Amortization_calculator

As a sanity check, we work out an example in Excel (Figure 217), using the Mount Diablo Fixed 30 pricing from Figure 215:

Mt Diablo Fixed 30		
P0	$	350,000
DownPct		20%
AnnRate		3.375%
PointsPct		2.00%
FeesAmt	$	799
n		360
Rate		3.375%
Points		2.000%
FeesAmt	$	799
r		0.281%
LoanAmt	$	357,799
DownAmt	$	71,560
Payment	$	1,581.82
P36	$	336,028
V	$	437,500
EquityPct		23.2%

Figure 217. Financial metrics calculation in Excel

The decision *RankedProducts* requires iterative invocation of *FinancialMetrics* for each lender product in *MatchingProducts* to create the relation *ProductMetrics*. Then, depending on the customer's stated objective, we select the appropriate FEEL *sort* function to rank the items in *ProductMetrics*.

The boxed expression is shown in Figure 218.

- *FinancialMetrics* is a function of a selected product from *MatchingProducts* in combination with the requested *loanAmount* and *DownPct*.

- *ProductMetrics* iteratively invokes *FinancialMetrics* for each item in *MatchingProducts*.

- The four *RankBy..* context entries each sort *ProductMetrics* by a different *precedesFunction* (see discussion of the FEEL *sort* function in Chapter 11).

- The final result box selects the proper *RankBy..* context entry as the decision output, based on the customer's stated objective.

RankedProducts			
FinancialMetrics	(product, Requested)		
	LenderName	product.LenderName	
	MortgageType	product.MortgageType	
	ConformanceType	product.ConformanceType	
	LoanAmt	Requested.LoanAmt * (1 + product.Points/100) + product.FeesAmt	
	DownPct	max(product.MinDown, Requested.DownPct)	
	DownAmt	LoanAmt * DownPct	
	Rate	product.Rate	
	Points	product.Points	
	FeesAmt	product.FeesAmt	
	r	product.Rate/12	
	Payment	LoanAmt * r / (1 - (1 + r)**-product.Term)	
	P36	LoanAmt * (1+r)**36 - Payment * ((1+r)**36 - 1) / r	
	V	Requested.LoanAmt / (1 - DownPct)	
	EquityPct	1 - P36/V	
ProductMetrics	for m in MatchingProducts return FinancialMetrics(m, Requested.LoanAmt)		
RankByRate	sort(ProductMetrics, precedesFunction(x,y) x.Rate<y.Rate)		
RankByPayment	sort(ProductMetrics, precedesFunction(x,y) x.Payment<y.Payment)		
RankByEquity	sort(ProductMetrics, precedesFunction(x,y) x.EquityPct>y.EquityPct)		
RankByDown	sort(ProductMetrics, precedesFunction(x,y) x.DownAmt<y.DownAmt)		
if Requested.Objective="Rate" then RankByRate else if Requested.Objective="Payment" then RankByPayment			
else if Requested.Objective="Equity" then RankByEquity else if Requested.Objective="Down" then RankByDown else null			

Figure 218. *RankedProducts* boxed expression

Customer Request and Decision Response

Let's take a look at the decision response for the customer request shown in Figure 219.

Requested	
MortgageType	Fixed 30
Objective	Equity
DownPct	20%
LoanAmt	350000
PropertyZIP	91001

Figure 219. Input data *Requested*

Based on the Equity objective, *LoanTypes* recommends considering a fixed 20-year loan in addition to the requested fixed 30-year loan. The result is a relation (Figure 220).

LoanTypes		
MortgageType	Conformance Type	DownPct
Fixed 20	Conventional	20%
Fixed 30	Conventional	20%

Figure 220. *LoanTypes* result

MatchingProducts selects from *Bankrates* the lender products matching *LoanTypes,* again a relation (Figure 221).

MatchingProducts								
LenderName	MortgageType	Conformance Type	MinDown	Term	APR	Rate	Points	FeesAmt
Mount Diablo Lending	Fixed 20	Conventional	20%	240	3.502%	3.500%	0	$ -
Linear Home Loans	Fixed 20	Conventional	20%	240	3.555%	3.500%	0	$ 795
AimLoan	Fixed 20	Conventional	20%	240	3.573%	3.500%	0	$ 1,995
America One	Fixed 30	Conventional	20%	360	3.577%	3.375%	2	$ 799
Mount Diablo Lending	Fixed 30	Conventional	20%	360	3.629%	3.625%	0	$ -
AimLoan	Fixed 30	Conventional	20%	360	3.682%	3.625%	0	$ 1,068
America One	Fixed 30	Conventional	20%	360	3.790%	3.750%	0	$ 799
IPL Mortgage	Fixed 30	Conventional	20%	360	3.796%	3.750%	0	$ 895
Kinecta	Fixed 30	Conventional	20%	360	3.808%	3.625%	1.125	$ 1,800
CalFed	Fixed 30	Conventional	20%	360	3.915%	3.875%	0	$ 795
Farmers and Merchants	Fixed 30	Conventional	20%	360	3.974%	3.875%	0	$ 795

Figure 221. *MatchingProducts* **result**

ProductMetrics iterates the *FinancialMetrics* calculation for each row in *MatchingProducts,* again producing a relation (Figure 222). Columns for the auxiliary context variables *DownPct, r, P36,* and *V* have been omitted.

ProductMetrics									
LenderName	MortgageType	Conformance Type	LoanAmt	DownAmt	Rate	Points	FeesAmt	Payment	EquityPct
Mount Diablo Lending	Fixed 20	Conventional	$ 350,000	$ 70,000	3.500%	0	$ -	$ 2,029.86	28.7%
Linear Home Loans	Fixed 20	Conventional	$ 350,795	$ 70,159	3.500%	0	$ 795	$ 2,034.47	28.6%
AimLoan	Fixed 20	Conventional	$ 351,995	$ 70,399	3.500%	0	$ 1,995	$ 2,041.43	28.3%
America One	Fixed 30	Conventional	$ 357,799	$ 71,560	3.375%	2	$ 799	$ 1,581.82	23.2%
Mount Diablo Lending	Fixed 30	Conventional	$ 350,000	$ 70,000	3.625%	0	$ -	$ 1,596.18	24.7%
AimLoan	Fixed 30	Conventional	$ 351,068	$ 70,214	3.625%	0	$ 1,068	$ 1,601.05	24.4%
America One	Fixed 30	Conventional	$ 350,799	$ 70,160	3.750%	0	$ 799	$ 1,624.60	24.4%
IPL Mortgage	Fixed 30	Conventional	$ 350,895	$ 70,179	3.750%	0	$ 895	$ 1,625.05	24.4%
Kinecta	Fixed 30	Conventional	$ 355,738	$ 71,148	3.625%	1.125	$ 1,800	$ 1,622.35	23.4%
CalFed	Fixed 30	Conventional	$ 350,795	$ 70,159	3.875%	0	$ 795	$ 1,649.57	24.3%
Farmers and Merchants	Fixed 30	Conventional	$ 350,795	$ 70,159	3.875%	0	$ 795	$ 1,649.57	24.3%

Figure 222. *ProductMetrics* **result**

Finally, *RankedProducts* sorts *ProductMetrics* by the objective metric, in this case *EquityPct* (Figure 223). This is the result returned to the customer.

| RankedProducts | | | | | | | | | |
LenderName	MortgageType	Conformance Type	LoanAmt	DownAmt	Rate	Points	FeesAmt	Payment	EquityPct
Mount Diablo Lending	Fixed 20	Conventional	$ 350,000	$ 70,000	3.500%	0	$ -	$ 2,029.86	28.7%
Linear Home Loans	Fixed 20	Conventional	$ 350,795	$ 70,159	3.500%	0	$ 795	$ 2,034.47	28.6%
AimLoan	Fixed 20	Conventional	$ 351,995	$ 70,399	3.500%	0	$ 1,995	$ 2,041.43	28.3%
Mount Diablo Lending	Fixed 30	Conventional	$ 350,000	$ 70,000	3.625%	0	$ -	$ 1,596.18	24.7%
AimLoan	Fixed 30	Conventional	$ 351,068	$ 70,214	3.625%	0	$ 1,068	$ 1,601.05	24.4%
America One	Fixed 30	Conventional	$ 350,799	$ 70,160	3.750%	0	$ 799	$ 1,624.60	24.4%
IPL Mortgage	Fixed 30	Conventional	$ 350,895	$ 70,179	3.750%	0	$ 895	$ 1,625.05	24.4%
CalFed	Fixed 30	Conventional	$ 350,795	$ 70,159	3.875%	0	$ 795	$ 1,649.57	24.3%
Farmers and Merchants	Fixed 30	Conventional	$ 350,795	$ 70,159	3.875%	0	$ 795	$ 1,649.57	24.3%
Kinecta	Fixed 30	Conventional	$ 355,738	$ 71,148	3.625%	1.125	$ 1,800	$ 1,622.35	23.4%
America One	Fixed 30	Conventional	$ 357,799	$ 71,560	3.375%	2	$ 799	$ 1,581.82	23.2%

Figure 223. *RankedProducts* **result**

Here the customer does not receive a single recommended product but a list, sorted in order of the stated objective. We see the 20-year loans have faster equity build, but also have higher monthly payment. In fact, of the matching products, the one with the lowest monthly payment also has the lowest equity build. The customer can now make a more informed choice.

This example shows the power of DMN's table manipulation features. You don't need to exit to SQL to select matching loan products or compute the metrics. It all can be done within DMN.

CHAPTER 16

Decision Analysis and Testing

A key advantage of model-based decision requirements compared to text-based equivalents is that models enable much more rigorous validation and analysis. Decision analysis and testing includes the following:

- **Completeness check.** Do the decision tables and other decision logic consider all possible combinations of input values? There should be no input combinations that are not considered.

- **Consistency check.** Does any decision table contain overlapping rules with different output entries?

- **Decision analysis.** Does the business decision as a whole give a sensible result in all cases? Do incremental changes in input data values result in sensible changes in the output?

Much of the "lore" of decision tables dates from a time when these tables were constructed by hand and validated by visual inspection. Good DMN tools today should be able to handle much of the job of checking completeness and consistency automatically. Checking whether the resulting business logic is sensible, however, cannot be fully automated. It requires development of *test cases,* simulation of the decision outcome in those cases, and careful analysis of the results.

Completeness

In a single-hit decision table, every possible combination of input values should be matched by a rule. That means the table is *complete.* A table for which certain combinations have no matching rule is *incomplete* and should be avoided. If some combination within the domain of allowed input values has no meaningful decision outcome, it should nevertheless be matched by a rule with *null* output. (In a multi-hit decision table that collects a list or possibly sums a score, only input combinations that contribute to the list or sum need to be considered, so completeness has less importance there.)

U	Applicant.Age	Applicant.IsExistingCustomer	CreditRiskScore	PrelimCreditRiskCategory
	Number	Boolean	Number	{Decline,High,Medium,Low,Very L...
1	< 18	-	-	Decline
2	≥ 18	= true	< 80	Decline
3	≥ 18	= false	< 100	High
4	≥ 18	= true	∈ [80..90)	High
5	≥ 18	= false	∈ [100..120)	Medium
6	≥ 18	= true	∈ (90..110]	Medium
7	≥ 18	= false	∈ [120..130]	Low
8	≥ 18	= true	> 110	Low

Check Decision Table

#	Rule	Description
1	---	No rule exists for (≥18, true, 90)

Figure 224. Completeness violation in Signavio Verify

Modern DMN tools should be able to test decision tables for completeness. For example, Figure 224 shows the result of the *Verify* function in the Signavio DMN Editor applied to a version of the *Pre-bureauRiskCategory* decision from the Lending example. It says there is no rule testing the combination *ApplicantData.Age>=18, ApplicantData.isExistingCustomer=true,* and *CreditRiskScore=90*, in other words, a gap. Analysis of the table reveals the problem. Rule 4 tests *CreditRiskScore<90* and Rule 6 tests *CreditRiskScore>90*, but there is no rule testing *CreditRiskScore=90*. We fix it by changing the input entry in Rule 4 from [80..90) to [80..90]. The open and closed endpoints of numeric ranges is one common source of gaps.

Another common source of inadvertent gaps stems from the fact that FEEL has no integer datatype, only number. So, for example, we might consider *ApplicantData.Age* an integer and have rules testing *ApplicantData.Age<=17* and *ApplicantData.Age>=18*. But technically this leaves a gap in the interval (17..18), numbers greater than 17 but less than 18. For an integer that makes no sense, but the completeness checker will report a gap. For that reason, rules should cover non-integer values, even when the input must be an integer.

To facilitate completeness verification, each decision table input should define a domain of allowed values. Even if the domain is specified in the item definition, it should be specified in the table input values as well. Any value in input values must, of course, be allowed by item definition.

Compared to other type languages like XSD, DMN/FEEL is somewhat limited in specifying constraints on the domain of allowed values. For example, a variable like *ZIPCode* is easily constrained in XSD to a 5-character string in which each character is a digit from 0 to 9, but in itemDefinition you would have to make it either any string or a number in the range [0..99999]. Neither of those is ideal. You could certainly define *tZIPCode* in XSD and have *typeRef* point to that definition, but your DMN tool completeness checker would have to support XSD import to make use of that.

Consistency

An *inconsistent* decision table has *overlapping* rules reporting different output values. A decision table with hit policy of *Unique* should never have overlapping rules. A decision table with hit policy of *Any* may have overlapping rules as long as all matching rules report the same outcome value. A table with hit policy of *Priority* or *First* typically has overlapping rules, but because of the hit policy is not inconsistent.

U	Applicant.Age		...ata.hasBankruptcy		...sExistingCustomer		CreditRiskScore		...u data.CreditScore	
	Number		Boolean		Boolean		Number		Number	
1	<	18		-		-		-		-
2	≥	18	=	true		-		-		-
3	≥	18	=	false		-		-	<	580
4	≥	18	=	false	=	false	<	120	∈	[580..590)
5	≥	18	=	false	=	false	<	120	∈	[590..610]
6	≥	18	=	false	=	false	<	120	>	610
7	≥	18	=	false	=	false	∈	[120..130]	<	600
8	≥	18	=	false	=	false	∈	[120..130]	∈	[600..625]
9	≥	18	=	false	=	false	∈	[120..130]	>	625
10	≥	18	=	false	=	false	>	130		-
11	≥	18	=	false	=	true	≤	100	∈	[580..600]
12	≥	18	=	false	=	true	≤	100	>	600

Check Decision Table

#	Rule	Description
1	Rule 3, 7	Overlapping rules: These rules apply for (≥18, false, false, ∈[120, 130], <580)
2	Rule 3, 10	Overlapping rules: These rules apply for (≥18, false, false, >130, <580)

Figure 225. Consistency violation in Signavio Verify

Modern DMN tools should be able to check decision table consistency automatically. Figure 225 shows Signavio's Verify function applied to *CreditRiskCategory*. When I first created this decision table, I thought it was correct, but the tool shows me otherwise. The consistency checking reports the overlapping rules and the overlap condition. We can fix it by changing the *CreditScore* input entry in Rule 7 to *[580..600)* and in Rule 10 to *>=580*. The corrected decision table is now shown in Figure 173.

Decision Analysis

Beyond basic completeness and consistency checking, analyzing the business logic requires examining test cases to see if the decision result makes sense.

U	Applicant.Age		...sExistingCustomer		CreditRiskScore		...limCreditRiskCategory
	Number		Boolean		Number		{Decline,High,Medium,Low,...
1	<	18				-	Decline
2	≥	18	=	true	<	80	Decline
3	≥	18	=	false	<	100	High
4	≥	18	=	true	∈	[80..90]	High
5	≥	18	=	false	∈	[100..120)	Medium
6	≥	18	=	true	∈	(90..110]	Medium
7	≥	18	=	false	∈	[120..130]	Low
8	≥	18	=	true	>	110	Low
9	≥	18	=	false	>	130	Very low

U	Applicant.Age		...ata.hasBankruptcy		...sExistingCustomer		CreditRiskScore		...u data.CreditScore		CreditRiskCategory
	Number		Boolean		Boolean		Number		Number		{Decline,High,Medium,Low,...
1	<	18		-		-		-		-	Decline
2	≥	18	=	true		-		-		-	Decline
3	≥	18	=	false		-		-	<	580	High
4	≥	18	=	false	=	false	<	120	∈	[580..590)	High
5	≥	18	=	false	=	false	<	120	∈	[590..610]	Medium
6	≥	18	=	false	=	false	<	120	>	610	Low
7	≥	18	=	false	=	false	∈	[120..130]	∈	[580..600]	High
8	≥	18	=	false	=	false	∈	[120..130]	∈	[600..625]	Medium
9	≥	18	=	false	=	false	∈	[120..130]	>	625	Low
10	≥	18	=	false	=	false	>	130	≥	580	Very Low
11	≥	18	=	false	=	true	≤	100	∈	[580..600]	Medium
12	≥	18	=	false	=	true	≤	100	>	600	Low
13	≥	18	=	false	=	true	>	100	∈	[580..590)	High
14	≥	18	=	false	=	true	>	100	∈	[590..615]	Medium
15	≥	18	=	false	=	true	>	100	>	615	Low

Figure 226. Comparison of *Pre-bureauRiskCategory* and *CreditRiskCategory* logic

For example, Figure 226 compares the decision logic for *Pre-bureauRiskCategory* and *CreditRiskCategory* from the Lending example. The basic difference is that the latter includes the credit bureau data. The relationship of the decision logic with and without credit bureau data should make sense from a business standpoint. Analyzing this, however, requires digging down into the details.

To do this, we need to understand how *Pre-bureauRiskCategory* and *CreditRiskCategory* affect the *Prequalification* and *Qualification* decisions, respectively. From Figure 168, we see that *Prequalification* is "Approve" without a credit score if *Pre-bureauRiskCategory* is "Very low," which occurs only when the applicant is not an existing customer and the *CreditRiskScore* is greater than 130. In *Qualification* (Figure 172), the result is "Approve" if *CreditRiskCategory* is not "Decline" or "High." From Figure 226, we see that is the case when any of the following are true:

- Not existing customer, *CreditRiskScore*<120, *CreditScore*>=590
- Not existing customer, *CreditRiskScore* in [120..130], *CreditScore*>600
- Not existing customer, *CreditRiskScore*>130, *CreditScore*>=580
- Existing customer, *CreditRiskScore*<=100, *CreditScore*>=580
- Existing customer, *CreditRiskScore*>100, *CreditScore*>=590

The application is sent to *Adjudication* if *CreditRiskCategory* is "High". This occurs when any of the following are true:

- *CreditScore*<=580
- Not existing customer, *CreditRiskScore*<120, *CreditScore* in [580..590)
- Not existing customer, *CreditRiskScore* in [120..130], *CreditScore* in [580..600]
- Existing customer, *CreditRiskScore*>100, *CreditScore* in [580..590)

Looking at this, you want to ask yourself, does it all make sense? Something looks funny to me here right away: For an existing customer, the *CreditScore* threshold for approval is actually higher for applicants with a *CreditRiskScore* of 590 than for those with a *CreditRiskScore* of 580. That does not make sense.

Something else that doesn't make sense is the difference in approval threshold for existing customers versus not-existing customers. An applicant with *CreditRiskScore* of 120 and *CreditScore* of 590 is *Approved* if an existing customer and *Referred* to *Adjudication* otherwise. But an applicant with a *CreditRiskScore* over 130 and a *CreditScore* of 585 is *Referred* to *Adjudication* if an existing customer and *Approved* otherwise. Why would existing customers have a higher approval threshold in some cases and a lower threshold in others? Anomalies like this suggest the detailed decision logic may require some adjustment.

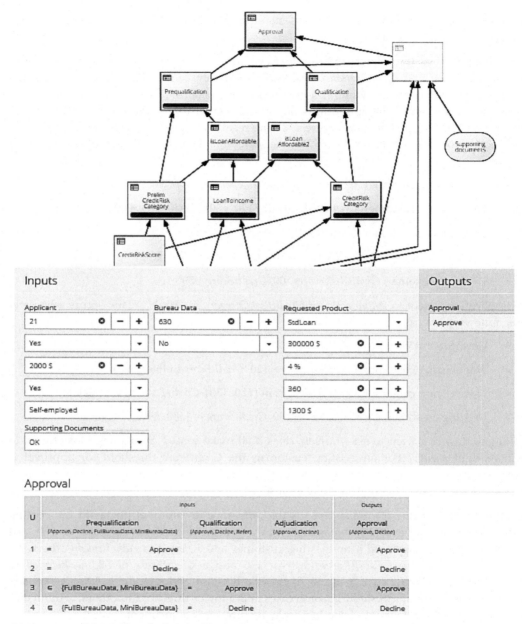

Figure 227. DMN Simulation in Signavio's BDM tool

To do this kind of analysis, you need to consider not just each decision in isolation, but the *entire chain of decision logic down to the input data.* If you do this by visual inspection, your head will be spinning in no time. It is very difficult. To do it effectively, you need assistance from your modeling tool. *Decision model simulation* (Figure 227) lets you enter values for the input data and see the result for any decision in the DRD. That is a big help in identifying inconsistencies in the end-to-end decision logic.

Figure 227 shows Signavio's DMN Simulation feature for the Lending decision we have been discussing. For the supplied input data values, the status of each decision node in the DRD is indicated by a bar. The top-level output value is displayed, and you can see the selected outputs of all the supporting decisions as well.

For more extensive testing of the end-to-end decision logic, Signavio provides a *Test Lab feature* (Figure 228). Modelers enter a list of *test cases* in the editor and the expected decision outcome of each one. The tool can even automatically generate a list of test cases, which can be imported into the Test Lab. The Save & Run button then executes all the test cases and compares the calculated result with the expected.

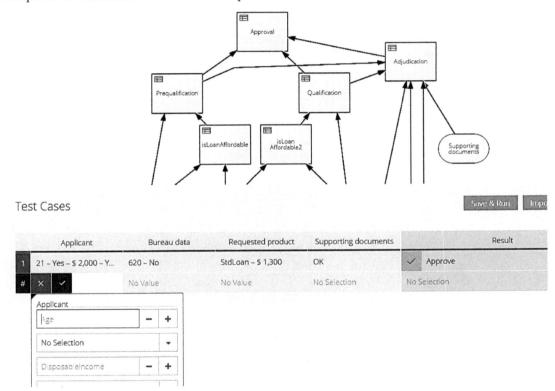

Figure 228. Signavio Test Lab feature

Analytics: Completing the Circle

In the end, decision analysis is more than finding minor inconsistencies in the logic. More important is the question, *Does this decision logic give us the best combination of opportunity, profitability, risk reduction, and compliance?* To answer that, we need to circle back to where we began in Chapter 1: *analytics*.

If you are a lender, you have data on loans you have made in the past, showing which ones have been profitable – timely payment, no default – and which have not. You have statistics on the difference between existing customers and others, the effect of the credit score, of applicant age, marital status, and employment, and the other factors that go into the end-to-end decision logic. Analytics tell you how various combinations of these factors correlate with past outcomes and may serve as predictors of future outcomes. The factors with the greatest correlation have the greatest predictive value and are normally the ones you use in your decision logic, determining, for example, the weights assigned in scoring, or the score cutoffs in classification. You can try a variety of rulesets on a sample set of transactions, compare their predictive ability, and select a Champion.

And because the decision logic is model-driven, it's easy to change. Suppose, in your analysis, you see some things that don't look right. You can change them! You can rerun your analytics models with the changes. If they look ok, you can try out a new Challenger decision model on a portion of your loan applications, and after some time period compare the results against the current Champion model. This is not magic. It's the way data-driven business works.

CHAPTER 17

The Road Ahead

In this book, I've tried to show you how DMN can play an important role in documenting, analyzing, automating, and improving the decision logic that drives your organization. As you've seen, DMN is a lot more than decision tables! It also provides a way to capture end-to-end decision logic of any size, even when it is executed in multiple steps separated in time. That end-to-end diagram, the DRD, reveals the dependencies among all the various decision elements and the required input data.

Moreover, DMN provides an executable expression language, so that *what you model is indeed what is executed*... without the need for programmers to translate it into another rule language. The default language, FEEL, is quite powerful, able to perform iteration, table lookups and joins, and data validation. Defenders of proprietary expression languages and tools may tell you FEEL is "too hard for business people." Don't believe it! If you can use Excel formulas (I'm not talking about macros!), you can use FEEL. It's just *an expression language*, not a programming language. When they tell business users it's "too hard," what they mean is, "Just write down your business requirements, and the programmers will take care of the rest." It doesn't have to be that way.

Best of all, DMN is an industry standard. The *meaning* of a DRD, decision table, or FEEL expression does not depend on the tool that created it or the modeler's personal interpretation. The meaning is defined in a tool-independent specification. That specification is available for free from the OMG website, but it is not easy reading. Part II of this book explains DMN a lot more clearly than the spec does. But to use DMN effectively, to create decision models that communicate the logic clearly and consistently, you need more than the information in the spec. You also need a methodology and best practices, such as DMN Method and Style.

In Part III, we provided Method and Style guidelines for element naming, decision table style, and decomposition of the end-to-end decision logic. Those are not official rules of DMN, just guidelines. Some experts find my rules too "dogmatic," but beginning modelers need the guidance of firm rules. Once they become more experienced, they will decide on their own which ones they want to break.

Choosing a DMN Tool

DMN does not assume paper-and-pencil decision modeling. It requires *modeling tools* that understand DMN concepts and enforces its rules, ideally tools that can not only model the decision logic but also execute it, at least for testing and validation purposes. DMN tools are now only beginning to appear. Many of them let you create DRDs and decision tables but not much else. That is not enough.

In the beginning of the book, we said that DMN *was five things*, not two:

1. DRD

2. Decision tables

3. XML export/import for standardized model interchange

4. Boxed expressions

5. FEEL

All DMN tools support the first two. The XML schema specification is now fixed and stable in DMN 1.1, so I am confident you will find tools supporting XML interchange of DMN models in the first half of 2016.

But tool vendor support for the last two, boxed expressions and FEEL, is less certain. It will require the urging of customers, people like you.

I mentioned earlier that FEEL is just an expression language, not a programming language. That means it does not have statements; it cannot create variables. So FEEL is fundamentally simpler than javascript, Python, or Visual Basic for Applications. But DMN *does* have a way to create statements and variables, *a graphical way*, more accessible to business users.

One part of that graphical way is the DRD itself, in which the chain of supporting decisions acts like a visual programming language. But a second and equally important part of the way is the *boxed expression*. Boxed expressions define graphically, in tables, the logic of any decision node in the DRD that requires more than a one-line literal expression. Boxed expressions have a defined format, usually two columns, a *name* and a *value expression*. The rows in a boxed expression for a *context* are like statements in a programming language, except they are simple, just name and expression.

A DMN tool vendor may think, "I don't really need boxed expressions. I can just use a large number of simple decision nodes in the DRD instead of a smaller number of decisions modeled with boxed expressions." But once you get beyond 30 decision nodes in a DRD, the experts tell us it becomes unmanageable. So boxed expressions are very important. They are *the business view of detailed decision logic*. You should urge your DMN tool vendor to support them.

Then there is the question of FEEL. It's a brand new language. Standard libraries for it don't yet exist, so to support it, tool vendors need to do more work than usual. Some hope to avoid that.

One challenge is simply parsing the expressions. We've discussed the problems of spaces in the names of variables and built-in functions. Another challenge is implementing FEEL's built-in functions and operators. In the examples of this book, we've seen the power of the iteration patterns, table query and join patterns, and data validation patterns that they enable. Today, *many first-generation DMN tools cannot implement those examples.* Some are hoping their customers never ask them to.

But think about it. If every DMN tool makes up its own expression language, would you really have a standard? The DRD may be interchangeable between tools, but the detailed decision logic would still be tool-dependent. Customers should demand more than that.

To be fair to the tool vendors, DMN is brand new. DMN 1.1, the first "implementable" version, was just published to OMG members in December 2015 and won't be officially released until mid-2016. So we need to give the vendors some time to implement it. But ultimately, when selecting a DMN tool, I would want one that supports not only DRDs and decision tables, but also:

- Structured data, not just simple types

- BKMs and boxed invocation

- The iteration patterns described in this book

- Data tables (relations) and the table query, join, and sorting patterns described in this book

- The validation patterns described in this book

- Boxed contexts

- Imports

- *null*

And then beyond features described by the DMN spec, ideally I would want also:

- Shared business glossary/fact type model

- Validation of decision table consistency and completeness

- Decision simulation and analysis capabilities

If your DMN tool does not provide a capability that you need, you must ask the vendor to provide it.

Improving the Standard

DMN 1.1 is pretty good, but far from perfect. It's the work of a committee, based on compromise and consensus. We probably won't even know all the parts of it that need improvement until we have wider adoption and tools that fully implement it. But OMG has an open process for revising the standard, and the RTF for DMN 1.2 has already been chartered. *If you are interested in improving DMN in some way, please join the RTF.* Contact OMG to find out how. If you're willing to do the work, you have a good chance of adding your bit to the standard.

Already I know a few things I would like to see considered in DMN 1.2:

- An alternative graphical representation of BKMs. Displaying both the calling decision node and the called BKM in the same level of the DRD adds visual clutter without much value. It would be better to indicate a decision that invokes a BKM with a special marker or border style, and combine the invocation mapping and BKM logic in a child-level diagram.

- A DRD representation of the iteration pattern, equivalent to FEEL *for..return* expressions. In the book we saw examples of Signavio's Multi-Instance Decision extension and a similar capability in Sapiens DECISION. DMN should standardize such a DRD pattern.

- A standardized mapping between a context and an equivalent DRD fragment. To me these are notational differences not semantic ones. Here is why it's important: In DMN 1.1, a bit of reusable decision logic is restricted to a single function definition, usually a BKM. If that reusable logic has any degree of complexity, it must be modeled as a context, which is less business-friendly than a DRD fragment. In other words, while a DRD fragment is not reusable, there is an obvious mapping between that fragment and a context, which is reusable. In general, the ability to represent complex decision logic as a DRD fragment makes it accessible to a wider base of CL2 modelers and tools. Conversely, the ability to collapse a DRD fragment into a single decision node enables high-level views of complex end-to-end decisions. Context and DRD fragment are two sides of the same coin, and DMN should treat them that way.

- Decision nesting, i.e., a decision that *contains* other decisions. This is not the same as a decision that *depends on* other decisions, which is all we have today. I am thinking of something similar to a subprocess in BPMN, an activity that contains other activities but could be viewed *collapsed* as a single node in the DRD. Such a construct would allow a high-level view of very complex end-to-end decision logic, while retaining the nested detailed logic in child-level diagrams. Decision services offer encapsulation of DRD fragments today, but they are just implementation-related overlays on the decision logic, not compositional elements of that logic.

- Dynamic function invocation. DMN 1.1 started on this path by allowing invocation to name its called function dynamically via an expression, but it did not complete the job, since the decision's knowledge requirement is still a static pointer. Allowing a decision to invoke different variations of its logic would be a useful thing.

- A metamodel and XML schema for the graphical elements, cross-referenced to the semantic model. This is part of BPMN, CMMN, and other OMG standards, where

---

diagram interchange has proven to be an important aspect of model interoperability. This is likely to be added in DMN 1.2.

- To support DMN in event processing, the metamodel should be extended to support a time dimension for aggregating and correlating events.

That's just my list as of today. You may have your own ideas. The RTF is always looking for people interested in doing the work. Please join us!

In closing, let me add that I have additional examples, XML serializations, and tools that would be helpful in understanding DMN but don't fit in a book. In the coming weeks, I hope to begin providing some of those things in my new website *methodandstyle.com*. Please have a look and feel free to contact me with your suggestions.

APPENDICES

Because DMN so closely links the DRD with an associated business process model, I provide here a very brief tutorial on BPMN. Those interested in more details on the standard itself or the BPMN Method and Style conventions are referred to my book.[103]

A *process* in BPMN is a sequence of actions, or more properly a network of possible sequences of actions leading from some initial state to some possible end state (Figure 229). Each *instance* of the process follows some path of *sequence flows*, the solid arrows, from the *start event* to some *end event*. Actions in the process are represented by rounded rectangles called *activities*, labeled Verb-object. Every activity is either a *task* or *subprocess*. A task is *atomic*, i.e., contains no subparts known to the model. A subprocess is *compound*; its subparts can be described as a process, a flow from start to end, typically in a separate hyperlinked diagram.

When an activity ends, the process continues on the outgoing sequence flow. If a choice of paths is available, a *gateway* evaluates some condition to determine which one to follow. The label on each *gate* – the gateway's outgoing sequence flows – suggests the condition value. In BPMN Method and Style, each distinct *end state* of the process is represented by a separate end event, labeled to indicate the end state.

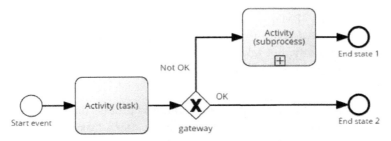

Figure 229. A simple BPMN process

---

[103] Silver, *BPMN Method and Style*

Figure 230. BPMN task types that can execute a decision

BPMN defines a number of task types, distinguished by an icon in the top left corner (Figure 230). Each of the task types shown in Figure 230 *may* represent execution of a DMN decision. Each task type signifies a different type of decision execution:

- Decision task. A *decision task*, technically called in BPMN 2.0 a *business rule task*, represents automated execution of a *decision service* on some kind of software engine. A decision service is *stateless*, meaning evaluation occurs at a single instant in time, with no wait states in the middle.

- User task. A *user task* represents a human activity, so a human decision would be represented in BPMN by a user task. It is inherently long-running, i.e., it takes time. Normally the decision logic of a human decision is *opaque*, not specified in DMN, although the supporting decisions and input data used to make the decision may be shown in the DRD.

- Service task. A *service task* represents execution of an automated service. Like a decision task, it is stateless and *synchronous*, meaning the task completes when the service returns its response. That means it is *short-running*, effectively instantaneous. Technically, a decision task is a particular kind of service task. To make best use of the notation, use service task for a *short-running external decision*. Here external means the decision logic is not defined by the decision model, but instead by some application system or external provider that returns a decision result quickly upon execution. Like a human decision, the decision logic of an external decision is typically opaque.

- Receive task. A *receive task* in BPMN waits for a response, such as from an external service provider. An *external decision that is long-running* – meaning the decision outcome is not returned instantly, but takes more than a second or two – would be modeled in BPMN as a receive task, typically following a *send task* that requests the decision from the external provider.

A gateway does not "make" a decision. It only applies a condition to process data to select a sequence flow to follow. Typically a gateway is placed immediately after a task representing a decision, with a gate for each possible value of the decision outcome.

Appendix B
Real-World Example: Dodd-Frank Regulatory Compliance

by Aaron Sayles

In the wake of the global financial crisis of 2008, regulatory regimes across the globe enacted sweeping changes to the reporting requirements of financial institutions large and small, vastly increasing the complexity of regulatory compliance. This has triggered wholesale changes in banks' risk management processes, requiring a new paradigm in risk and regulatory reporting, which often must unify and consolidate source data from systems in many different countries.

Moreover, the requirements for transparency and auditability of both quantitative and qualitative aspects of risk management and reporting have become far more stringent. Today, simply providing the "answer", the final outcome of a risk metric, is no longer enough. The entire process of determining that metric is under regulatory scrutiny.

These enhanced standards have introduced a host of functional, operational, and technical challenges that remain an ongoing struggle for many institutions. By applying transparent, verifiable, and auditable business logic to financial risk reporting, *business decision management* offers a lifeline to these institutions, even though they may not have considered this a matter of "decisions".

In the US, the Dodd-Frank *Wall Street Reform and Consumer Protection Act* was signed into law on July 21, 2010. This legislation applies advanced prudential standards to bank holding companies and foreign banking organizations, particularly those with global consolidated assets of $50 Billion or more. It set forth rigorous reporting standards for both capital adequacy and liquidity risk, including the *Comprehensive Capital Adequacy Review* (CCAR) and the *Liquidity Coverage Ratio* (LCR) requirements, along with their related regulatory filings, the FR Y-14 series and FR 2052a. These enhanced standards required a level of data sourcing, aggregation, and organizational integration not previously seen in a regulatory reporting context.

Comprehensive Capital Adequacy Review

CCAR and related regulatory reports are intended to provide regulators with greater clarity as to the institution's capital adequacy on a consolidated basis, under varying levels of macroeconomic stress. Banks must demonstrate the ability to *forecast their capital position* out nine quarters under macroeconomic scenarios ranging from adverse to severely adverse; and must integrate the results of this analysis into a *capital plan*. The capital plan, which is submitted to the Federal Reserve for approval, effectively impacts all capital actions at the bank, from dividends to executive bonuses. Fed approval is predicated on both the resulting capital ratios (quantitative) and the robustness of the decision logic and associated process for determining capital adequacy (qualitative). The latter has actually proven the bigger challenge. Eight of the nine capital plan rejections since 2014 have been due to these qualitative deficiencies.[104]

Liquidity Coverage Ratio

The final rule of the *Liquidity Coverage Ratio: Liquidity Risk Measurement Standards*, which outlines required liquidity risk monitoring practices, was enacted in October of 2014. The rule requires banks to maintain an adequate level of *high quality liquid assets* (HQLA) to cover net cash outflows for a 30 day period on a consolidated basis, as measured by the ratio HQLA/Net Cash Outflows. HQLA consists of three categories, or levels: 1, 2a, and 2b. Each level is comprised of specific assets that must have specific attributes. Cash inflows and outflows are determined by regulator-prescribed assumptions and are netted to yield Net Cash Outflows. An example of an outflow could be a maturing certificate of deposit, while an inflow could be a maturing of a fixed income security.

For banks, Dodd-Frank makes proper classification of both HQLA and Net Cash Flows a critical business decision. It involves applying specific criteria – rules – to all the underlying contracts, which requires consolidating context-sensitive data from disparate systems in different jurisdictions. It is a difficult job. Best practice is to create a *logic-based classification framework* that can apply clear and consistent classification rules to the pertinent data, as opposed to simply flagging individual assets as a specific HQLA level.

This approach also adapts more easily to changes in the regulations. For example, consider classification of an *equity asset*, that is, a quantity of stock. Let's say that previously a requirement for a certain HQLA level was inclusion of that stock in the Russell 1000 index, but now the regulation has become more stringent and the stock must be in the S&P 500. It is far easier – and less prone to error – to update the classification framework than to individually re-flag all the equity assets. The logic of this framework – that is, the decision logic – would be the focus of the regulator's scrutiny, as it dictates the classification process. By making this logic clear and transparent, and formulating it in business terms, DMN thus

---

[104] http://www.federalreserve.gov/bankinforeg/ccar.htm,
http://www.federalreserve.gov/newsevents/press/bcreg/20140326a.htm

provides great benefit to the bank, both by calculating the LCR metrics more efficiently and accurately, and by demonstrating to the regulators a robust classification process.

To do the classification, the Bank must first translate the stated requirements into decision logic. It will need to make various assumptions and interpretations of the requirements, and those assumptions need to be transparent and auditable. Once the high-level classification logic is understood in detail, it then must be reverse-engineered to identify the attributes of the source data required by the decision logic. The mapping of disparate source data to those uniform attributes can be modeled as *supporting decisions* in the classification. Because this too is transparent and auditable, a decision modeling language like DMN shows *how* the Bank formulated its classifications, essential to demonstrating the *qualitative* aspects of compliance.

Example: HQLA Level 2B Classification

Consider the regulatory requirements for a security to be considered *HQLA Level 2B*:

(i) Included in:
    (A) The Russell 1000 Index; or
    (B) An index that a [BANK]'s supervisor [i.e., regulator] in a foreign jurisdiction recognizes for purposes of including equity shares in level 2B liquid assets under applicable regulatory policy, if the share is held in that foreign jurisdiction;

(ii) Issued in:
    (A) U.S. dollars; or
    (B) The currency of a jurisdiction where the [BANK] operates and the [BANK] holds the common equity share in order to cover its net cash outflows in that jurisdiction, as calculated under subpart D of this part;

(iii) Issued by an entity whose publicly traded common equity shares have a proven record as a reliable source of liquidity in repurchase or sales markets during stressed market conditions, as demonstrated by:
    (A) The market price of the security or equivalent securities of the issuer declining by no more than 40 percent during a 30 calendar-day period of significant stress, or
    (B) The market haircut demanded by counterparties to securities borrowing and lending transactions that are collateralized by the publicly traded common equity shares or equivalent securities of the issuer increasing by no more than 40 percentage points, during a 30 calendar day period of significant stress;

(iv) Not issued by a financial sector entity and not issued by a consolidated subsidiary of a financial sector entity;

(v) If held by a depository institution, is not acquired in satisfaction of a debt previously contracted (DPC); and

(vi) If held by a consolidated subsidiary of a depository institution, the depository institution can include the publicly traded common equity share in its level 2B liquid assets only if the share is held to cover net cash outflows of the depository institution's consolidated subsidiary in which the publicly traded common equity share is held, as calculated by the [BANK] under subpart D of this part.[105]

These rules, as specified by the LCR standards, determine the attributes that must be applied to equity assets held around the world. We can see that some rules leave a bit to the Bank's own judgment, such as the selection of a "period of significant stress." Overall, the decision logic required for the classification framework typically results in the need to enhance and unify the data model for the Bank's asset holdings. By starting from the required decisions first, the principles of BDM make this effort manageable.

---

[105] http://www.gpo.gov/fdsys/pkg/FR-2014-10-10/pdf/2014-22520.pdf

Index

action subtable, xvii, 146, 170, 171, 207, 208
acyclic, 43
allowed values, 5, 18, 25, 54, 57, 62, 64, 68, 76, 98, 104, 114, 115, 118, 126, 128, 142, 143, 149, 158, 161, 174, 180, 208, 209, 233, 234, 237, 238, 239, 249, 250, 267, 278
and function, 82
append function, 82
authority requirement, 43, 175
backward chaining, 36, 37, 38, 179, 207, 217
Boolean, 9, 21, 54, 55, 56, 58, 62, 74, 75, 76, 78, 82, 83, 84, 114, 118, 130, 155, 160, 161, 189, 197, 209, 210, 215, 234, 247, 249, 250, 252
boxed expression, xiii, xiv, xvi, xvii, xviii, 20, 22, 23, 24, 57, 69, 71, 72, 73, 74, 75, 88, 89, 95, 99, 109, 186, 192, 197, 235, 272, 273, 286
BPMN, x, xi, xii, xiii, xiv, xv, xvi, xviii, 3, 8, 9, 18, 23, 25, 26, 29, 30, 31, 32, 33, 34, 36, 38, 46, 47, 50, 52, 75, 76, 91, 92, 93, 106, 110, 113, 119, 157, 174, 175, 176, 177, 178, 179, 180, 194, 195, 196, 213, 217, 218, 221, 247, 288, 293, 294
BPMN Method and Style, xii, xvi, 32, 93, 178, 247, 293
business decision as a whole, xv, xvii, 20, 30, 31, 32, 33, 34, 36, 37, 38, 44, 47, 89, 91, 93, 161, 168, 173, 174, 175, 176, 177, 178, 179, 180, 196, 211, 212, 213, 214, 218, 229, 241, 247, 266, 277, 283, 284, 285, 288
business decision management (BDM), xvi, xviii, xix, 1, 3, 4, 5, 6, 7, 8, 9, 10, 237, 282, 295, 298

business glossary, xvii, 6, 24, 111, 154, 157, 158, 174, 176, 180, 233, 237, 238, 239, 287
business knowledge model (BKM), 20, 21, 25, 38, 39, 42, 43, 48, 49, 52, 58, 60, 61, 68, 69, 73, 74, 75, 86, 91, 94, 95, 96, 97, 98, 99, 101, 103, 105, 106, 110, 111, 112, 113, 119, 120, 124, 125, 130, 155, 164, 165, 185, 186, 192, 210, 225, 239, 256, 257, 258, 259, 260, 266, 267, 271, 288
business rule engine (BRE), ix, x, 40, 51, 76, 148
business rule management system (BRMS), ix, x, 51
category-score pattern, 191, 222, 223, 230
ceiling function, 83
cell merging, 95, 139, 154, 162
classification, xvii, 29, 161, 180, 187, 188, 191, 202, 211, 215, 222, 223, 284, 296, 297, 298
CODASYL, 41, 173
Collect Hit policy, 47, 66, 74, 93, 98, 196, 198, 255, 269
collection, 74, 75, 79, 114, 192, 195, 234
completeness, xv, xviii, 18, 24, 40, 51, 66, 138, 142, 154, 155, 156, 162, 165, 167, 181, 187, 191, 224, 277, 278, 279, 280, 287
compound decision table, 60, 64, 128, 138, 150, 152, 155, 162, 169, 170, 293
concatenation, 57, 61, 79, 82
conditional computation, 187
Conformance Level, xvii, 39, 40, 51, 53, 69, 71, 100, 166, 198
contains function, 81

context, 4, 22, 23, 32, 39, 49, 72, 73, 74, 75, 76, 77, 84, 87, 89, 99, 100, 101, 102, 119, 124, 130, 158, 164, 177, 178, 180, 183, 184, 185, 186, 192, 194, 197, 200, 202, 205, 206, 222, 231, 235, 239, 254, 257, 258, 259, 272, 274, 286, 288, 295, 296

context entry, 23, 39, 72, 73, 74, 75, 76, 87, 89, 99, 124, 185, 186, 192, 197, 200, 205, 206, 239, 258, 259, 272

contraction, 138, 139, 141, 150, 154, 156, 163, 164, 173, 297

count function, 81

Crosstab orientation, 67, 68, 142, 143, 145, 150, 161

data model, xvii, 24, 77, 86, 144, 145, 174, 180, 233, 234, 238, 239, 298

data object (BPMN), 47, 92

datatype, 6, 53, 62, 74, 78, 84, 86, 112, 114, 118, 120, 165, 180, 208, 233, 234, 235, 238, 239, 278

date function, 57, 79

decimal function, 83

decision analysis, xii, xv, xviii, 3, 175, 181, 191, 219, 277, 282, 283, 284, 287, 296

decision discovery, 36, 178, 179, 180, 216, 217, 218, 223, 247

decision logic, ix, x, xii, xiv, xv, xvi, xvii, xix, 4, 5, 6, 8, 9, 11, 15, 16, 17, 18, 19, 20, 21, 22, 23, 25, 26, 27, 28, 29, 30, 31, 32, 33, 35, 36, 37, 38, 39, 40, 41, 42, 43, 44, 47, 48, 49, 51, 53, 54, 55, 64, 68, 71, 72, 73, 75, 76, 79, 88, 89, 91, 92, 93, 94, 95, 96, 97, 100, 101, 103, 104, 105, 106, 112, 116, 130, 137, 139, 140, 141, 143, 144, 147, 149, 150, 159, 162, 165, 167, 174, 176, 177, 178, 179, 180, 183, 187, 190, 191, 192, 194, 195, 196, 208, 211, 212, 216, 217, 218, 219, 221, 222, 224, 225, 229, 231,233, 235, 247, 249, 250, 253, 254, 255, 256, 257, 258, 260, 265, 269, 277, 280, 281, 282, 283, 284, 285, 286, 287, 288, 294, 296, 297, 298

Decision Management Manifesto, xviii, 3, 42, 49

decision point, 32, 46, 47, 175, 176, 180, 212, 218

Decision Requirements Analysis (DRA), 42, 175, 176, 177, 178, 179, 180, 233

Decision Requirements Diagram (DRD), x, xi, xii, xiii, xiv, xv, xvii, xviii, 5, 6, 9, 19, 20, 21, 25, 26, 28, 29, 30, 31, 33, 34, 36, 37, 38, 41, 42, 43, 44, 45, 46, 47, 48, 49, 51, 52, 53, 55, 56, 59, 64, 68, 76, 86, 91, 93, 94, 95, 100, 103, 106, 107, 109, 110, 118, 119, 146, 147, 149, 150, 151, 159, 160, 161, 168, 169, 173, 174, 175, 176, 178, 179, 180, 183, 184, 195, 207, 211, 212, 213, 214, 216, 217, 218, 222, 226, 227, 228, 229, 230, 231, 241, 242, 248, 250, 253, 254, 256, 257, 261, 266, 277, 283, 285, 286, 287, 288, 293, 294

Decision Requirements Graph (DRG), 20, 41, 43, 96, 111, 160, 239

decision rule, 4, 7, 15, 16, 17, 21, 25, 39, 56, 64, 141, 142, 149, 167, 207

decision service, xv, 29, 30, 33, 34, 36, 38, 47, 93, 149, 150, 174, 175, 176, 177, 178, 195, 212, 218, 229, 230, 265, 294

decision table, xiii, xiv, xv, xvi, xvii, xviii, 15, 16, 17, 18, 19, 20, 21, 22, 25, 26, 27, 28, 29, 34, 35, 36, 38, 39, 40, 41, 47, 48, 51, 52, 55, 56, 57, 58, 59, 60, 61, 62, 63, 64, 65, 66, 67, 68, 69, 71, 72, 74, 77, 79, 91, 94, 95, 96, 97, 98, 99, 100, 104, 105, 109, 122, 126, 129, 130, 137, 138, 139, 140, 141, 142, 143, 144, 145, 146, 147, 149, 150, 152, 154, 155, 156, 159, 160, 161, 162, 163, 164, 165, 167, 168, 169, 170, 171, 173, 179, 180, 187, 188, 189, 190, 191, 196, 198, 199, 207, 208, 217, 218, 220, 222, 224, 225, 226, 227, 228, 229, 237, 247, 250, 251, 252, 253, 255, 258, 259, 268, 269, 277, 278, 279, 285, 286, 287

decision task (BPMN), 9, 10, 19, 25, 33, 47, 52, 92, 93, 175, 194, 294

decision tree, 27, 36, 37, 137, 138

Decker, Gero, xix

declarative, 9, 17, 26, 30, 36, 65, 76, 141, 145, 146, 179

decomposition, xv, xvii, 152, 176, 178, 179, 180, 183, 212, 213, 214, 215, 216, 217, 222, 223, 226, 227, 228, 229, 230, 247, 248, 250, 256, 260, 261, 285 default output entry, 64, 155, 167

distinct values function, 82, 88, 89, 198

DMN Method, xiv, xv, xvi, xvii, 6, 31, 32, 33, 36, 38, 49, 89, 97, 98, 135, 137, 139, 159, 160, 161, 162, 165, 166, 167, 173, 175, 176, 177, 178, 179, 180, 181, 183, 188, 214, 216, 218, 238, 241, 247, 265, 285

DMN Style, xv

Dodd-Frank, 295, 296

duration, 54, 57, 58, 59, 76, 77, 78, 79, 80, 118, 209, 234, 239

ends with function, 81

external decision, xv, 21, 30, 150, 175, 176, 177, 218, 294

fact model, 158, 248

FEEL, xii, xiii, xiv, xvi, xvii, xviii, 20, 22, 23, 38, 40, 51, 53, 54, 55, 56, 57, 58, 61, 63, 71, 73, 75, 76, 77, 78, 79, 83, 86, 87, 88, 89, 99, 100, 101, 104, 109, 110, 112, 113, 118, 130, 132, 159, 166, 167, 183, 187, 192, 194, 197, 198, 199, 200, 201, 202, 203, 204, 205, 208, 209, 224, 233, 234, 235, 236, 237, 239, 241, 248, 257, 261, 265, 272, 278, 285, 286, 287, 288

filter expression, 71, 74, 75, 79, 87, 88, 89, 197, 198, 199, 202, 203

final result box, 23, 73, 99, 184, 186, 202, 210, 258, 259, 272

Fish, Alan, xii, xv, xviii, 5, 30, 31, 38, 42, 48, 49, 97, 151, 156, 162, 175, 176, 179, 187, 188, 189, 190, 225

flatten function, 82

floor function, 83

for..return, 83, 88, 89, 192, 193, 194, 195, 196, 200, 201, 202, 205, 210, 257, 259, 261, 288

forward chaining, 36, 37, 179

function definition, 39, 43, 48, 61, 68, 73, 74, 85, 88, 101, 120, 185, 186, 187, 192, 193, 200, 201, 202, 205, 206, 239, 271, 288

function invocation, 69, 73, 74, 186, 187, 192, 202, 288

function library, 49, 77, 113, 186, 187

gateway (BPMN), 9, 93, 180, 293, 294

Goldberg, Larry, xiii, xv, xviii, 31, 32, 36, 37, 147, 148, 152, 158, 173, 174, 238

Hallmark, Gary, xiii, xviii, 55, 75, 76, 88, 205, 235

hit policy, 36, 62, 64, 65, 66, 68, 74, 91, 94, 97, 98, 104, 138, 140, 141, 147, 150, 152, 154, 156, 162, 187, 188, 189, 190, 191, 198, 251, 253, 255, 269, 279

hyphen (irrelevant), 35, 63, 95, 129, 138, 147, 149, 150, 188, 190, 220

if..then, 16, 57, 59, 73, 83, 99, 100, 101, 187, 210

import, 54, 85, 86, 87, 112, 113, 114, 123, 132, 186, 279, 286

index of function, 82

information requirement, 16, 20, 23, 28, 42, 43, 47, 48, 49, 52, 53, 58, 59, 61, 64, 68, 86, 87, 94, 95, 99, 100, 106, 151, 155, 164, 174, 175, 179, 183, 195, 197, 223

input data, xii, xv, 6, 7, 20, 23, 24, 25, 28, 29, 30, 31, 32, 33, 34, 36, 37, 38, 41, 42, 43, 44, 46, 47, 52, 53, 55, 56, 59, 68, 72, 76, 79, 86, 87, 88, 89, 91, 92, 95, 96, 99, 101, 104, 106, 151, 158, 159, 160, 168, 170, 175, 179, 180, 183, 184, 187, 191, 196, 197, 198, 201, 204, 205, 208, 209, 212, 215, 216, 217, 218, 220, 229, 231, 235, 236, 237, 239, 247, 248, 249, 251, 253, 257, 265, 267, 270, 273, 277, 282, 283, 285, 294

input entry, 17, 21, 56, 58, 59, 62, 63, 68, 79, 91, 95, 96, 100, 138, 139, 156, 162, 165, 166, 171, 190, 220, 278, 279

input expression, 17, 18, 21, 28, 56, 58, 59, 60, 61, 62, 68, 69, 77, 79, 84, 91, 98, 100, 138, 150, 155, 164, 165, 166

input values, xv, 9, 15, 18, 21, 25, 26, 61, 62, 64, 66, 68, 98, 115, 120, 138, 139, 143, 144, 147, 150, 155, 162, 163, 165, 167, 183, 187, 191, 224, 237, 277, 278

insert before function, 82

Internet of Things, xvi, 10, 11

invocation, 39, 43, 48, 52, 68, 69, 72, 73, 86, 91, 95, 96, 97, 98, 99, 100, 101, 104, 105, 118, 119, 120, 124, 125, 157, 165, 185, 186, 192, 200, 222, 272, 287, 288

item component, 54, 78, 234, 236, 239

item definition, 54, 62, 78, 85, 86, 98, 208, 224, 234, 235, 236, 237, 239, 267, 278 iteration, xvii, 22, 72, 83, 88, 180, 192, 193, 194, 196, 200, 202, 207, 210, 241, 250, 253, 256, 257, 259, 261, 271, 285, 287, 288

iteration pattern, xvii, 83, 88, 180, 192, 193, 194, 200, 210, 241, 287, 288

JSON, 77

Kay, Alan, 81, 83

Knowledge Automation, xii, xv, xviii, 30, 38, 42, 48, 156, 175, 179, 188, 191

knowledge requirement, 20, 43, 48, 49, 52, 68, 86, 100, 288

knowledge source, 20, 24, 42, 43, 213

Lending decision example, xiv, 33, 45, 49, 91, 94, 97, 151, 191, 214, 215, 216, 223, 225, 227, 278, 280

limited-entry decision table, 138

list contains function, 81

literal expression, 22, 23, 38, 40, 52, 55, 58, 59, 68, 69, 71, 72, 73, 74, 77, 83, 84, 87, 99, 100, 101, 128, 130, 160, 167, 180, 183, 184, 185, 186, 187, 192, 195, 209, 210, 222, 251, 253, 254, 258, 286

lower case function, 80

matches function, 81

max function, 61, 63, 166, 194, 202, 207

mean function, 194

metamodel, xiv, xvi, xvii, xviii, 19, 20, 23, 24, 36, 38, 51, 66, 71, 96, 109, 110, 112, 115, 116, 118, 120, 122, 123, 124, 159, 177, 237, 239, 288, 289

min function, 194, 202, 203, 207

model interchange, 18, 19, 20, 24, 109, 113, 286, 289

model-driven, xiii, 6, 8, 11, 284

namespace, 54, 78, 86, 87, 110, 111, 112, 113, 114, 118, 123, 186, 187, 235, 237, 239

naming convention, 160

Normal Form, 152, 153, 163, 164

normalization, 149, 151, 152, 156, 173

null, 35, 77, 78, 79, 80, 81, 82, 104, 145, 165, 166, 167, 168, 169, 187, 197, 208, 209, 210, 219, 220, 226, 230, 247, 277, 287

Object Management Group (OMG), x, xii, xiii, xiv, xix, 9, 18, 20, 23, 25, 26, 27, 39, 42, 45, 46, 48, 52, 60, 65, 67, 68, 69, 72, 74, 92,

94, 97, 98, 99, 100, 101, 102, 103, 105, 106, 107, 109, 119, 144, 151, 157, 159, 161, 173, 175, 189, 214, 236, 285, 287, 288

optimization, xvii, 3, 5, 25, 173, 176, 203, 205, 207

or function, 82

output component, 60, 155, 169, 180

output entry, 18, 21, 61, 64, 91, 142, 146, 158, 167, 170, 187, 190, 207

output label, 60, 126, 155

output values, 15, 26, 33, 37, 61, 62, 64, 65, 66, 93, 97, 98, 104, 165, 189, 218, 223, 279

parameter, 39, 43, 48, 49, 52, 58, 61, 68, 69, 72, 73, 74, 77, 88, 95, 96, 99, 105, 125, 185, 186, 192, 193, 200, 201, 202, 205, 239, 248, 265, 266

path expression, 75, 77, 79, 87

pattern, xvi, xvii, xix, 22, 52, 57, 71, 72, 74, 81, 84, 88, 149, 150, 154, 162, 180, 183, 187, 188, 189, 191, 192, 197, 202, 209, 211, 215, 222, 237, 271, 287, 288

precedesFunction, 85, 203, 272

predictive analytics, xii, xvi, 3, 7, 8, 20, 43, 211, 215, 223, 283, 284

Priority Hit policy, 62, 65, 66, 97, 104, 147, 150, 154, 156, 162, 187, 188, 189, 190, 219, 220, 221, 225, 230, 251, 279

process logic, 6, 9, 29, 31, 35, 174, 180, 194

process model, x, xi, xiii, xv, xviii, 8, 9, 15, 19, 25, 30, 38, 44, 46, 92, 106, 119, 145, 174, 176, 177, 178, 179, 180, 212, 218, 219, 221, 293

qualified name, 23, 54, 55, 60, 61, 63, 69, 77, 78, 79, 86, 96, 110, 112, 118, 164, 166, 186, 235, 238, 239

relation, 39, 75, 79, 83, 84, 85, 87, 88, 123, 131, 132, 192, 193, 194, 196, 197, 198, 200, 201, 202, 203, 204, 205, 206, 210, 235, 271, 272, 273, 274

remove function, 82

replace function, 81

requirements document, x

reverse function, 82

Ronen, Gil, xviii, 265

Ross, Ron, xv, xix, 4, 141, 142, 143, 144, 145, 146, 154, 155, 156, 158, 167, 227
rule family, 149, 150, 151, 174, 196
Rules-as-rows orientation, 21, 142, 143, 150, 154
Sapiens, xiii, xviii, 147, 196, 238, 265, 288
Sayles, Aaron, xix, 295
scope, 5, 15, 19, 53, 61, 64, 72, 77, 118, 120, 130, 142, 143, 144, 150, 154, 155, 165, 167, 168, 176, 186, 197, 239
score pattern, 29, 34, 35, 36, 69, 79, 93, 98, 104, 144, 160, 191, 211, 219, 223, 227, 243, 244, 257, 258, 259, 277, 281, 284
S-FEEL, xvii, 39, 40, 51, 54, 55, 56, 57, 58, 61, 62, 63, 69, 73, 99, 113, 118, 130, 160, 167, 183, 184
Signavio, xviii, xix, 5, 62, 195, 196, 257, 261, 262, 263, 278, 279, 282, 283, 288
single-sourcing, 142, 143, 144, 227, 231
some..satisfies, 84
sort function, xvii, 71, 85, 203, 287
spaces, variables contain, 55, 76, 77, 112, 114, 159, 160, 165, 235, 287
starts with function, 81
Steinert, Bastian, xix
string length function, 80, 209
Structured Business Vocabulary and Rules (SBVR), 24, 144, 157, 158
sublist function, 82
substring after function, 81
substring before function, 80
substring function, 80
sum function, 79, 209
table query patterns, xvii, 72, 74, 88, 180, 197, 198, 199, 200, 201, 202, 250, 258, 269, 271, 287
TableSpeak, xv, 141, 142, 143, 144, 145
Taylor, James, xiii, xviii, 3, 4, 7, 8, 10, 42
tDMNElementReference, 86, 110, 118, 119, 122
The Decision Model (TDM, xiii, xv, xviii, 36, 37, 95, 98, 147, 148, 152, 173, 174
The Decision Model (TDM), xiii, xiv, 30, 31, 38, 138, 147, 148, 149, 150, 151, 152, 153, 154,

155, 156, 158, 162, 163, 164, 173, 174, 175, 176, 177, 178, 179, 180, 196, 233, 237, 238
top-level decision, 31, 33, 36, 38, 168, 169, 175, 176, 178, 179, 211, 213, 215, 218, 219, 220, 221, 229, 230, 248
type language, 53, 54, 113, 234, 239, 278
typeRef, 53, 54, 62, 78, 87, 114, 116, 118, 120, 122, 126, 128, 131, 165, 234, 235, 239, 279
unary tests, 62, 165
unconditional computation, 59, 183, 187
union function, 82
Unique Hit policy, xviii, 65, 66, 68, 94, 97, 138, 140, 141, 152, 154, 156, 162, 187, 188, 189, 190, 191, 198, 225, 251, 279
upper case function, 80
user task (BPMN), 47, 93, 106, 294
validation patterns, xvii, 30, 84, 109, 143, 180, 208, 209, 210, 277, 285, 286, 287
Vanthienen, Jan, xv, xviii, 41, 137, 138, 139, 140, 146, 152, 154, 156, 157, 162, 170, 173, 187, 188
variable, 16, 22, 33, 39, 42, 43, 44, 49, 52, 53, 54, 55, 56, 59, 60, 61, 62, 63, 64, 69, 72, 73, 74, 75, 76, 77, 78, 83, 84, 86, 87, 88, 91, 95, 96, 98, 99, 110, 112, 114, 115, 116, 118, 120, 122, 125, 126, 128, 130, 131, 132, 146, 149, 150, 154, 155, 159, 160, 164, 165, 166, 174, 180, 192, 193, 194, 195, 197, 200, 201, 205, 218, 234, 238, 239, 278
von Halle, Barbara, xiii, xv, 36, 37, 147, 148, 152, 158, 173, 174, 238
XML Schema, xiii, xiv, xvi, xvii, xviii, 19, 24, 66, 71, 86, 109, 110, 113, 114, 115, 117, 118, 120, 121, 122, 123, 124, 125, 126, 127, 128, 129, 130, 131, 235, 237, 286, 288
XML Schema (XSD), 20, 24, 53, 54, 57, 78, 85, 86, 87, 109, 110, 112, 113, 114, 118, 125, 126, 234, 235, 236, 239, 278
XPATH, 55, 75, 76, 77, 78, 79, 81, 83, 87, 123, 133, 197, 201
zero-input decision, 197, 231

About the Author

Bruce Silver is Principal at Bruce Silver Associates, provider of consulting and training in the areas of business process management and business decision management. In addition, he is founder and Principal of BPMessentials, a global provider of BPM training and certification. His book *BPMN Method and Style* is now in its second edition, and has been translated into German, Japanese, and Spanish. He served on the technical committee in OMG that drafted the BPMN 2.0 standard, and currently serves on the DMN Revision Task Force. His website methodandstyle.com focuses on process and decision modeling using the Method and Style approach.

Prior to founding Bruce Silver Associates in 1994, he was Vice President in charge of workflow and document management at the analyst firm BIS Strategic Decisions, now part of Forrester Research. He has Bachelor and PhD degrees in Physics from Princeton and MIT, and four US Patents in electronic imaging.

To contact the author, email bruce@brsilver.com.

Appendix B Author

Aaron Sayles is a Senior Functional Implementation Consultant and has assisted numerous large financial institutions with Risk and Regulatory Reporting data management initiatives.

CPSIA information can be obtained
at www.ICGtesting.com
Printed in the USA
LVOW02s0757071216

516057LV00016B/364/P